D0567807

Successful Strategies in Supply Chain Management

Chi Kin Chan
The Hong Kong Polytechnic University, Hong Kong

H.W.J. Lee
The Hong Kong Polytechnic University, Hong Kong

IDEA GROUP PUBLISHING

Hershey • London • Melbourne • Singapore

Acquisitions Editor:	Mehdi Khosrow-Pour
Senior Managing Editor:	Jan Travers
Managing Editor:	Amanda Appicello
Development Editor:	Michele Rossi
Copy Editor:	Bernie Kieklak
Typesetter:	Jennifer Wetzel
Cover Design:	Lisa Tosheff
Printed at:	Integrated Book Technology

Published in the United States of America by
      Idea Group Publishing (an imprint of Idea Group Inc.)
      701 E. Chocolate Avenue, Suite 200
      Hershey PA 17033
      Tel: 717-533-8845
      Fax: 717-533-8661
      E-mail: cust@idea-group.com
      Web site: http://www.idea-group.com

and in the United Kingdom by
      Idea Group Publishing (an imprint of Idea Group Inc.)
      3 Henrietta Street
      Covent Garden
      London WC2E 8LU
      Tel: 44 20 7240 0856
      Fax: 44 20 7379 3313
      Web site: http://www.eurospan.co.uk

Library of Congress Cataloging-in-Publication Data

Successful strategies in supply chain management / Chi Kin Chan and H.W.J. Lee, editors.
    p. cm.
  Includes bibliographical references and index.
  ISBN 1-59140-303-0 (h/c) -- ISBN 1-59140-304-9 (s/c) -- ISBN 1-59140-305-7 (ebook)
1. Business logistics. I. Chan, Chi-Kin, 1959- II. Lee, H. W. J. (Heung Win J.)
  HD38.5.S83 2005
  658.7'2--dc22
                        2004021988

British Cataloguing in Publication Data
A Cataloguing in Publication record for this book is available from the British Library.

All work contributed to this book is new, previously-unpublished material. The views expressed in this book are those of the authors, but not necessarily of the publisher.

In Memoriam

Brian G. Kingsman 1939-2003

Professor Brian G. Kingsman passed away in Lancaster on August 30, 2003. He was an excellent supervisor who guided his students, from various countries, with countless innovative ideas. He made an enormous contribution in research with remarkable breakthroughs. He was a pioneer in production planning for make-to-order manufacturing industries. Professor Kingsman was a British scholar with a great sense of humour and kindness. He always displayed his gifted ability as a problem solver all throughout his productive and influential career. His untimely death at the age of 64 brought great shock to all of his students, colleagues and acquaintances. We will miss Professor Kingsman for his enthusiasm, spirit of collegiality, and friendship which motivated all those who had the pleasure of working with and learning from him.

Chapter I of this book was co-authored by Professor Brian G. Kingsman and he played a very important role in originating the idea and writing that chapter. At the early stage of preparing this book, he also promised to contribute another chapter on his own. Very sadly, this "another chapter" will never arrive.

Chi Kin Chan
H.W.J. Lee
May 2004

Successful Strategies in Supply Chain Management

Table of Contents

Foreword

Supply Chain Management (SCM) is one of the fastest growing research areas and of interest to both academics and professionals. In recent years, due to the demand driven by globalization and the introduction of electronic commerce, supply chain management has become more interdisciplinary as well as more polarized. On one hand, numerical/quantitative techniques developed in other research areas have been adopted to solve SCM problems and, on the other hand, many qualitative arguments have been surfaced to discuss the modeling of the problems. Readers will find that the book covers many recently identified interdisciplinary research areas of SCM and presents many prevailing qualitative discussions of SCM modeling. We very much hope that in this way the book will be of interest to a much wider readership. Inevitably, some of the chapters are more mathematically involved.

During the preparation of the manuscript, many colleagues have discussed with us different topics for presentation in the book. We were not able to include them all, but would like to express our special gratitude to them. All chapters were refereed. We would like to extend our thanks to the authors and the reviewers for their excellent contributions. Finally, we would like to thank the Idea Group Publishing staff for their patience and their support for this work.

Chi Kin Chan
H.W.J. Lee
May 2004

Preface

In modern organisational/corporate management, the area of Supply Chain Management (SCM) has been considered as a competitive strategy for integrating suppliers and customers with the objective of improving responsiveness and flexibility of manufacturing/service organisations. The optimal design of a supply chain is therefore a crucial issue of SCM researchers and practitioners. An effective supply chain policy can reduce average holding inventory level as well as expected cost. Significant advances have recently been made in the theory and in applications under the drive of the inevitable prevailing trend of globalisation and today's competitive knowledge-based economy. Undoubtedly, the introduction of e-commerce/e-business has sped up this process simply because the flow of information is far too fast and geographical boundaries with respect to the information flow become less and less important. On the other hand, it is still essential to focus on the SCM as an integrated system with physical flow of materials, manufacturing planning and control, and physical distribution. The development of models and approaches for SCM has become a challenging topic toward the optimisation of supply chain priorities. There are numerous articles and reports published in the areas of SCM.

The objective of this book is to promote, exchange, and disseminate information and research results on optimisation models and approaches of SCM. This book will address problems of SCM from modeling, conceptual and practical perspectives such that researchers and practitioners in SCM can keep up with the development of this field and have a better understanding and collaboration among them. Review articles, conceptual and analytical and empirical analysis on SCM are also included.

Effective coordination plays an important role in the successful operation of modern manufacturing and inventory systems. If no such coordination exists, then the vendor and the buyer will act independently to make decisions that maximise their respective profits or minimise their costs. This may not be optimal if one considers the supply chain as a whole. How best to achieve effective coordination between the suppliers and the buyers is both a current managerial concern and an important research issue. Chapter I considers coordination in a single-vendor multi-buyer supply chain by synchronising ordering and production cycles. The synchronisation is achieved by scheduling the actual ordering days of the buyers and coordinating it with the vendor's production cycle while allowing the buyers to choose their own lot sizes and order cycle.

A supply chain or network may be considered to be a set of linked processes connecting downstream customers to upstream suppliers, factories, distribution centers and retailers.

It was reported in recent work that productive efficiencies between stages in a serial linkage of processes were modeled so that linear programming could be used to determine optimal throughput. Chapter II proposes how these theoretical results might be extended and applied to supply chain management, especially to the monitoring of chains and supply networks for efficiency, capacity and continuous improvement. Moreover, discussions on possible applications of this study to the upcoming and important area of e-business are provided.

Significant advances have been made in the computational studies of optimisation and optimal controls. A number of efficient computational techniques are now available for solving various classes of optimisation and optimal control problems numerically. Despite the development of advanced information technology and significant advances in the computational studies of optimisation and optimal controls, there are still many issues which need to be addressed with a view to enhance the application of SCM in real life environments and further theoretical development. In Chapter III, a single echelon supply chain problem is posed as an optimal control problem of a system with time delays, and thus solved by adopting techniques from the theory of computational optimal controls. An illustrative numerical example is also provided to demonstrate the effectiveness of the novel technique.

It is inevitable for SCM to be affected by the life cycle of products. In Chapter IV, a systematic and in-depth discussion of three main interrelated life cycles affecting the dynamics of supply chain associated with products is presented, namely, innovation, the market, and the location. References to real-world products are also given in the chapter for readers to relate the theory.

Literature on supply chain management has acknowledged the effects of forecasting techniques, lot sizing rules, centralising information systems, vendor managed inventory, and various biases and noises on order variability or bullwhip effect. In Chapter V, the order variability from a buyer is shown to be affected by the payment terms offered by the supplier. A new mathematical model is proposed and numerical simulation results are presented to demonstrate the substantial effects of payment terms.

In Chapter VI, lengthy discussions on globalisation on SCM and the resulting ideas of two different schools of thoughts, namely, standardisation and adaptation of products, are presented. This chapter has laid the theoretical groundwork for a strategy that captures the advantages of both schools, and has given the suggestion of a delayed adaptation strategies that may profitably address the efficiencies required by competition and the product features demanded by increasingly discerning customers.

In Chapter VII, a detailed comparison between Genetic Algorithm (GA) and other meta-heuristics are given for solving SCM problems which are potentially very complex and very size-formidable, with thousands of variables. The weakness of GA is also addressed in the chapter. Readers having a background of computational optimisation would find this chapter interesting.

One of the most interesting aspects of supply chains is their intrinsic dynamic behaviour. Dynamic interactions can cause unexpected and undesirable results. There are both external and internal reasons for this. In Chapter VIII, some of the principal dynamics features of supply chains are reviewed. A study of the relationship between the competitiveness of the supply chain and its intrinsic dynamics is provided, for both positive and negative aspects.

In order to achieve a successful implementation of electronic commerce (EC), it is necessary to review and restructure the logistics activities of the enterprise. In Chapter IX, such a review, defined as *re-engineering*, is provided. Four stages of EC — and the links between — are presented: Brochureware, e-commerce, e-Business, and e-Enterprise. A self-diagnosis tool is also provided, which is the first detailed checklist for a systematic analysis of a company's processes. It is the first step in the re-engineering of logistics activities for EC since it allows a company to evaluate its situation within the EC framework.

It is well known that traditional inventory models that assume the inventory can all be used to fulfill the future demands are no longer applicable for perishable products. Many authors have contributed to the area in the literature. In Chapter X, a detailed literature review is presented for these works on the interaction and coordination in supply chains with perishable products. Professionals and researchers may find this chapter useful.

The topics are discussed with sufficient detail to enable the readers to follow the procedure and calculations quite easily. The book is directed toward graduate students interested in the conceptual, analytical and empirical analysis on SCM. To avoid the necessity of frequent and disruptive cross-referencing, the chapters are designed to be as independent of each other as possible, and are self-contained. The mathematical requirements for most of the chapters are at the first-year graduate level.

Chapter I

A Co-Ordinated Single-Vendor Multi-Buyer Supply Chain Model:
Synchronisation of Ordering and Production Cycles

Chi Kin Chan, The Hong Kong Polytechnic University, Hong Kong

Brian G. Kingsman, Lancaster University, UK

Abstract

This chapter considers the co-ordination in a single-vendor multi-buyer supply chain by synchronising ordering and production cycles. The synchronisation is achieved by scheduling the actual ordering days of the buyers and co-ordinating it with the vendor's production cycle whilst allowing the buyers to choose their own lot sizes and order cycle. A mathematical model for our proposed co-ordination is developed and analysed. Our results show that the synchronised cycles policy works better than independent optimisation or restricting buyers to adopt a common order cycle. Some illustrative examples demonstrate that there are circumstances where both the vendor and the buyers gain from such synchronisation without the need for price and quantity discount incentives.

Introduction

Effective co-ordination plays an important role in the successful operation of modern manufacturing and inventory systems. If no such co-ordination exists then the vendor and the buyer will act independently to make decisions that maximise their respective profits or minimise their costs. This may not be optimal if one considers the supply chain as a whole. How best to achieve effective co-ordination between the suppliers and the buyers is both a current managerial concern and an important research issue. This chapter considers the problem of co-ordinating ordering and inventory holding in a supply chain consisting of one vendor supplying many buyers.

A number of researchers, including Goyal (1976), Monahan (1984), Banerjee (1986a, 1986b), Goyal (1987, 1988, 1995), Lee and Rosenblatt (1986), Joglekar (1988), Lu (1995), Hill (1997) and Pan and Yang (2002), have shown that under the scenario of a vendor supplying a product to a single buyer, a co-ordinated inventory replenishment policy is more desirable from a total system perspective than each party operating its individual optimal policy. These papers have generally compared joint lot sizing decision models with independent ordering. Some research, for example Pujawan and Kingsman (2002), has shown that synchronising the order times and agreeing on the delivery lot size, allowing the buyer to determine the order quantity and the supplier the production lot size independently, is virtually as good as jointly agreeing on the relevant lot sizes. The general result of the above research is that integrated lot sizing models reduce the total system cost. However, while they reduce the costs to the vendor, they increase the costs to the buyer. Attention has been thus put on examining mechanisms for the vendor to share the savings by offering price or quantity discounts to encourage the buyer to purchase larger quantities.

Integrated inventory models for the one-vendor multi-buyer case have also been discussed by a number of other authors, such as Lal and Staelin (1984), Joglekar (1988), Lal and Staelin (1984) and Dada and Srikanth (1987).

Joglekar and Tharthare (1990) proposed an individually responsible and rational decision (IRRD) approach to economic lot sizes for one vendor and many purchasers. They argued that the co-operation proposed by earlier authors was antithetical to the free enterprise system and they strongly argued in favour of allowing each party to adopt its own independently derived optimal replenishment policy. They advocated making the purchasers pay for the order processing cost they impose on the vendor every time they order. Because the vendor is not incurring certain costs he will have otherwise incurred, he can now afford to lower his price per unit (not a quantity discount, but a simple price revision). The purchaser now sees a lower price and consequently a lower carrying cost per unit. The author showed that the system costs under IRRD are lower than the system cost under the joint economic lot sizing approach.

Joglekar and Tharthare (1990) suggested that in the presence of multiple buyers with unequal order sizes, their timings might not be known deterministically. Therefore, the vendor should seek to minimise its own costs by resorting to the classical production lot size (PLS) model. Through a series of deterministic simulation experiments, Banerjee and Burton (1994) showed that, in such a case, the actual results for the vendor and the buyers were different from the ones obtained from the standard lot size models. In particular, stock outs might occur, even under deterministic conditions, in the absence of an adequate production reorder point policy. They therefore pointed out that discrete and unequally spaced depletions from the vendor's inventories violated the assumption of uniform usage in the PLS seriously enough to call into question the appropriateness of the use of the IRRD approach under such conditions. As an alternative, Banerjee and Burton (1994) developed an integrated production/inventory model for a vendor and multiple buyers under deterministic conditions, with the objective of minimizing total system cost incurred by all parties. Their model was based on the concept of a delivery cycle time, common to all buyers, and a supplier's manufacturing cycle time that is an integer multiple of it. If all the parties involved agree to co-operate in implementing such a system, they found that such co-ordination was more desirable than independent optimisation.

Banerjee and Banerjee (1994) further developed an analytical model for co-ordinated inventory control between a vendor and multiple buyers dealing with a single product under stochastic demands and lead times through a common cycle approach. They focused their attention on the use of electronic data interchange (EDI). They argued that EDI makes it feasible for multiple buyers and the supplier to be linked together on a real-time basis and it is possible for the supplier to monitor the consumption pattern of the buyers, if so desired. As a result, it is not necessary for the buyers to place an order but the supplier can send the needed material based on a prearranged decision system. In their paper, they also assumed that the parties involved dealt with a single product and had agreed to shipments at fixed intervals common to all buyers and the vendor shipped at regular intervals to each buyer a quantity that would make the quantity on hand and on shipment equal to a predetermined replenish-up-to quantity. A major implication of Banerjee and Banerjee (1994) was that the vendor assumed full responsibility for all inventory-related decisions of the buyers.

Lu (1995) made an interesting observation that all the previous studies assumed that the vendor must have the knowledge of buyer's holding and ordering costs, which are very difficult to estimate unless the buyer is willing to reveal the true values. Therefore, Lu considered another circumstance in which the objective is to minimise the vendor's total annual cost subject to the maximum cost that the buyer may be prepared to incur.

More recently, Viswanathan and Piplani (2001) proposed a model to study and analyze the benefit of co-ordinating supply chain inventories through the use of common replenishment epochs (CRE) or time periods. A one-vendor multi-buyer supply chain for a single product was considered. Under their strategies, the vendor specifies common replenishment periods and requires all buyers to replenish only at those time periods. However, the authors did not include any inventory costs of the vendor in the model. Woo et al. (2001) considered an integrated inventory model where a single vendor purchases and processes raw materials in order to deliver finished items to multiple buyers at a common cycle. The vendor and all buyers are willing to invest in reducing the ordering cost (e.g., establishing an electronic-data-interchange-based inventory control system) in order to decrease their joint total cost. Their work is an extension of the model of Banerjee and Banerjee (1994) in which the vendor makes replenishment decisions for all buyers to optimise the joint total cost.

This chapter takes a different approach that takes into account the comment of Lu (1995) that neither the vendor nor the buyers may have knowledge of each other's cost. We examine the situation where each partner in the supply chain determines their lot sizes independently, but that they synchronise their ordering and production times. Each buyer in determining the size for their order also fixes the intervals between their orders. The buyers then allow the vendor to schedule exactly when their ordering days will occur, subject to the ordering interval fixed by the buyer. All the parties accept some regularity in their policies of making their ordering intervals an integer multiple of some basic period, say days or weeks. We develop a model for the total system cost assuming that each partner operates as a rational decision maker seeking to minimise its costs. However, if the vendor wished to co-ordinate its supply chain in such a way in practice, it would only need to know the buyers' order sizes and not their costs. Compared to the common cycle for all buyers' approach of Bannerjee and Burton (1994), we permit each buyer to have its own cycle which must be an integer multiple of some basic time period and an integer factor of the vendor's cycle time.

Independent Policies for Buyers and Vendor

We assume that each of the n buyers faces a deterministic demand at rate d_i per unit time, incurs an ordering cost A_i each time it places an order on the vendor and incurs an inventory holding cost h_i per unit per unit time held. If the buyers and the supplier operate independently, then each buyer will order a quantity Q_i at time intervals of T_i units apart, which are determined only on the basis of the costs and demands of the ith buyer. The total costs per unit time for the ith buyer can thus be expressed as

$$k_i(T_i) = \frac{A_i}{T_i} + \frac{h_i d_i T_i}{2} \tag{1}$$

where $Q_i = d_i T_i$. This is the simple standard EOQ model so that the costs per unit time are minimised where

$$T_i = \sqrt{\frac{2A_i}{h_i d_i}} \ . \tag{2}$$

The vendor is faced with orders from each of the n buyers based on demand rates of $d_1, d_2, ..., d_n$ per unit time. Thus the vendor has to satisfy a demand that occurs at an average rate of D per unit time, where

$$D = d_1 + d_2 + \ldots\ldots + d_n .$$

The vendor produces new items at a rate P per unit time. We assume that the vendor incurs a set-up cost S_v for each production run and incurs a holding cost of h per unit held per unit time. If the vendor operates independently of the buyers and aims to satisfy the average demand rate D per unit time, then we have the simple EBQ model where the vendor starts a production run every T_v units of time and produces a total lot size of Q_v, where $Q_v = DT_v$. The costs per unit time for the vendor are given by

$$K_v(T_v) = \frac{S_v}{T_v} + \frac{hDT_v}{2}\left(1 - \frac{D}{P}\right) + \sum_{i=1}^{n} \frac{C_i}{T_i} . \qquad (3)$$

The last term in equation (3) covers the order processing and fixed shipment costs in supplying the order quantities $Q_i = d_i T_i$ to each of the buyers. These depend only on the T_i, which are determined by the buyers and outside the control of the vendor, so they do not affect the determination of the T_v and Q_v for the vendor. Equation (3) becomes the simple EBQ model where the costs of the vendor per unit time are minimised by

$$T_v = \sqrt{\frac{2S_v}{hD\left(1 - \dfrac{D}{P}\right)}} .$$

The above is standard inventory theory, but details can be found in Banerjee and Burton (1994).

The above model for the vendor assumes that the buyers' demand occurs continuously at the average rate D. However, the demands made on the vendor actually occur as aggregated orders $Q_1, Q_2, \ldots\ldots, Q_n$. So the above model for the vendor cannot guarantee that there will never be any stockouts, failure to meet the buyers' demands on time. The maximum demand that can occur at any time is when all buyers require a delivery order at the same time. So to ensure that all demands are satisfied on time, then the vendor should not have less than $Q_1 + Q_2 + \ldots\ldots + Q_n$ in stock at the time the vendor starts a new production run.

This will be the case for instantaneous delivery. This quantity $Q_1+Q_2+......+Q_n$ becomes the re-order level. Thus an extra term

$$h\sum_{i=1}^{n}Q_i$$

needs to be added to equation (3) to give the true costs per unit time for the vendor if the vendor is to have zero stockouts. If the vendor starts a production run with a stock level less than $Q_1+Q_2+......+Q_n$ then stockouts are certain to occur.

If the vendor provides products on a delivery time basis, rather than instantaneously, where part of the lead time allows for partial production after orders are received, the situation is more complicated. If L is the part of the delivery lead time used for production then approximately $(P-D)L$ can be produced to meet the maximum delivery at any time. So the re-order level will be

$$\text{re-order level} = \sum_{i=1}^{n}Q_i - (P-D)L. \qquad \textbf{(4)}$$

Note however if the whole of the delivery time is required for the transportation of items between the vendor and the buyers then $L = 0$. This introduction of a re-order level to determine when to start each new production run does not affect the determination of the minimum cost vendor production lot size. It just increases the costs for the vendor and hence the total system cost. Using the optimal order intervals and order quantities for the vendor and the buyers, the total system cost ensuring that no stockouts occur becomes

$$K(T_v,T_1,T_2,......,T_n) =$$

$$\sqrt{2S_vDh\left(1-\frac{D}{P}\right)} + h\left(\sum_{i=1}^{n}Q_i - (P-D)L\right) + \sum_{i=1}^{n}\left(C_i\sqrt{\frac{h_id_i}{2A_i}} + \sqrt{2A_id_ih_i}\right).$$

Banerjee and Burton (1994) used a deterministic simulation approach, rather than analysis, to the problem of determining the re-order level for the vendor. These simulation experiments showed that there will be significant amounts of stockouts (late deliveries in their case) if the vendor uses a re-order level to start a new production run at a value below that given in (4).

It is not completely clear from their research what is the true value for L, which is about when stock levels are reduced by a buyer's order. It is stated that the delivery lead time is $L = 2$, the production $P = 2D = 116$. The sum of the order quantities (see Table 1 of the paper) is 955 units. Assuming $L = 2$ in (4), then

$$\sum_{i=1}^{n} Q_i - (P-D)L = 955 - DL = 955 - 116 = 839.$$

Thus the extra inventory holding cost will be $0.005 \times 839 = 4.195$. If this is added to the cost for their ZERO option, starting a new vendor production run when the vendor stock is zero, then the new cost becomes $28.20 + 4.195 = 32.395$. This is quite close to the value of 32.62 given by Banerjee and Burton (1994) for a re-order level equal to the sum of the order quantities.

Co-Ordinated Ordering and Production Policies

Clearly in the previous situation where the vendor and the buyers are operating independently, the vendor needs to carry a large stock of items to satisfy all demands on time, or the buyers will have to suffer stockouts and late deliveries. Co-ordinating the timing of orders of the buyers with the production policy of the vendor may enable the stock needed in the system to avoid stockouts to be reduced. Banerjee and Burton (1994) and others proposed that the buyers all adopt a common order cycle of placing order every T periods of time apart. In order to meet these scheduled demands the vendor will have to use a production cycle that is some integer multiple of T, say NT.

However, forcing all buyers to use the same common cycle time T will be costly for both the small buyers, forced to carry higher stocks than they would wish, and the large buyers, forced to place more orders than they would wish. It would be more economic to have small cycle times for the low demand buyers and large cycle times for the high demand buyers. This can be achieved by having some basic cycle time, T, and insisting that each buyer use an integer multiple of that basic cycle time, say k_iT for the ith buyer. Let the vendor production cycle time be denoted by NT, where N is also an integer. The idea is closely akin to the Extended Basic Period approach for the Economic Lot Scheduling Problem introduced by Haessler (1979), etc.

For simplicity we assume that delivery to the buyers is instantaneous, or more exactly that buyers' orders are received and deducted from the vendor's inventory at regular intervals T apart. The result of the co-ordination will be a set of demands $D_1, D_2, D_3, \ldots\ldots, D_N$ over the NT periods of the vendor production cycle, where each demand is some subset of the buyers' order quantities. To determine the vendor's stock holding cost we first need to consider how to meet these given demands and then secondly consider how to allocate the individual buyer's orders to the successive demands $D_1, D_2, D_3, \ldots\ldots, D_N$. If two buyers order every two periods, we can allocate both to periods 1, 3, 5, etc., or to periods 2, 4, 6, etc., or allocate one buyer to periods 1, 3, 5, and the other buyer to periods 2, 4, 6, $\ldots\ldots$

A Model for Optimisation of the Co-Ordinated System

Let us assume that the vendor cycle starts at time 0, immediately after having satisfied the last demand in the previous cycle. Let a production run start at time $-ST$, a time ST before the start of the vendor cycle, where S may be positive or negative. Production continues, building up stock at a constant rate P, and meeting demand D_1 at time T, D_2 at time $2T$, D_3 at time $3T$, etc. Production stops at time FT, where F is not necessarily an integer. Let b be the nearest integer below F. Stock remains constant from FT until $(b+1)T$, at which it is decreased by demand D_{b+1} at $(b+1)T$. Thereafter stock decreases in a series of steps at times $(b+2)T$, $(b+3)T$ until the last demand in the vendor cycle, which is D_N at time NT after which the stock is zero. The stock development over time is shown in Figure 1. There are four different types of areas under the inventory curve to be considered, denoted by polygons (A), (B), (C) and (D) in Figure 1. Let us define

Figure 1. Inventory level of vendor

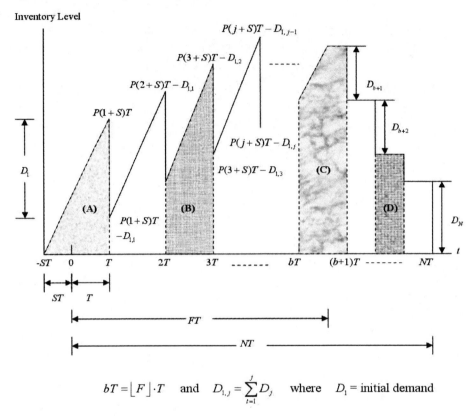

$$bT = \lfloor F \rfloor \cdot T \quad \text{and} \quad D_{1,j} = \sum_{t=1}^{j} D_j \quad \text{where} \quad D_1 = \text{initial demand}$$

$$D_{1,j} = \text{cumulative demands over time } T, 2T, \ldots\ldots, jT = \sum_{i=1}^{j} D_i .$$

Considering each of the polygons in turn, the area, χ, under the inventory curve can be calculated (see Chan and Kingsman, 2003). The final result is that, since the vendor's production cycle is of length NT, the average stock held by the vendor is

$$\frac{\chi}{NT} = \frac{1}{NT} \left\{ \sum_{j=1}^{N} (j-1) D_j T + (1+S) D_{1,N} T - \frac{D_{1,N}^2}{2P} \right\} \qquad (5)$$

where $D_{1,N}$ is the total demand on all the buyers (and hence on the vendor, over the full cycle NT).

The final stage is to allocate individual buyer's orders to each vendor demand period. Assume buyer i orders every k_i periods. Then let us define

$$\delta_{i,t} = \begin{cases} 1 & \text{buyers i order in period tT} \\ 0 & \text{otherwise} \end{cases}.$$

Since the buyer orders every $k_i T$ units of time

$$\delta_{i,t+k_i} = \delta_{i,t}.$$

The buyer orders only once in each set of successive k_i periods, so

$$\sum_{j=0}^{k_i-1} \delta_{i,t+j} = 1.$$

Over the NT vendor production cycle, the buyer orders $\dfrac{NT}{k_i T} = \dfrac{N}{k_i}$ times. Thus

$$\sum_{t=1}^{N} \delta_{i,t} = \frac{N}{k_i}.$$

With this notation the demand, i.e., orders on the vendor at time tT, will be

$$D_t = \sum_{i=1}^{n} \delta_{i,t} k_i d_i T.$$

Hence

$$D_{1,N} = \sum_{t=1}^{N} D_t = \sum_{t=1}^{N}\sum_{i=1}^{n}\delta_{i,t}k_i d_i T = \sum_{i=1}^{n}\left\{\left(\sum_{t=1}^{N}\delta_{i,t}\right)k_i d_i T\right\}$$

$$= \sum_{i=1}^{n}\frac{N}{k_i}k_i d_i T = NT\sum_{i=1}^{n} d_i = NDT$$

where D is the total outside demand on the system per unit time. Also

$$\sum_{t=1}^{N}(t-1)D_t = \sum_{t=1}^{N}(t-1)\left(\sum_{i=1}^{n}\delta_{i,t}k_i d_i T\right) = \sum_{i=1}^{n} k_i d_i T\left\{\sum_{t=1}^{N}(t-1)\delta_{i,t}\right\}.$$

No shortages are allowed at the vendor, so the production over the time $-ST$ to T must be at least sufficient to meet the first demand in the full cycle, D_1 at time T. Let us define ψ as the surplus stock above the demand D_1 at time T, then

$$(1+S)PT = \Psi + D_1.$$

Substituting these into the expression (5) for the vendor's average stock level following some simplification gives

Vendor's Average Stock

$$= \frac{1}{NT}\left\{T^2\sum_{i=1}^{n}k_i d_i\left\{\sum_{t=1}^{N}(t-1)\delta_{i,t}\right\} + \frac{\Psi}{PT}NDT^2 + \frac{D_1}{PT}NDT^2 - \frac{N^2 D^2 T^2}{2P}\right\}$$

$$= T\left\{\frac{1}{N}\sum_{i=1}^{n}\left\{k_i d_i\left(\sum_{t=1}^{N}(t-1)\delta_{i,t}\right)\right\} + \frac{\Psi D}{PT} + \frac{D}{P}\sum_{i=1}^{n}\delta_{i,1}k_i d_i - \frac{ND^2}{2P}\right\}.$$

Hence, the *Vendor's Holding Cost* is given by

$$= hT\left\{\frac{1}{N}\sum_{i=1}^{n}\left\{k_i d_i\left(\sum_{t=1}^{N}(t-1)\delta_{i,t}\right)\right\} + \frac{\Psi D}{PT} + \frac{D}{P}\sum_{i=1}^{n}\delta_{i,1}k_i d_i - \frac{ND^2}{2P}\right\}.$$

In addition to the Vendor's Holding Cost, the other relevant costs of the co-ordinated vendor-buyer system to be included are:

$$\text{Vendor's Setup Cost} = \frac{S_v}{NT}$$

$$\text{Vendor's Order Processing and Shipment Cost} = \sum_{i=1}^{n} \frac{C_i}{k_i T}$$

$$\text{Buyers' Ordering Cost} = \sum_{i=1}^{n} \frac{A_i}{k_i T}$$

$$\text{Buyers' Holding Cost} = \frac{1}{2} \sum_{i=1}^{n} h_i d_i k_i T .$$

Summing up all the relevant costs, remembering that d_i is the demand per unit time for buyer i and D the total demand on the system per unit time, this gives the total relevant cost of the vendor-buyer system as

Total Relevant Cost

$$= hT \left\{ \frac{1}{N} \sum_{i=1}^{n} \left\{ k_i d_i \left(\sum_{t=1}^{N} (t-1)\delta_{i,t} \right) \right\} + \frac{\Psi D}{PT} + \frac{D}{P} \sum_{i=1}^{n} \delta_{i,1} k_i d_i - \frac{ND^2}{2P} \right\}$$

$$+ \frac{1}{2} \sum_{i=1}^{n} h_i d_i k_i T + \left\{ \frac{S_v}{N} + \sum_{i=1}^{n} \frac{(C_i + A_i)}{k_i} \right\} \frac{1}{T} . \qquad (6)$$

Since the vendor must produce sufficient stock over the N-period cycle to meet the demands $D_1, D_2, \ldots\ldots, D_N$, total production must equal total demand over a cycle. Hence

$$(F+S)PT = \sum_{j=1}^{N} D_j = D_{1,N} = NDT$$

where, as before, D is the demand rate per unit time of all the buyers. Also, since no stockouts or late deliveries are permitted

$$(S+1)PT \geq D_{1,1} = D_1$$

$$(S+j)PT \geq D_{1,j} \qquad \text{for all } j = 1, 2, \dots, b.$$

Substituting the surplus stock Ψ at time D_1 by replacing $(1+S)PT$ by $\psi + D_1$, the constraints now become

$$(1+S)PT = \Psi + D_1 \geq D_1$$

$$(j+S)PT = \Psi + D_1 + (j-1)PT \geq D_{1,j} \qquad j = 2, \dots, b$$

i.e.,

$$\Psi \geq 0$$

$$\Psi + (j-1)PT \geq \sum_{i=1}^{n} \left\{ k_i d_i T \left(\sum_{t=2}^{j} \delta_{i,t} \right) \right\} \qquad 2 \leq j \leq b. \qquad (7)$$

The objective is now to find the non-negative values for N, k_i, $\delta_{i,t}$ and ψ that minimise the cost expression (6) subject to satisfying the constraints (7).

A Synchronised Cycles Algorithm to Solve the Model

If buyer i, who orders every k_i periods apart, and places its orders as early as possible in each of its order cycles then $\delta_{i,1} = 1$ and $\delta_{i,rk+1} = 1$ for $r = 1$ to $N/k_i - 1$. If this happens for every buyer then it can be shown that $\Psi = 0$ and the total relevant cost can be written as

Total relevant cost =

$$\left\{ \frac{S_v}{NT} + \left[\frac{hD}{2} - \frac{hD^2}{2P} \right] NT \right\} + \left\{ \sum_{i=1}^{n} \left(\frac{C_i + A_i}{k_i T} + d_i \left[\frac{h}{P} \sum_{i=1}^{n} d_i - \frac{1}{2}(h - h_i) \right] k_i T \right) \right\}.$$

This is a function of NT and $k_i T$. Thus we can arbitrarily set $T = 1$. However, the k_i are a function of N or vice versa, since k_i have to be multiples of N. So we can use this expression to find the k_i for a given N. We cannot use it to find the optimal N. For fixed N and T, it can be shown that when

$$\frac{h}{P} d_i \sum_{i=1}^{n} d_i - \frac{1}{2}(h - h_i) d_i > 0,$$

the total relevant cost above is a convex function of k_i and we need to search for the minimum point. However, if

$$\frac{h}{P} d_i \sum_{i=1}^{n} d_i - \frac{1}{2}(h - h_i) d_i \leq 0,$$

the total relevant cost is a monotone decreasing function of k_i and the optimal solution should be as large as possible, i.e., $k_i = N$. Hence, a simple sub-algorithm can be used to search for optimal k_i for fixed N and T. Clearly we have to ensure that the k_i values found are multiples of the current N.

We can embed this procedure to determine the k_i given N within a systematic search over all values of N from 1 to 365. For each value of N, a sub-algorithm determines the optimal values for k_i for each buyer for that N on a cost minimisation basis, but only allowing values of k_i that are factors of N. The complete algorithm is as follows:

Synchronised Cycles Algorithm

Step 1: Set $N = 1$ and $T = 1$.

Step 2: Use Sub-Algorithm to find the optimal k_i^* values for fixed N and T.

Step 3: If $N < 365$, then set $N = N + 1$ and go back to *Step 2*.

Step 4: Take the N which gives the least total relevant cost.

Sub-Algorithm to find Optimal k_i for fixed N and T

Step 1: Find all factors of N.

Step 2: If $\dfrac{h}{P}d_i \sum_{i=1}^{n} d_i - \dfrac{1}{2}(h - h_i)d_i > 0$, then go to *Step 3*. Otherwise set $k_i^* = N$ & exit.

Step 3: Calculate $\quad \Phi = \dfrac{C_i + A_i}{\left[\dfrac{hD}{P} - \dfrac{1}{2}(h - h_i) \right] \times d_i T^2}$

Step 4: Find $\quad k_i^*(k_i^* - 1) \le \Phi \le k_i^*(k_i^* + 1)$

Step 5: If $N \le k_i^*$, then set $k_i^* = N$ and exit.

Step 6: If k_i^* is a factor of N, then exit. Otherwise go to *Step 7*.

Step 7: Find two consecutive integers k_i^a and k_i^b, which are factors of N and

$$k_i^a \le k_i^* \le k_i^b$$

Step 8: If $f(k_i^a) < f(k_i^b)$, then set $k_i^* = k_i^a$. Otherwise set $k_i^* = k_i^b$

$$\text{where} \quad f(k_i) = \frac{C_i + A_i}{k_i T} + d_i \left(\frac{h}{P} \sum_{i=1}^{n} d_i - \frac{1}{2}(h - h_i) \right) \times k_i T$$

We have applied the synchronised cycles algorithm assuming $T = 1$. It is simple to extend it to search over other values of T below 1. These should all be of the form $T = 1/\text{integer}$.

Common Cycle Solution

This is a special case of the general synchronised cycles algorithm. If all buyers adopt a common order cycle placing orders every kT periods of time apart (e.g., Banerjee & Burton, 1994), it is equivalent to setting $\delta_{i,1} = 1$, $T = 1$ and $k_i = k$ for all i in our proposed model. The main algorithm is the same. The sub-algorithm is applied in the same way to work out only one value, the common cycle value for k. Step 3 needs to be modified to redefine Φ as follows

$$\Phi = \frac{\displaystyle\sum_{i=1}^{n}(C_i + A_i)}{\displaystyle\sum_{i=1}^{n} d_i \left[\frac{hD}{P} - \frac{1}{2}(h - h_i) \right]}$$

and $f(k_i)$ in step 8 modified similarly.

Results

Some numerical experiments have been carried out to illustrate the performance of the synchronised cycles algorithm. These results have compared with those obtained from the common cycle method as well as with that of buyers and a supplier operate independently. Three examples are used in our experiments. The data are shown in Appendix A. Example 1 is that used by Banerjee and Burton (1994) (see their Table 1.). Since this example has only five buyers, data were randomly generated for 30 buyers and 50 buyers in example 2 and example 3, respectively. This enables us to see if the results for the many buyer case differ from those with only a few buyers. As can be seen from the objective function, expression (6), of the problem, the vendor's holding cost as well as total relevant cost depends directly on the ratio D/P, the ratio of the system demand per period to the vendor's production rate per period. Different values of D/P may have different effects on different models. We therefore also include a full range of different values of D/P from 0.1, 0.2, ..., up to 0.9 for comparisons in our experiments.

The results enable us to see how allowing each buyer to have its own individual cycle rather than follow a common cycle performs. These results are shown in Table 1, 2 and 3 for Example 1, Example 2 and Example 3, respectively. The independent model has been adjusted as proposed in Section 2 to carry a safety stock so as to ensure that the vendor never has a shortage, nor failure to meet any buyer's order on time. Thus all three models are compared on the same basis of satisfying all demand on time.

For Example 1, it can be seen from Table 1 that the performances of our synchronised cycles algorithm and the common cycle model of Banerjee and Burton (1994) are approximately the same and both of them outperform the independent policy over the whole range of D/P. The improvement of the synchronised cycles algorithm over the independent policy ranges from 20% to 37%. As D/P increases, the improvement decreases. For D/P equal to 0.1 and 0.2, the synchronised cycles solution is as good as that of the common cycle method and the planning horizon (i.e., NT) suggested by the two models are virtually the same. For D/P ranging from 0.3 to 0.9, the synchronised cycles solution is slightly better by an average of about 1%. The NT of the synchronised cycles solution is shorter when $D/P = 0.4$ and 0.5 but longer for other D/P values. It can also be observed that when D/P increases, the planning horizon of both of the co-ordinated models tends to increase. In the independent policy, the total relevant cost decreases as D/P increases. This is to be expected as the vendor's holding costs are proportional to $1 - D/P$. However, the total relevant cost of the synchronised cycles solutions only increases as D/P increases from 0.1 to 0.5 (or 0.6), and then decreases as D/P increases further. The change of the total relevant cost along with the change of D/P is data and solution dependent (i.e., d_i, k_i, N), this can be verified from expression (6).

For the results of Example 2, Table 2 shows that the performance of the synchronised cycles algorithm is better than the common cycle method by an average of about 9%. The synchronised cycles algorithm also performs better than the independent policy over the whole range of D/P by an average of about 4.5%. However, the common cycle method performs worse than the independent policy by an average of about 5%. As the case in Example 1, the improvement of the synchronised cycles algorithm over the independent policy decreases as D/P increases. The decrease is from 6.1% down to 3%. When D/P increases, the planning horizon of the two co-ordinated models increases while the total relevant cost decreases. The total relevant cost of both of the two co-ordinated models decreases by about 10% when D/P increases from 0.1 to 0.9.

Table 1. Results of Example 1

$\alpha = D/P$	Synchronised Cycles Algorithm		Common Cycle Method Banerjee and Burton (1994)			Independent Policy
	N	Total Relevant Cost	N	T	Total Relevant Cost	Total Relevant Cost
0.1	45	23.19	1	44.7645	23.19	36.58
0.2	44	23.83	1	43.5617	23.83	35.92
0.3	56	24.25	1	42.4510	24.45	35.23
0.4	56	24.43	2	31.8049	24.78	34.48
0.5	56	24.61	2	31.8049	24.78	33.67
0.6	78	24.60	2	31.8049	24.78	32.77
0.7	78	24.31	3	28.5255	24.70	31.75
0.8	78	24.02	3	29.0154	24.29	30.54
0.9	144	23.16	5	27.1426	23.51	28.96

Table 2. Results of Example 2

$\alpha = D/P$	Synchronised Cycles Algorithm		Common Cycle Method Banerjee and Burton (1994)			Independent Policy
	N	Total Relevant Cost	N	T	Total Relevant Cost	Total Relevant Cost
0.1	24	99.02	5	5.24389	108.32	105.45
0.2	24	98.43	5	5.28060	107.56	104.27
0.3	30	97.53	5	5.31809	106.51	103.01
0.4	30	96.62	6	5.20255	105.97	101.65
0.5	36	95.62	6	5.25197	104.98	100.18
0.6	36	94.43	7	5.19496	103.84	98.55
0.7	48	93.11	8	5.17656	102.48	96.70
0.8	60	91.22	10	5.14003	100.78	94.50
0.9	60	88.88	14	5.11872	98.41	91.64

Table 3. Results of Example 3

$\alpha = D/P$	Synchronised Cycles Algorithm		Common Cycle Method Banerjee and Burton (1994)			Independent Policy
	N	Total Relevant Cost	N	T	Total Relevant Cost	Total Relevant Cost
0.1	48	729.36	19	2.82723	814.15	767.43
0.2	60	723.68	20	2.82822	808.28	760.89
0.3	60	717.41	21	2.83257	802.00	753.94
0.4	60	711.06	23	2.82549	795.21	746.46
0.5	72	703.71	25	2.82571	787.77	738.34
0.6	84	695.88	28	2.82283	779.46	729.35
0.7	96	686.46	32	2.82294	769.94	719.15
0.8	120	674.75	40	2.81600	758.52	707.04
0.9	180	660.23	56	2.81553	743.43	691.27

The results for Example 3, presented in Table 3, also have the synchronised cycles algorithm performing better than that of the common cycle method. On average, the synchronised cycles algorithm is better by 10.7%. The synchronised cycles model is better than the independent policy over the whole range of D/P by an average of 4.7%. As in Example 2, the common cycle model is always worse than the independent policy, and the average is 6.7%. Contrary to the results for Example 1 and 2, the improvement of the synchronised cycles algorithm over the independent policy does not decrease as D/P increases. Instead, the improvement stays rather stable over the range of 4.5% to 5%.

Solutions were also derived for the three examples allowing T to take lower values than 1. For examples 1 and 2, the solutions for T = 0.5 and T = 0.25 were exactly the same as for T = 1. For example 3, there were further noticeable savings on those given for T = 1. The major change was to decrease the number of orders placed by the buyers so saving on the vendor's order processing and shipment costs. So obviously in some circumstances it is worthwhile to include a search over T in the general algorithm. However, one should point out that fractional values for T would only be applied in practice if the periods were weeks or months. Fractional values for days cannot be implemented, unless $k_i T$ is an integer for all buyers.

The synchronised cycles algorithm is a heuristics based on particular properties of the objective function and the constraints. An estimate of the "optimal" solution and cost can be found by using some more general heuristics search method, such as simulated annealing or genetic algorithms.

Conclusions

From the results shown in Table 1, 2 and 3, it can be seen that the synchronised cycles algorithm of allowing each buyer to adopt his own order cycle can work better than restricting them to adopt a common order cycle placing order every kT periods of time apart. For a problem with a small number of buyers (e.g., five), the minimum cost solution for the synchronised cycles algorithm is only slightly better than the common cycle method of Banerjee and Burton (1994). But our synchronised cycles algorithm is significantly better for a problem of a moderately large size (e.g., 15 and 30 buyers). Adopting a common order cycle appears worse than the independent policy when the number of buyers is as large as 15 and 30, however, a large number of experiments would be needed to confirm if this is generally true. The reasons for this can be seen if we examine the way the system costs are made up in the different model solutions, in

Table 4. Costs for the buyers and for the vendor - Example 1

$\alpha = D/P$	Synchronised Cycles Algorithm			Common Cycle Method Banerjee and Burton (1994)			Independent Policy		
	Buyers' Cost	Vendor's Cost	Total Relevant Cost	Buyers' Cost	Vendor's Cost	Total Relevant Cost	Buyers' Cost	Vendor's Cost	Total Relevant Cost
0.1	12.54	10.30	22.84	12.49	10.70	23.19	7.95	28.63	36.58
0.2	12.33	10.93	23.26	12.24	11.59	23.83	7.95	27.97	35.92
0.3	10.37	13.22	23.59	12.00	12.45	24.45	7.95	27.28	35.23
0.4	10.37	13.21	23.58	9.95	14.83	24.78	7.95	26.53	34.48
0.5	10.37	13.18	23.55	9.95	14.83	24.78	7.95	25.72	33.67
0.6	9.37	14.27	23.64	9.95	14.83	24.78	7.95	24.82	32.77
0.7	9.37	13.80	23.17	9.39	15.31	24.70	7.95	23.80	31.75
0.8	9.37	13.32	22.69	9.47	14.82	24.29	7.95	22.59	30.54
0.9	9.01	11.98	20.99	9.18	14.33	23.51	7.95	21.01	28.96

Table 5. Costs for the buyers and for the vendor - Example 2

$\alpha = D/P$	Synchronised Cycles Algorithm			Common Cycle Method Banerjee and Burton (1994)			Independent Policy		
	Buyers' Cost	Vendor's Cost	Total Relevant Cost	Buyers' Cost	Vendor's Cost	Total Relevant Cost	Buyers' Cost	Vendor's Cost	Total Relevant Cost
0.1	77.70	21.32	99.02	86.67	21.65	108.32	76.60	28.85	105.45
0.2	77.70	20.73	98.43	86.69	20.87	107.56	76.60	27.67	104.27
0.3	77.21	20.32	97.53	86.72	20.09	106.51	76.60	26.41	103.01
0.4	77.21	19.41	96.62	86.64	19.33	105.97	76.60	25.05	101.65
0.5	77.20	18.42	95.62	86.67	18.31	104.98	76.60	23.58	100.18
0.6	77.10	17.33	94.43	86.64	17.20	103.84	76.60	21.95	98.55
0.7	77.01	16.10	93.11	86.63	15.85	102.48	76.60	20.10	96.70
0.8	76.84	14.38	91.22	86.62	14.16	100.78	76.60	17.90	94.50
0.9	76.84	12.04	88.88	86.62	11.79	98.41	76.60	15.04	91.64

Table 6. Costs for the buyers and for the vendor - Example 3

$\alpha = D/P$	Synchronised Cycles Algorithm			Common Cycle Method Banerjee and Burton (1994)			Independent Policy		
	Buyers' Cost	Vendor's Cost	Total Relevant Cost	Buyers' Cost	Vendor's Cost	Total Relevant Cost	Buyers' Cost	Vendor's Cost	Total Relevant Cost
0.1	505.33	224.03	729.36	570.34	243.81	814.15	476.05	291.38	767.43
0.2	504.91	218.76	723.67	570.38	237.90	808.28	476.05	284.84	760.89
0.3	504.43	212.97	717.40	570.59	231.41	802.00	476.05	277.89	753.94
0.4	504.43	206.63	711.06	570.26	224.95	795.21	476.05	270.41	746.46
0.5	505.48	198.23	703.71	570.27	217.50	787.77	476.05	262.29	738.34
0.6	504.88	191.00	695.88	570.13	209.33	779.46	476.05	253.30	729.35
0.7	505.33	181.13	686.46	570.14	199.80	769.94	476.05	243.10	719.15
0.8	502.74	172.01	674.75	569.82	188.70	758.52	476.05	230.99	707.04
0.9	503.18	157.05	660.23	569.80	173.63	743.43	476.05	215.22	691.27

particular the division of the system costs between the vendor and the buyers. This is shown in Tables 4, 5 and 6.

Comparing both the synchronised cycles and the common cycle policies with the independent policy shows that both make a significant reduction in the vendor's cost compared to the independent policy. However, the cost to all the buyers is significantly increased. This appears to be a general result that applies in all analyses of co-ordinated ordering, inventory and production planning models. The vendor is motivated to seek to co-ordinate decisions in the whole supply chain but the buyers are not. Hence, the interest in examining what price and quantity discounts are needed from the vendor to motivate the buyers to change their policies to allow the savings from co-ordination to be achieved.

On average the common cycle policy for all buyers increases their costs by 32.2%, 13.1% and 19.8% for examples 1, 2 and 3, respectively, compared to the independent policy. It saves on average 45%, 22.7% and 17.4% on the vendor's costs. In example 1, the buyers' costs for the independent policy are under one third of the vendor's costs. Since the vendor incurs around three quarters of the system cost in example 1, the large saving for the vendor more than outweighs the increase in cost for the buyers so that there is overall a moderate saving for the system compared to the independent policy. In example 2, the buyers' costs in total make up 77% of the system cost whilst in example 3 it is 65%. Thus in both these examples the increases in the buyers' costs of 13.1% and 19.8% are far greater than the savings of 22.7% and 17.4% in the vendor's costs, for examples 2 and 3, respectively. Thus a tentative conclusion, which of course needs much more experimentation, is that the common cycle method for co-ordination in a supply chain will only be advantageous compared to the independent policy if the vendor's costs make up the greater proportion of the total supply chain ordering and inventory holding costs. This will apply if there are few buyers in the system.

In the many buyers examples 2 and 3, the buyers' costs in the independent policy made up 77% and 65% of the total system costs. In addition there was a wide range of buyer demands per period, from 2 to 39 units in example 2 and 1 to 50 units in example 3. In these circumstances forcing the buyers to adopt a common ordering cycle will be a long way away from their independent optimal intervals so increasing the costs for both the large and the small demand buyers particularly. Hence in these two examples the common cycle policy was much worse than the independent policy.

By contrast, the synchronised cycles policy had a much smaller increase in the buyers' costs, as it was designed to do, than the common cycle policy but also gave a larger reduction in the vendor's cost also. It is the combination of these two factors that gave the synchronised cycles policy over the common cycle policy over all of the examples studied.

The number of k_i which can be varied in the synchronised cycles algorithm is limited by the number of buyers in the problem. Obviously, when the number of buyers is small, the improvement obtained by the synchronised cycles algorithm is rather limited. However, when the number of buyers increases, the synchronised cycles algorithm has a larger freedom of varying the k_i's such that the total relevant cost can be decreased further and the performance can therefore be much better than restricting all k_i to a common value.

These three examples show that the benefits of co-ordination through synchronisation of ordering will depend on the specific situation pertaining to a supply chain. Serendipitously, they cover a range of situations and actions needed to obtain the savings in practice. For example 1, it can be seen from Table 4 that the total system cost for the synchronised cycles algorithm solution is sometimes less than the vendor's cost alone in the independent cycles policy. Thus if the vendor in this case implemented a vendor managed inventory system, of managing and replenishing the stock at the buyers' premises, it would reduce the costs to the vendor. This is provided that the vendor pays no extra holding costs for storing items at the buyers' premises compared to storage at its own factory. In the case of example 2, see Table 5, the buyers' costs only increased by an average of about 0.8%. The buyers are unlikely to notice such a small increase and so would probably accept the order day schedule imposed by the vendor that the algorithm would suggest. In the case of example 3, see Table 6, the buyers' costs are increased on average by 6%. The vendor makes a large saving. Thus the vendor would need to offer some incentive to the buyers to adopt the order day schedule indicated by the algorithm. The vendor would need to offer a price or quantity discount to the buyers, which has been suggested in recent literature as a workable device. Thus an interesting by-product of this research is that co-ordination in supply chains can achieve savings for both the vendor and the buyers without having to work out complicated schemes to share the benefits between the partners.

This analysis, albeit on a very limited range of examples, shows that the synchronised cycles model can be used to plan the ordering intervals in a one-vendor many-buyer supply chain so as to significantly reduce the system costs compared to each partner operating completely independently. The precise impact on each partners' costs and therefore what motivation the vendor will need to offer the buyers to change will depend on the particular circumstances of that supply chain. The cost reductions achieved by co-ordination across the supply chain by this model do not depend upon the vendor dictating what the order quantities for each buyer should be. The buyers can freely choose these. The use of this synchronised cycles model would seem to be a fruitful way for the partners in a supply chain to seek to co-ordinate their activities without any one partner forcing the others to change their activities to suit that partner's interest.

Acknowledgments

This research is supported by the Research Committee of The Hong Kong Polytechnic University.

References

Banerjee, A. (1986a). On a quantity discount pricing model to increase vendor profit. *Management Science, 32*, 1513-1517.

Banerjee, A. (1986b). A joint economic lot-size model for purchaser and vendor. *Decision Sciences, 17*, 292-311.

Banerjee, A., & Banerjee, S. (1994). A coordinated order-up-to inventory control policy for a single supplier and multiple buyers using electronic data interchange. *International Journal of Production Economics, 35*, 85-91.

Banerjee, A., & Burton, J.S. (1994). Coordinated vs. independent inventory replenishment policies for a vendor and multiple buyers. *International Journal of Production Economics, 35*, 215-222.

Chan, C.K., & Kingsman, B.G. (2003). *Co-ordination in a single-vendor multi-buyer supply chain by synchronizing ordering and production cycles.* Working Paper, Department of Applied Mathematics, The Hong Kong Polytechnic University, Hong Kong.

Dada, M., & Srikanth, K.N. (1987). Pricing policies for quantity discounts. *Management Science, 33*, 1247-1252.

Goyal, S.K. (1976). An integrated inventory model for a single supplier-single customer problem. *International Journal of Production Research, 15*(1), 107-111.

Goyal, S.K. (1987). Comment on generalized quantity discount pricing model to increase supplier's profits. *Management Science, 33*, 1635-1636.

Goyal, S.K. (1988). A joint economic-lot-size model for purchaser and vendor: A comment. *Decision Sciences, 19*, 236-241.

Goyal, S.K. (1995). A one-vendor multi-buyer integrated inventory model: A comment. *European Journal of Operational Research, 82*, 209-210.

Haessler, R. (1979). Improved extended basic period procedure for solving the Economic Lot Scheduling Problem. *AIIE Trans., 11*(4), 336-340.

Hill, R.M. (1997). The single-vendor single-buyer integrated production-inventory model with a generalised policy. *European Journal of Operational Research, 97*, 493-499.

Joglekar, P.N. (1988). Comments on a quantity discount pricing model to increase vendor profits. *Management Science, 34*, 1391-1398.

Joglekar, P.N., & Tharthare, S. (1990). The individually responsible and rational decision approach to economic lot sizes for one vendor and many purchasers. *Decision Sciences, 21*(3), 492-506.

Lal, R., & Staelin, R. (1984). An approach for developing an optimal discount pricing policy. *Management Science, 30*, 1524-1539.

Lee, H.L., & Rosenblatt, M.J. (1986). A generalized quantity discount pricing model to increase supplier's profits. *Management Science, 32*, 1177-1185.

Lu, L. (1995). A one-vendor multi-buyer integrated inventory model. *European Journal of Operational Research, 81*, 312-323.

Monahan, J.P. (1984). A quantity discount pricing model to increase vendor profits. *Management Science, 30*, 720-726.

Pan, J.C.H., & Yang, J.S. (2002). A study of an integrated inventory with controllable lead time. *International Journal of Production Research, 40*(5), 2002.

Pujawan, I.N., & Kingsman, B.G. (2002). Joint optimisation of timing synchronization in a buyer supplier inventory system. *International Journal of Operations and Quantitative Management* (under review).

Viswanathan, S., & Pipkani, R. (2001). Coordinating supply chain inventories through common replenishment epochs. *European Journal of Operational Research, 129*, 277-286.

Woo, Y.Y., Hsu, S. L., & Wu, S. (2001). An integrated inventory model for a single vendor and multiple buyers with ordering cost reduction. *International Journal of Production Economics, 73*, 203-215.

Appendix A

Example 1

Buyer i	d_i	C_i	A_i	h_i
1	8	40	20	0.008
2	15	40	15	0.009
3	10	40	6	0.010
4	5	40	10	0.010
5	20	40	18	0.007

Total demand rate of all the buyers: D = 58
Vendor's setup cost: S_v = 250
Vendor's holding cost: h = 0.005

Example 2

Buyer i	d_i	C_i	A_i	h_i
1	21	1	9	0.076
2	25	1	14	0.050
3	25	1	23	0.046
4	26	1	16	0.069
5	15	1	19	0.011
6	6	1	10	0.091
7	2	1	24	0.011
8	27	1	8	0.067
9	6	1	16	0.026
10	10	1	6	0.059
11	20	1	8	0.068
12	39	1	20	0.065
13	28	1	21	0.039
14	31	1	6	0.051
15	37	1	19	0.040

Total demand rate of all the buyers: D = 318
Vendor's setup cost: S_v = 250
Vendor's holding cost: h = 0.003

Example 3

Buyer i	d_i	C_i	A_i	h_i
1	33	2	2	0.120
2	25	12	10	0.273
3	10	1	38	0.424
4	4	3	31	0.298
5	35	9	28	0.064
6	31	4	16	0.715
7	41	27	29	0.183
8	4	7	1	0.214
9	46	8	7	0.284
10	33	12	31	0.245
11	28	27	16	0.028
12	18	5	5	0.332
13	42	29	14	0.200
14	40	11	11	0.376
15	43	13	34	0.461

Buyer i	d_i	C_i	A_i	h_i
16	47	3	29	0.186
17	26	6	16	0.763
18	29	19	32	0.007
19	11	1	23	0.126
20	22	15	34	0.184
21	11	14	18	0.474
22	3	17	26	0.421
23	45	12	30	0.433
24	34	17	32	0.171
25	50	28	24	0.197
26	42	5	18	0.577
27	5	14	6	0.037
28	45	27	6	0.315
29	50	7	35	0.161
30	10	19	17	0.594

Total demand rate of all the buyers: D = 863
Vendor's setup cost: S_v = 3000
Vendor's holding cost: h = 0.0028

Chapter II

Multi-Stage Efficiency Tools for Goal Setting and Monitoring in Supply Chains

Marvin D. Troutt, Kent State University, USA

Paul J. Ambrose, University of Wisconsin - Milwaukee, USA

Chi Kin Chan, The Hong Kong Polytechnic University, Hong Kong

Abstract

This chapter discusses the extension and potential application of some recent theoretical results on efficiency monitoring and throughput rate optimization for serial processes. In particular, we consider the relevance and adaptation of these results for use in monitoring and continuous improvement uses in supply chains or networks, with particular emphasis on the importance to e-business. Linear programming models based on ideas from Data Envelopment Analysis have been developed for maximizing the throughput of serial input-output processes in which one or more outputs of an upstream process become inputs to a successor process. We consider their adaptation to supply chain monitoring. We also propose some additional research needs in this area.

Introduction

A supply chain or network may be considered to be a set of linked processes connecting downstream customers to upstream suppliers, factories, distribution centers and retailers. Chopra and Meindl (2003) discuss a point of relevance to supply chain management of efficiency frontiers. In particular, they note that the supply chain should ideally operate on the cost-responsiveness efficiency frontier. In this chapter, we explore several other efficiency connections in supply chain links.

Some basic theory in this area has been developed in Troutt et al. (2001a). In that work, productive efficiencies between stages in a serial linkage of processes were modeled so that linear programming could be used to determine optimal throughput. This chapter proposes how these theoretical results might be extended and applied to supply chain management, especially to the monitoring of chains and supply networks for efficiency, capacity and continuous improvement.

This chapter is organized as follows. The second section discusses the importance of efficiency in the context of supply chains for e-business. The concepts of e-business and supply chains are reviewed. A particular form of e-business, the value net integrator, which focuses on supply chain management, is presented since the optimization model developed in this paper may have direct relevance to the operations of this e-business. In the next section, we review the previous theory results. In particular, a number of efficiency related issues that are relevant to optimal functioning of supply chains are raised, and salient LP models developed in previous research to address the issue of optimal throughput in supply chains are presented and extended. The chapter then considers how these results may be modified and extended to supply networks. Here, the application of the models developed is discussed with particular reference to centralized supply chains. Appropriate strategies for handling uncertainty when optimal value changes from period to period and efficiency bottlenecks are discussed. The fifth section provides a discussion with opportunities and needs for further research. Application of data envelopment analysis and stochastic programming to extend the research is discussed.

Further research to address issues such as variable returns to scale, efficiency bottlenecks, and multiple inputs/outputs across multiple processes is urged. The chapter concludes where the relevance of the research to e-businesses managing supply chains is discussed.

Importance from e-Business Perspective

The commercialization of the Internet in the mid-1990s saw the advent of new opportunities for organizations to market products and services to customers. Organizations are now able to access hitherto untapped markets for existing products and services. For example, Barnes and Noble, through its online store, is now able to reach markets not serviced by its physical stores. The Internet permits organizations to develop new technology enabled products or services, and increases the extent to which customer needs are fulfilled through personalization of the marketing message and customization of products and services. For example, priceline.com has implemented a "name-your-price" reverse auction system to sell airline tickets. Dell.com lets customers configure their computers to their needs. Amazon.com is able to provide instant recommendations based on past purchase patterns.

The use of the Internet to support various business activities that a firm may engage in is termed e-business. Weill and Vitale (2001) provide a formal definition of e-business as, "Marketing, buying, selling, delivering, servicing, and paying for products, services, and information across (nonproprietary) networks linking an enterprise and its prospects, customers, agents, suppliers, competitors, allies, and complementors." This broad-based definition captures the essence of e-business, which is doing business using open, non-proprietary electronic networks such as the Internet. The various types of e-businesses that exist can be classified as B2B (businesses selling to businesses), B2C (businesses selling to individual consumers), C2C (individuals selling to individual consumers), and C2B (individuals selling to businesses).

B2Cs are the most visible forms of e-businesses. However, in terms of value transacted, B2Bs are much larger than B2Cs. In 2002 in the U.S., $800 billion was transacted in B2Bs as compared to $78 billion in B2Cs (eMarketer, 2003). The B2B is characterized by various business models. A business model is a set of planned business activities designed to generate profits for an organization (Laudon & Traver, 2003). B2B business models include direct-to-customer (selling directly to customers), intermediary (bringing buyers and sellers together), and models that electronically manage the supply chain (Weill & Vitale, 2001). Of particular importance are models that manage supply chains discussed next.

A supply chain consists of a set of business entities that are involved in the design and development of new products and services, their manufacture through procurement of raw materials and transformation to finished goods, and the distribution of goods to end customers (Swaminathan & Tayur, 2003). Supply chain management (SCM) refers to the efficient management of the end-to-end process of designing, planning and forecasting, sourcing though complex supplier networks, manufacturing, and distributing products from raw material to the end customer, and the final disposal of the product by the customer (Smock, 2003; Swaminathan & Tayur, 2003). The goals of SCM include reducing costs, standardizing, simplifying, and reducing inventories, and maximizing profits from assets by responding efficiently to customer requirements. This involves rapid and accurate response to customer needs with no waste and with zero defects.

Supply chain management has its roots in the 1950s research on inventory management (Graves, Kan, & Zipkin, 1993). However, the emergence of the concept of supply chain management can be traced to the 1980s when Chrysler revolutionized the role of purchasing materials to reflect managed material flow from raw materials to finished products (Smock, 2003). Over the years, research on supply chains has evolved from inventory management from a centralized perspective to a contemporary focus on analyzing supply chain coordination problems, modeling the integration of information availability across the supply chain, modeling supply contracts and demand forecasting, and modeling the integration of product design with supply chain management (Graves & de Kok, 2003).

While logistics and product distribution are vital to supply chain management, the actual benefits emerge through optimized demand forecasting, supplier management, and product development (Smock, 2003). Thus, successful SCM focuses on understanding and managing customer demand, the front end of a supply chain, rather than on improving logistics or the backend of the supply chain. SCM purports to answer questions such as how much inventory of different semi-finished and finished goods should be stored to realize expected service levels, and should suppliers be required to deliver goods just-in-time. A failure to anticipate customer demand and appropriately manage inventory leads to supply chain inefficiencies such as poor inventory utilization, information distortion (bullwhip effect), high stock-outs, non-responsive supply chains, and poor customer service (Fisher, Hammond, Obermeyer, & Raman, 1994; Lee & Tang, 1997; Lee & Billington, 1992; Swaminathan & Tayur, 1998; Swaminathan & Tayur, 2003).

However, accurate end-customer demand forecasting is not easy. Uncertainty surrounds demand forecasting, as it is difficult to obtain and model all relevant information that is required for accurate demand forecasting. In addition, accurate demand forecasting requires adjusting demand based on real-time data, which again is difficult to obtain. Consequently, demand is often over- or under-forecasted leading to inefficiencies in the supply chain. The advent of the Internet has greatly contributed to better demand forecasting. The use of the Internet to collect, synthesize, and share information required for forecasting has helped reduce uncertainty. While the Internet has helped reduce uncertainty, it has not eliminated it. However, the Internet has increased the ability to capture and model real-time data, and share the forecasted demand in real-time with the various supply chain entities. This has helped improve the overall efficiency of supply chains.

Management of information flow across the supply chain is also known as *virtual* supply chain management in contrast to *physical* supply chain management, which focuses on the flow of goods and services across the supply chain (Rayport & Sviokla, 1995). Since the mid-1990s several firms such as Cisco and Seven Eleven Japan have entered into the business of virtual supply chain management, made possible largely by the commercial use of the Internet

Figure 1: Value Net Integrator

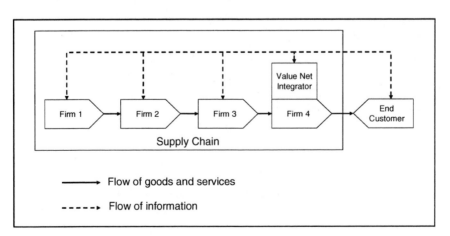

(Weill & Vitale, 2001). These e-businesses are typically the key entity in a supply chain that has the best access to information required for the various supply chain entities. The business model on which these e-businesses operate is known as "Value Net (or Supply Chain) Integrator" (Weill & Vitale, 2001), and Figure 1 depicts this business model.

Figure 1 depicts the value net integrator as an extension of firm 4. Typically the firm closest to the end customer has the maximum information about the end customer, and firms such as Seven Eleven and Cisco have capitalized on this access to expand into managing the virtual supply chain. However, value net integration can be done by any supply chain entity or even by an independent firm. Figure 1 shows a simplified, linear representation of the supply chain, which in reality would be a network of entities.

The value net integrator helps coordinate the supply chain by gathering, synthesizing, and distributing information to improve supply chain operations. The success of these e-businesses would largely depend on the ability to rapidly gather, synthesize, and distribute accurate static and real-time information to enable both strategic and tactical decision-making by supply chain entities. The ability to synthesize information will be greatly enhanced by the availability of analytical models that can synthesize information to yield useful metrics that can be used in procurement-, production-, and distribution-related decision-making. In this paper we present one such analytical model that will help coordinate the flow of goods and services across the supply chain. We develop a model that will help optimize the outputs of each entity in the supply chain so that they match the inputs required by the entity that consumes the outputs as inputs. The model developed helps determine the optimal throughput in a supply chain and establish the minimal levels of inventory to be held in the buffers between the successive producing and consuming entities.

Review of Basic Theory Results

Some basic theory results on optimal throughput were proposed in Troutt et al. (2001a). These results considered an abstract, serially linked set of input-output processes representative generally of the value chain or a supply chain (Chopra & Meindl, 2003), as in Figures 2 and 3.

These results concentrated on what may be called optimal monetary throughput planning. This approach determines the relative proportions and levels of outputs to target for production at each stage or process during a cycle in order to maximize the output value at the end of the chain. Two programming models were proposed, depending on whether buffers were permitted between stages. These models were for strictly serial chains in which exactly one process follows or precedes each process in the sequence. However, most chains fall into the general serial model depicted in Figure 2. Namely, the overall supply chain may be considered as a sequence of processes and buffers in which the outputs of one process become the inputs of the next process. In fact, more abstractly, the value chain itself may be regarded as a connected series of input-output processes as in Figure 4.

Supply chains can usually be described similarly to the value chain, but with more detail at each stage. That is, each stage of the value chain can be subdivided into further detailed stages. New product development requires monetary inputs of capital and expenses and then yields outputs of materials and labor, which in turn yield outputs of new products. These new products

Figure 2. Serial process model

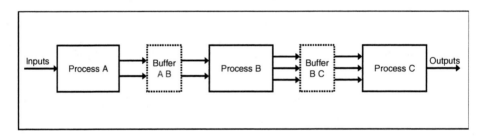

Figure 3. A link with scalar initial inputs and final outputs

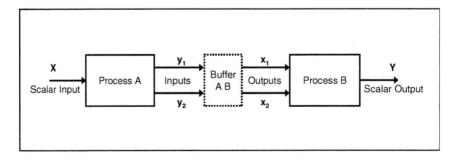

Figure 4. Value chain as based on Chopra and Meindl (2003, p. 28).

become inputs to the suite of products available for marketing and sales. With this set of products and other monetary inputs, marketing and sales produces a stream of orders. The generated orders, along with additional capital and expenses, forecasts and warehouse usages, become inputs to operations, which in turn produce outputs of completed orders, scrap and rework, warrantee repair, and inventory changes. Capital and expenses, orders, and completed sales become inputs to service operations which yield completed sales transactions, and finally profits. Other examples of multiple input and output links are given in Table 1 of Troutt et al. (2001a).

Each of the processes may have differing productive efficiencies. In view of this, a number of questions arise. For example:

- Are the outputs and inputs being produced in a congruent manner? That is, are there imbalances between the stages and sub-stages that lead to inefficiencies or bottlenecks?

- How do the differences in productivity impact the buffers? Are the buffers balanced and stable and, ideally, decreasing in sizes?

- How does the overall productive efficiency of the whole chain depend on that of the individual sub-process?

- Are there exploitable opportunities created by estimating the productivity differences? For example, inefficient sub-processes may signal needs for outsourcing, capacity expansion, or process re-engineering, while highly efficient ones may be targets for separate services, marketing or shifting of resources.

- Given available monetary inputs, what inputs and outputs should be targeted or planned-for at successive processes in order to maximize throughput value?

Modeling Results

The basic ideas of the optimal throughput model can best be introduced with a simple direct link of two processes: A and B. Let there be a scalar input to Process A and a scalar output to Process B. Further, suppose that Process A has two outputs, which in turn are the two inputs to Process B. Next, define:

X_t = input to Process A

y_{1t} = output 1 for Process A

y_{2t} = output 2 for Process A

x_{1t} = input 1 for Process B

Figure 5. Normalized scatter diagram and efficient frontier for process A outputs

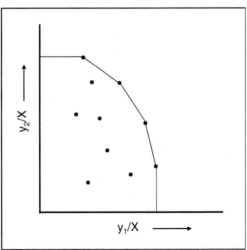

Figure 6. Normalized scatter diagram and efficient frontier for process B inputs

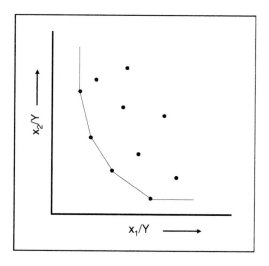

x_{2t} = input 2 for Process B

Y_t = output for Process B

In the case that no buffer is permitted between the processes, we have:

$$y_{1t} = x_{1t} \text{ and } y_{2t} = x_{2t}.$$

We assume that data on these inputs and outputs have been collected over periods $t = 1,...,T$. Consider the scatter diagram of the data pairs $(y_{1t}/X_t, y_{2t}/X_t)$. These data represent the output rates of y_1 and y_2 per unit of X. The scatter diagram will be of the form suggested in Figure 5 and may be called the normalized output of Process A.

The line connecting the extreme points represents the Pareto boundary, also called the efficient frontier. In the case of multiple inputs and outputs, the frontier is the Pareto-Koopmans boundary. For the scalar input case, all points on this frontier are assumed to be possible production pairs for a unit level of X. The efficient frontier points might be determined using Data Envelopment Analysis (DEA) (Charnes et al., 1994). However, due to the special structure of the problem, it will not be necessary to determine these efficient frontiers in advance. Similarly, the data for Process B can be represented by Figure 6.

Figure 7. Correspondence of input-output efficiency frontiers (The inputs of a downstream process (B) are the outputs of an immediately upstream process (A).)

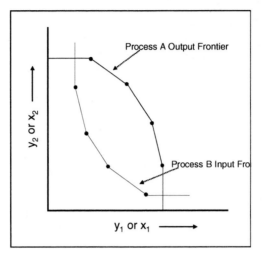

Figure 8. Optimal tangency of efficiency frontiers in the single input upstream and single output downstream process link

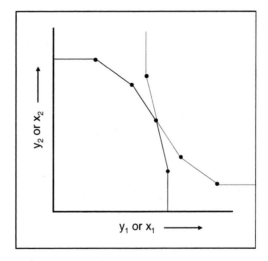

Intuitively, it appears that the output vectors of the upstream process should match the input vectors of the downstream process at the technically efficient boundaries (Figure 7 and Figure 8).

With these basic ideas, we may now state the general model. Let H^k, $k = 1$, ..., K be the set of observed input-output vectors available at the time of

Table 1. Hypothetical process data

Observed Data											
H^1			H^2					H^3			
Input	Outputs		Inputs		Outputs			Inputs			Output
x_1	y_1	y_2	X_1	x_2	y_1	y_2	y_3	x_1	x_2	x_3	y_1
110	25	36	20	24	4	4	9	5	3	8	351
108	18	35	19	25	5	3	7	5	4	5	294
121	27	34	31	40	6	7	10	6	5	11	315
141	30	41	20	35	6	10	8	7	6	12	407
114	26	37	27	30	7	5	10	8	8	10	396
119	29	32	24	37	6	7	11				
113	21	36	18	34	5	4	8				
115	25	38									

planning for the next cycle. Table 1 illustrates hypothetical data of the kind required. Thus, H^k is the set of vector pairs of the form $(x^{i,k}, y^{i,k})$, where $i = 1, \ldots, n\_k$ is the number of observed vectors for process k; with $x^{i,k} \in \Re^{k_1}$, and $y^{i,k} \in \Re^{k_2}$. Let $j = 1, \ldots, k_1$ index the coordinates of the $x^{i,k}$, and similarly $l = 1, \ldots, k_2$ index the coordinates of the $y^{i,k}$. In addition, we assume the components of these vectors are non-negative.

The set H^k defines the observed feasible technology for Process-k. We next utilize the concept of intensities. These are nonnegative multipliers of the input-output pairs

$(x^{i,k}, y^{i,k})$. They may be used to describe points on or inside the production possibilities sets in terms of linear combinations of the observed pairs (see, for example, Färe et al., 1985; Charnes et al., 1994). If $\lambda^k \geq 0$, $k = 1, \ldots, K$ are the intensities, then:

$$\left(\sum_{i=1}^{n\_k} \lambda_i^k x^{i,k}, \ \sum_{i=1}^{n\_k} \lambda_i^k y^{i,k} \right) \tag{1}$$

represents potentially feasible input and output vectors for Process-k that are formed as linear combinations of the existing data. Here, $\sum_{k=1}^{K} \lambda^k$ is unrestricted, which reflects constant returns to scale assumption. Since the output vector for Process-k becomes the input vector for Process-$(k+1)$, then the assumption of no buffers requires that

$$\sum_{i=1}^{n\_k} \lambda^k y^{i,k} = \sum_{i=1}^{n\_{k+1}} \lambda^{k+1} x^{i,k+1} \quad \text{for } k = 1, \ldots, K\text{-}1. \tag{2}$$

It should be noted that (2) is a vector equation, which holds for each coordinate. By requiring:

$$\sum_{i=1}^{n\_1} \lambda_i^1 x^{i,1} = 1, \tag{3}$$

we may propose a linear programming model to maximize throughput per unit of input at the first process. The resulting model, SLP is given as follows:

SLP: $\qquad \max \sum_{i=1}^{n\_K} \lambda_i^K y^{i,K}$ \hfill (4)

s. t. $\qquad \sum_{i=1}^{n\_k} \lambda_i^k y^{i,k} = \sum_{i=1}^{n\_{k+1}} \lambda_i^{k+1} x^{i,k+1}$, for each coordinate and

$$\text{for } k = 1, \ldots, K\text{-}1 \tag{5}$$

$$\sum_{i=1}^{n\_1} \lambda_i^1 x_i^1 = 1 \tag{6}$$

$\lambda_i^k \geq 0$ for all i and for all k.

In order to expand this model to the more realistic nonzero-buffer case, we consider maximal throughput planning for the series of processes at the beginning of a cycle. Here we also suppose that buffer vectors s^k exist between Processes-$(k$-$1)$ and k, with s^1 being the initial vector of inputs available at Process-1. Vector s^k is of the same dimension as the input vector for Process-k, $k = 1, \ldots, K$. This vector, or a portion p^k, with $p^k \leq s^k$, in each coordinate, can be used as input to Process-k. Thus, model SLP becomes model NSLP given by:

NSLP: $\qquad \max \ \sum_{i=1}^{n\_K} \lambda_i^K y^{i,K}$ $\qquad\qquad$ (7)

s. t. $\qquad \sum_{i=1}^{n\_k} \lambda_i^k y^{i,k} + p^{k+1} = \sum_{i=1}^{n\_{k+1}} \lambda_i^{k+1} x^{i,k+1}$ for each coordinate and

$\qquad\qquad\qquad\qquad\qquad\qquad\qquad$ for $k = 1, \ldots, K\text{-}1$ $\qquad$ (8)

$\qquad\qquad 0 \le p^{k+1} \le s^{k+1}$ $\qquad\qquad$ for each coordinate and

$\qquad\qquad\qquad\qquad\qquad\qquad\qquad$ for $k = 1, \ldots, K\text{-}1$ $\qquad$ (9)

$\qquad\qquad \sum_{i=1}^{n\_1} \lambda_i^1 x_i^1 = s^1$ $\qquad\qquad\qquad\qquad$ (10)

$\lambda_t^k \ge 0$ and $p^{k+1} \ge 0$ for all components, for all i, and for $k = 1, \ldots, K$.

In Troutt et al. (2001a), an illustration of model NSLP was developed using Table 1 data for the case in which the buffer vectors were: $s^1 = 130$, $s^2 = (1, 2)$, and $s^3 = (2, 4, 3)$. For that scenario, the model solution indicated that an optimal output level of 718.9817 at Process-3 could be obtained using the following intensities and portion vectors:

$\lambda^{1*} = (0,\ 0,\ 1.171171,\ 0,\ 0,\ 0,\ 0,\ 0)$

$\lambda^{2*} = (0,\ 0,\ 0,\ 0.100271,\ 0.929537,\ 0,\ 0.306595)$

$\lambda^{3*} = (1.636312, 0.491959, 0, 0, 0)$

$p^{1*} = 130$

$p^{2*} = (1.000000,\ 2.000000)$

$p^{3*} = (2.000000,\ 0,\ 3.000000).$

Our interpretation of this model solution is as follows. First, we note that that the data are rates per period, namely, rates of input usages and output rates. Thus, the solution above would require, with respect to Process-1, that the third observed data rate in H^1, be used by itself at an intensity of $\lambda_3^{1*} = 1.171171$. From Table 1, that observation is associated with input of 121 and outputs of 27 and 34, respectively. Namely, the ideal solution would strive to achieve outputs in the ratio of 27 and 34, and attempt to scale the pace of the operation or process up by a factor of about 17%, so that all the available input (here, $s^1 = 130$) is consumed. Thus, this plan would call for an increase in productive intensity or capacity, or a combination of both of these. That is, in addition to targeting outputs in the stated ratio, the pace of this process would need increased by 17% to utilize fully the available input of 130. Similarly, it will be noted that the sum of components in the optimal intensity vectors λ^{2*} and λ^{3*} also exceed unity, with similar interpretations. Such short-run intensity or capacity increases may or may not be possible.

A more conservative goal-setting plan could be developed by assuming that capacities must not exceed those that have been observed in the data represented in Table 1. For this approach the NSLP model would need modified by inclusion of constraints on the sum of the intensity vectors at each stage. In particular, for the most conservative plan formulation, the following constraints would need to be added:

$$\sum_{i=1}^{n\_1} \lambda_i^1 = 1 \ , \quad \sum_{i=1}^{n\_2} \lambda_i^2 = 1 \ , \quad \text{and} \quad \sum_{i=1}^{n\_3} \lambda_i^3 = 1. \tag{11}$$

More generally, the right-hand sides in (11) might be adjusted to $1 + c^k, k = 1, \ldots, K$, where c^k indicates the planner's belief about the maximal scale increase that is possible for Process-k.

We may also note that constraint (10) can be relaxed to an inequality. Namely, in view of the maximization objective, all of the available input is expected to be consumed without need for directly forcing equality, as in the solution shown above, for which $p^{1*} = s^1 = 130$.

Applications to Supply Chains and Networks

We concentrate on centralized supply chains in this chapter, as this case facilitates the collection of the kind of data and monitoring of processes relevant to the present topic, and which may be more problematic in the decentralized case. Also, supply chains associated with very short product life-cycles, as for example, discussed in Higuchi and Troutt (2004), may not be able to generate sufficient data in time to utilize the present type of model.

We assume that observations have been collected over periods of intervals convenient to the supply chain. Thus, data such as that exhibited in Table 1 may be obtained at daily, weekly or other suitable intervals. For planning of optimal throughput, a complete cycle from materials and supplier receipts to completed sales appears to be a natural choice for a planning horizon. The situation is similar to aggregate production planning (APP) (see for instance, Chopra & Meindl, 2003; Silver et al., 1998; Vollman et al., 1997; Nam & Logendran, 1992; Dubois & Oliff, 1991; Hax & Candea, 1984). However, the choice of number of periods in the planning horizon is influenced differently in the present efficiency-based modeling approach. In APP, the number of periods in the horizon is usually governed by the number of periods for which reliable forecasts are available. Uncertainty in APP models arises because of unknown demand forecast errors. As first period demands become known, the planning model can be solved again in what is called rolling horizon planning. By analogy to the APP problem, we regard the rolling horizon assumption as also appropriate for the present planning model. That is, the model can be updated after each period with new output targets based on the buffers that result from implementing the plan in the first period of the last plan.

In the present model, uncertainty might be said to occur in that fully efficient outputs at the various stages tend to vary from trial to trial in a way that can be modeled probabilistically, leading to differing effects on the buffers. This kind of productivity variation has been discussed and modeled in Troutt et al. (2000, 2001c, 2003a, 2003b, 2003c). In particular, such efficiency variations can often be modeled based on transformations of probability density function models like the gamma or Weibull (see, for example, Law & Kelton, 1982). These two distributions have shape and scale parameters. The smaller is the shape parameter, the more heavily concentrated is the distribution on its mode, which corresponds to the ideal efficiency score of unity. Similarly, the scale parameter is related to variance of the distribution, with smaller being better. Process improvement can therefore be signaled by continual decrease of one or both of these parameters in such a way that the mean, corresponding to a mean deviation from full (unity) efficiency score, is also decreasing.

We note further that while technical efficiency of the various stages appears to be associated with optimal throughput, allocative efficiency also appears to play a role. As can be seen in Figure 8, the frontiers of adjacent stages may need to meet at a particular point. This may be called congruency between the stages. *Efficiency bottlenecks* may be said to occur in cases such as represented in Figure 7. Here, there is an overlap of frontiers, indicating a situation in which one or both of the adjacent stages have not operated at full efficiency.

The NSLP model may be used in a variety of different views. For example, the model might be applied at a micro-level such as to a single factory or facility, or a process such as shipping from a distribution center. More generally, the network may be cut (Ford & Fulkerson, 1962) in such a way as to combine stages or sub-processes into two or more input-output stages. Also, separate operational or financial views might be developed depending on whether the flows feature materials or monetary sums. In addition, a combined financial and operational view might be developed based on Figure 9.

Figure 9. Combined financial and operational view (Financial cost flows to the sub-processes may have further divisions such as material, labor, systems, etc., which are not shown.)

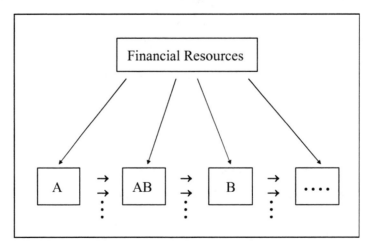

Discussion and Areas for Further Study

Data Envelopment Analysis (DEA) (Charnes et al., 1994) might be used to identify efficient frontiers. As seen here, the special structure of the present formulation permits computation of maximal throughput without prior identification of the efficient frontier. The DEA reduction may be useful in the case of larger data sets and may help reduce computation times, an issue for further study.

By permitting $l^k, k = 1, \ldots, K$, to be unrestricted in sum, the scale or intensity of the kth process is allowed to vary. This is subject to the requirement that the outputs plus any buffer amounts are to be used as the inputs for the succeeding process. A tacit assumption was that returns to scale are constant for each process. The case of variable returns to scale should be useful for further research. In general, we may expect continual improvement in process performances, so that efficient frontiers will tend to expand outward in the output sense or be reduced toward lower values in the input sense. This raises the possibility that targets on the right-hand sides in (11) might be set in anticipation of such improvements. That is, the c^k-values in (11) might be optimized, if information on the rate of process improvements and scale returns for the stages and processed can be gathered. By simulation, or simulation-optimization (Troutt et al., 2001c), optimal values of the c^k might be proposed. Also, values of c^k greater than zero may be useful for motivational goals or incentives with the aim of forcing such efficiency improvements. However, another viewpoint might be considered. If the efficiency variations are modeled by probability distributions, then throughput becomes stochastic and a stochastic programming (see, for example, Birge & Louveaux, 1997) analog of the NSLP model might be possible and worthy of further study.

A linear programming model has been proposed in Troutt et al. (2001b) for bottleneck analysis in networks. That approach concentrated on material flows and did not recognize the possibility of efficiency variations. Also, it focused on flows in network processes in which little flexibility existed in input mixes or output targets. For example, chemical mixing processes do not permit very much variation from a set proportion of ingredients or materials. At the same time, that work considered the possibility of nonzero constant yield losses. Similar considerations may apply in various supply chains so that a combination of that modeling approach with the present one may be useful for further research.

As in simple LP models for production planning, there may exist technological coefficient matrices A^k such that $A^k y \leq x$ is a required relationship between the inputs x, and outputs y, of Process-k. Model NSLP could be readily modified by inclusion of the appropriate constraints. Evidently, the inclusion of any such constraints must tend to lower the overall throughput rate of the network. Such constraints might already be expected to be known from either the design or operational experience with a particular process. However, recent work in Troutt et al. (2003a) has proposed an approach for estimating such constraints in the linear case.

As noted above, maximal throughput is expected to be associated with technical efficiency at each process, as suggested in particular by Figure 7 for the special case of just two processes and zero buffer amounts. It should be noted that tangency of the frontiers can be easily illustrated in that case because the upstream process has a single input and the downstream one has a single output. The case in which both processes have multiple inputs and outputs cannot easily be illustrated. Thus, it remains for further research to characterize general optimal throughput rate solutions.

Conclusions

This chapter has shown how certain linear programming models may be applied to improve the output rate of a supply chain or network when the outputs of an upstream stage or process become inputs to an adjacent downstream stage or process. The model may be used to establish output targets or goals for each process in order to achieve a maximum throughput rate for the whole chain or network. Updating based on the evolving data permits continuous adjustment of these goals in the manner of rolling horizon plan usage. Along with reductions of process variability and efficiency deviations from their maximal value, improvements of the stage-to-stage output targets provide a further dimension for continuous productivity improvement of the supply chain.

At present, e-businesses that manage supply chains, such as the value net integrator, provide aggregated information that is relevant to supply chain entities. However, the value net integrator can add value by providing focused information as to how much quantity each entity should produce to optimally meet customer demand. The dot-com bust of 2000 has forced e-businesses to rethink their online business strategies. E-businesses are no longer technology-

and revenue-focused. Instead, they are now emphasizing profit maximization by streamlining operations. For example, Amazon.com in 2000 hired a team of mathematicians to figure how to cut costs by developing models for inventory management, order consolidation, and fulfillment errors reduction (Laudon & Traver, 2003). Appropriate extensions of the linear programming models developed in this paper can thus help better manage e-business supply chains.

References

Birge, J. R. & Louveaux, F. (1997). *Introduction to stochastic programming.* New York: Springer.

Charnes, A., Cooper, W. W, Lewin, A. Y., & Seiford, L. M. (Eds.) (1994). *Data envelopment analysis: Theory, methodology, and application.* Boston: Kluwer Academic Publishers.

Chopra, S., & Meindl, P. (2003). *Supply chain management: Strategy, planning and operation (2nd ed.).* Upper Saddle River, NJ: Pearson Prentice Hall.

Dubois, F., & Oliff, M.D. (1991). Aggregate production-planning in practice. *Production and Inventory Management Journal, 32*(3), 26-30.

eMarketer, Inc. (2003, April). E-commerce trade and B2B exchanges.

Färe, R., Grosskopf, S., & Lovell, C. A. K. (1985). *The measurement of efficiency of production.* Boston: Kluwer-Nijhoff.

Fisher, M. L., Hammond, J. H., Obermeyer, W. R., & Raman, A. (1994). Making supply meet demand in an uncertain world. *Harvard Business Review, 72*(3), 83-92.

Ford, L. R., & Fulkerson, D. R. (1962). *Flows in networks.* Princeton, NJ: Princeton University Press.

Graves, S. C., & de Kok, A. G. (2003). *Supply chain management: Handbook of OR/MS.* Amsterdam, The Netherlands: North-Holland.

Graves, S. C., Kan, R., & Zipkin, P. H. (1993). *Logistics of production and inventory: Handbook of OR/MS.* Amsterdam, The Netherlands: North-Holland.

Hax, A.C., & Candea, R. (1984). *Production and inventory management.* Englewood Cliffs, NJ: Prentice-Hall.

Higuchi, T., & Troutt, M. D. (2004). Dynamic simulation of the supply chain for a short life cycle product: Lessons from the Tamagotchi case. *Computers & Operations Research* (forthcoming).

Laudon K. C., & Traver, C. G. (2003). *E-commerce: Business, technology, society (2nd ed.)*. Boston: Pearson Addison-Wesley.

Law, A. M., & Kelton, W. D. (1982). *Simulation modeling and analysis*. New York: McGraw-Hill.

Lee, H. C., & Tang, C. S. (1997). Modeling the costs and benefits of delayed product differentiation. *Management Science*, *43*(1), 40-53.

Lee, H. L., & Billington, C. (1992). Managing supply chain inventories: Pitfalls and opportunities. *Sloan Management Review*, *33*(3), 65-77.

Nam, S. J., & Logendran, R. (1992). Aggregate production-planning: A survey of models and methodologies. *European Journal of Operational Research*, *61*, 255-272.

Rayport, J., & Sviokla, J. (1995). Exploiting the virtual value chain. *Harvard Business Review*, *73*(6), 75-85.

Silver, E.A., Pyke, D. F., & Peterson, R. (1998). *Inventory management and production planning and scheduling (3rd ed.)*. New York: John Wiley & Sons.

Smock, D. (2003). Supply chain management: What is it? *Purchasing*, *132*(13), 45-49.

Swaminathan, J. M., & Tayur, S. R. (1998). Managing broader product lines through delayed differentiation using vanilla boxes. *Management Science*, *44*(12), 161-172.

Swaminathan, J. M., & Tayur, S. R. (2003). Models for supply chains in e-business. *Management Science*, *49*(10), 1387-1406.

Troutt, M.D., Ambrose, P. J., & Chan, C. K. (2001a). Optimal throughput for multistage input: Output processes. *International Journal of Operations and Production Management*, *21*(1), 148-158.

Troutt, M.D., Gribbin, D.W., Shanker. M., & Zhang. A. (2000, Fall). Cost efficiency benchmarking for operational units with multiple cost drivers. *Decision Sciences*, *31*(4), 813-832.

Troutt, M.D., Gribbin, D.W., Shanker. M., & Zhang. A. (2003c). Maximum performance efficiency approaches for estimating best practice costs. In J. Wang (Ed.), *Data mining: Opportunities and challenges* (pp. 239-259). Hershey, PA: Idea Group Publishing.

Troutt, M. D., Nersesian, R. L., & Weinroth, G. J. (2001c). *Plausible efficiency score adjustments using data augmentation and simulation-optimization.* Working paper, under publication review, Department of Management & Information Systems. Kent State University, Kent, Ohio.

Troutt, M.D., Pang, W. K. & Hou, S. H. (2003b). *Vertical density representation and its applications.* Singapore: World Scientific Publishing.

Troutt, M.D., Tadisina, S.K., Sohn, C., & Brandyberry, A. A. (2003a). Linear programming system identification. *European Journal of Operational Research* (forthcoming).

Troutt, M.D., White, G.P., & Tadisina, S.K. (2001b). Maximal flow network modeling of production bottleneck problems. *Journal of the Operational Research Society, 52,* 182-187.

Vollman, T.E., Berry, W.L., & Whybark, D.C. (1997). *Manufacturing planning and control systems (4th ed.).* Homewood, IL: Irwin.

Weill, P., & Vitale, M. R. (2001). *Place to space: Migrating to e-business models.* Boston: Harvard Business School Press.

Chapter III

Optimal Feedback Production for a Supply Chain

K. H. Wong, University of the Witwatersrand, South Africa

H.W.J. Lee, The Hong Kong Polytechnic University, Hong Kong

Chi Kin Chan, The Hong Kong Polytechnic University, Hong Kong

Abstract

In this chapter, we modeled the dynamics of a supply chain considered by several authors. An infinite-horizon, time-delayed, optimal control problem was thus obtained. By approximating the time interval [0, ∞] by [0, T_f], we obtained an approximated problem ($P(T_f)$) which could be easily solved by the control parameterization method. Moreover, we could show that the objective function of the approximated problem converged to that of the original problem as $T_f \to \infty$. Several examples have been solved to illustrate the efficiency of our method. In these examples, some important results relating the production rate to demand rate have been developed.

Introduction

Several authors have modeled the dynamics of a supply chain (Bellman & Cooke, 1963; Forrester, 1961, 1973; Hafrez et al., 1996; Macdonald, 1978; Sterman, 1987; Sterman, 1989; Towill, 1991, 1992; Towill & Del Velcchio, 1994). Forrester (1961, 1973) modeled and simulated supply chains using differential equations. A highly nonlinear model of a supply chain was derived using repeated coupling of first-order differential equations. Riddals and Bennet (2000, 2002) obtained conditions for the stability of time-delay differential equations for supply chain models. Wikner et al. (1991) considered smoothing of supply chain models.

In this chapter, we used the model considered by Riddals and Bennet (2002) to develop an optimal control problem. We considered a single echelon supply chain, such as a furniture manufacturer and assumed that orders for furniture were placed continuously. We also assumed that the state variables were the rate of production and the inventory level, which followed the same dynamics as that given by Riddals and Bennet (2002). We further identified the control variables as the management's magic numbers, $\alpha^i(t)$ and $\alpha^{WIP}(t)$, which were the measures of the importance attached to the inventory level and the amount of work in process. The objective function to be minimized was simply an integral consisting of the sum of all costs (production cost plus storage cost plus shortage cost), possible incorporating future or present value calculations. By minimizing the objective function with respect to $\alpha^i(t)$ and $\alpha^{WIP}(t)$, given some past production parameter and of course the past and future demand, we could compute an optimal open-loop production schedule.

Due to the delay differential equations, it could not be transformed to any canonical form soluble by the package MISER described by Jennings et al. (1990). However, Kaji and Wong (1994), Teo et al. (1984), Wong et al. (1984) and Wong et al. (2001) have established the theoretical framework for solving this time-delayed control problem.

Problem Statement

Let $i(t)$ be the inventory level at time t, $p(t)$ be the production rate, $D(t)$ be the demand rate, $\alpha^i(t)$ be the inventory adjustment parameter and $\alpha^{WIP}(t)$ be the work in process adjustment factor. The production rate at any time t can be expressed as

$$p(t) =$$

$$\frac{1}{T}\int_{t-T}^{t} D(s)ds + \alpha^{i}(t)(\bar{i} - i(t)) + \alpha^{WIP}(t)\left[\frac{\hat{h}}{T}\int_{t-T}^{t} D(s)ds - \int_{t-h}^{t} p(s)ds\right], \quad t \in [0,\infty).$$

$$(1)$$

The first term of (1) is the expected demand rate over the period $[t-T, t]$; the second term is the inventory discrepancy term, where $\bar{i}$ is the ideal inventory level; the last term is the work in progress term, where $\hat{h}$ and h are respectively the lead time in the demand supply and the production respectively.

Also, the rate of change of the inventory satisfies the following equation

$$\frac{di(t)}{dt} = p(t-h) - D(t), \quad t \in [0,\infty). \tag{2}$$

By assuming that both $\alpha^{i}(t)$ and $\alpha^{WIP}(t)$ are step functions with

$$0 \le \alpha^{i}(t) \le 1, \quad t \in [0,\infty) \tag{3}$$

$$0 \le \alpha^{WIP}(t) \le 1, \quad t \in [0,\infty), \tag{4}$$

we can easily obtain from equations (1) and (2) that

$$\begin{aligned}
\frac{dp(t)}{dt} = &-\alpha^{WIP}(t)p(t) - \left(\alpha^{i}(t) - \alpha^{WIP}(t)\right)p(t-h) \\
&+ \frac{1}{T}\left(\alpha^{WIP}(t)\hat{h} + 1 + \alpha^{i}(t)T\right)D(t) \\
&- \frac{1}{T}\left(\alpha^{WIP}(t)\hat{h} + 1\right)D(t-T) \qquad a.e. \text{ on } [0,\infty)
\end{aligned} \tag{5}$$

Moreover, we also need to impose the following constraint

$$p(t) \geq 0, \quad t \in [0, \infty) . \tag{6}$$

The pair of step-functions $(\alpha^i(t), \alpha^{WIP}(t))$ satisfying (3), (4) and (6) is called a feasible control.

Now, we define the objective function to be minimized as

$$J(\alpha^i(t), \alpha^{WIP}(t)) = \int_0^\infty e^{-\beta t} \{c_p p(t) + c_i \max[i(t) - \bar{i}, 0] + c_D \max[-i(t), 0]\} dt . \tag{7}$$

Here, the term $c_p p(t)$ is the production cost at time t; the term $c_i \max[i(t) - \bar{i}(t), 0]$ is the storage cost at time t; the term $c_D \max[-i(t), 0]$ is the shortage cost at time t, assuming that all the demand not satisfied at time t can be backlogged and satisfied at a later time; the term $e^{-\beta t} (\beta > 0)$ is due to capital depreciation at time t.

Feedback Production Law

At any time $t = \hat{t}$, we wish to find $\alpha^i(\hat{t})$ and $\alpha^{WIP}(\hat{t})$ so that $p(\hat{t})$ can be calculated from (1). Without loss of generality, we can always choose $\hat{t} = 0$. By using $\bar{i} = 0$ in (1), we have

$$p(0) = \bar{D}(0) - \alpha^i(0)i(0) + \alpha^{WIP}(0)[\hat{h}\bar{D}(0) - h\bar{p}(0)], \tag{8}$$

where

$$\bar{D}(0) = \frac{1}{T} \int_{-T}^{0} D(t)dt \tag{9}$$

and

$$\bar{p}(0) = \frac{1}{h}\int_{-h}^{0} p(t)dt. \tag{10}$$

Since $\bar{D}(0)$ and $\bar{p}(0)$ are functions of $\{D(t), t \in [-T,0]\}$ and $\{p(t); t \in [-h,0]\}$ together with $i(0)$, equation (1) provides a feedback law for $p(0)$ in terms of $\{D(t): t \in [-T,0]\}, \{p(t): t \in [-h,0]\}$ and $i(0)$. The optimal control problem, denoted by (P), can be stated as follows:

Subject to the system

$$
\begin{aligned}
\frac{dp(t)}{dt} = & -\alpha^{WIP}(t)p(t) - \left(\alpha^i(t) - \alpha^{WIP}(t)\right)p(t-h) \\
& + \frac{1}{T}\left(\alpha^{WIP}(t)\hat{h} + 1 + \alpha^i(t)T\right)D(t) \\
& - \frac{1}{T}\left(\alpha^{WIP}(t)\hat{h} + 1\right)D(t-T), \quad a.e. \quad \text{on } [0,\infty)
\end{aligned}
\tag{11}
$$

$$\frac{di(t)}{dt} = p(t-h) - D(t), \qquad t \in [0,\infty) \tag{12}$$

$$p(t) = \omega(t), \qquad t \in [-h,0) \tag{13}$$

$$D(t) = \gamma(t), \qquad t \in [-T,0] \tag{14}$$

$$i(0) = i_0, \tag{15}$$

$$p(0) = \bar{D}(0) - \alpha^i(0) \times i_0 + \alpha^{WIP}(0)[\hat{h}\bar{D}(0) - h\bar{p}(0)], \tag{16}$$

$$\bar{D}(0) = \frac{1}{T}\int_{-T}^{0} \gamma(t)dt \tag{17}$$

$$\overline{p}(0) = \frac{1}{h} \int_{-h}^{0} \omega(t) dt ,$$

(18)

$(\omega(t) \geq 0, t \in [-h, 0]$ and $\gamma(t) \geq 0, t \in [-T, 0]$ are given functions) find feasible control $(\alpha^i(t), \alpha^{WIP}(t))$ such that the following objective function $J^\infty(\alpha^i(t), \alpha^{WIP}(t))$ is minimized over the set of feasible controls, where

$$J^\infty(\alpha^i(t), \alpha^{WIP}(t)) =$$

$$\int_0^\infty e^{-\beta t} \{ c_p p(t) + c_i \max[i(t), 0] + c_D \max[-i(t), 0] \} dt .$$

(19)

Since $\gamma(t), \omega(t), i_0$ with $\gamma(t) \geq 0$ and $\omega(t) \geq 0$ are given, the above problem (P) belongs to a special type of time-delayed optimal control problem with an infinite time horizon, where the initial condition of the state variable $p(t)$ is a function of the control variables at time zero (i.e., $\alpha^2(0)$ and $\alpha^{WIP}(0)$).

Finite Time Approximation

Let us solve the problem (P) by using finite time approximation. Let T_f be a positive number. The approximated problem $(P(T_f))$ can be described as follow:

Subject to the system

$$\frac{dp(t)}{dt} =$$

$$-\alpha^{WIP}(t)p(t) - \left(\alpha^i(t) - \alpha^{WIP}(t)\right)p(t-h) + \frac{1}{T}\left(\alpha^{WIP}(t)\hat{h} + 1 + \alpha^i(t)T\right)D(t)$$

$$-\frac{1}{T}\left(\alpha^{WIP}(t)\hat{h} + 1\right)D(t-T), \quad a.e. \quad \text{on } [0, T_f)$$

(20)

$$\frac{di(t)}{dt} = p(t-h) - D(t), \qquad t \in [0, T_f) \tag{21}$$

$$p(t) = \omega(t), \qquad t \in [-h, 0) \tag{22}$$

$$D(t) = \gamma(t), \qquad t \in [-T, 0] \tag{23}$$

$$i(0) = i_0 \tag{24}$$

$$p(0) = \bar{D}(0) - \alpha^i(0)i_0 + \alpha^{WIP}(0)[\hat{h}\bar{D}(0) - h\bar{p}(0)] \tag{25}$$

$$\bar{D}(0) = \frac{1}{T} \int_{-T}^{0} \gamma(t)dt \tag{26}$$

$$\bar{p}(0) = \frac{1}{h} \int_{-h}^{0} \omega(t)dt \,, \tag{27}$$

find feasible controls $(\alpha^i(t), \alpha^{WIP}(t))$ such that the following objective function $J^{T_f}(\alpha^i(t), \alpha^{WIP}(t))$ is minimized over the set of feasible controls, where

$$J^{T_f}(\alpha^i(t), \alpha^{WIP}(t)) =$$

$$\int_{0}^{T_f} e^{-\beta t}\{c_p p(t) + c_i \max[i(t), 0] + c_D \max[-i(t), 0]\}dt \,. \tag{28}$$

Now, we wish to establish some convergence result of the problem $(P(T_f))$ as T_f approaches infinity.

Lemma 1. Suppose that the input demand $D(t) \geq 0$ is a non-decreasing function for all $t \in [0, \infty)$. Then there exist feasible controls $(\alpha^{WIP}(t), \alpha^i(t))$ such that the states $p(\alpha^{WIP}, \alpha^i)(t)$ and $i(\alpha^{WIP}, \alpha^i)(t)$ corresponding to the above controls satisfy

$$p(\alpha^{WIP}, \alpha^i)(t) \geq 0, \quad t \in [0, \infty) \tag{29}$$

$$p(\alpha^{WIP}, \alpha^i)(t) \leq \frac{1}{T} \int_0^t D(s)ds + \bar{D}(0), \quad t \in [0, \infty) \tag{30}$$

$$\left| i\left(\alpha^{WIP}, \alpha^i\right)(t) \right| \leq \bar{D}(0) \times t + |i_0| +$$

$$\frac{1}{T} \int_0^t \int_0^{t_1} D(s)ds dt_1 + \int_{-h}^0 w(s)ds + \int_0^t D(s)ds, \quad t \in [0, \infty) \tag{31}$$

Proof. By choosing $\alpha^i(t) = \alpha^{WIP}(t) = 0$ for all $t > 0$, we get from (11) and (16) that

$$\frac{dp(t)}{dt} = \frac{D(t) - D(t-h)}{T} \tag{32}$$

$$p(0) = \bar{D}(0). \tag{33}$$

Thus, $p(t) \geq 0$ follows easily from the fact that $D(t)$ is non-decreasing function and the fact that $p(0) = \bar{D}(0) \geq 0$. Now from (32), we get

$$\frac{dp(t)}{dt} \leq \frac{D(t)}{T}. \tag{34}$$

Thus, from (34) and (33), we get

$$p(t) \leq \frac{1}{T} \int_0^t D(s)ds + \bar{D}(0). \tag{35}$$

From (12) and (15), we get

$$\left|\frac{di(t)}{dt}\right| \le |p(t-h)| + |D(t)| \tag{36}$$

and

$$|i(0)| = |i_0|. \tag{37}$$

From (36), (37), (34), (13) and (15), we can easily obtain (31).

Remark 1. Suppose $D(t) \ge 0$ is any piecewise continuous function, then Lemma 3.1 remains valid provided that $\bar{D}(0) + \int_0^t \frac{D(s) - D(s-h)}{T} ds$ is always non-negative.

Remark 2. The assumption imposed by Remark 1 is really not too restrictive in real-life problems. In fact, if the manager knows that the future demand always decreases, then probably he will consider closing up shop!

Lemma 2. Suppose that the input demand $D(t) \ge 0$ is a non-decreasing function for all $t \in [0, \infty)$ or the assumption imposed on Remark 1 holds. Suppose further that $D(t) \le Kt^n$ for all $t \in [0, \infty)$, where K is a positive constant. Then there exists feasible controls $(\alpha^{WIP}(t), \alpha^i(t))$ such that $J^\infty(\alpha^{WIP}(t), \alpha^i(t))$ is finite.

Proof. In view of Lemma 1, by choosing $\alpha^{WIP}(t) = 0$ and $\alpha^i(t) = 0$, $t \in [0, \infty)$ we have

$$J^\infty\left(\alpha^{WIP}(t), \alpha^i(t)\right) \le \int_0^\infty e^{-\beta t} \left\{ c_p \left[\frac{Kt^{n+1}}{(n+1)T} + \bar{D}(0) \right] \right.$$

$$\left. + (c_i + c_D) \left[\frac{Kt^{n+2}}{(n+1)(n+2)T} + \frac{Kt^{n+1}}{n+1} + |i_0| + \int_{-h}^0 \omega(s)ds + \bar{D}(0) \times t \right] \right\} dt \tag{38}$$

Thus, there exists a positive constant K_1 such that

$$J^\infty(\alpha^{WIP}(t), \alpha^i(t)) \le \int_0^\infty K_1 e^{-\beta t} t^{n+3} dt = \frac{K_1(n+3)!}{\beta^{n+4}}. \tag{39}$$

It is clear from (39) that $J^\infty(\alpha^{WIP}(t), \alpha^i(t))$ is finite.

Theorem 1. Suppose that the assumptions imposed on $D(t)$ of Lemma 2 holds.

Let $u^{T_f}(t) = (\alpha^{WIP, T_f}(t), \alpha^{i, T_f}(t))$ be optimal control of the problem $(P(T_f))$. Let $u^\infty(t) = (\alpha^{WIP, \infty}(t), \alpha^{i, \infty}(t))$ be optimal control of the problem (P). Then we have

$$\lim_{T_f \to \infty} J^{T_f}(u^{T_f}) = J^\infty(u^\infty) \tag{40}$$

Proof. Let $\{T_f(j), j = 1, 2, ..., \infty\}$ be a sequence of monotonically increasing real numbers. Then we have

$$\begin{aligned}
&J^{T_f(j+1)}(u^{T_f(j+1)}) - J^{T_f(j)}(u^{T_f(j)}) \\
&= J^{T_f(j)}(u^{T_f(j+1)}) - J^{T_f(j)}(u^{T_f(j)}) \\
&+ \int_{T_f(j)}^{T_f(j+1)} e^{-\beta t} \{c_p p(u^{T_f(j+1)}(t)) \\
&+ c_i \max[i(u^{T_f(j+1)}(t)), 0] + c_d \max[-i(u^{T_f(j+1)}(t)), 0]\} dt,
\end{aligned} \tag{41}$$

where $p(u^{T_f(j+1)}(t))$ and $i(u^{T_f(j+1)}(t))$ are the states correspond to the optimal control $u^{T_f(j+1)}$.

Now, since $u^{T_f(j)}$ is the optimal control for the problem $(P(T_f(j)))$, we have

$$J^{T_f(j)}(u^{T_f(j+1)}) - J^{T_f(j)}(u^{T_f(j)}) \ge 0. \tag{42}$$

Since u^{T_f} is feasible, $p(u^{T_f(j+1)})(t) \geq 0$ for all $t \in [0, \infty)$.

Thus, the integral term of (41) is also non-negative. Thus, from (41) and (42), we get

$$J^{T_f(j+1)}(u^{T_f(j+1)}) \geq J^{T_f(j)}(u^{T_f(j)}). \tag{43}$$

Thus, $\{J^{T_f(j)}(u^{T_f(j)})\}, j = 1, 2, \dots \infty\}$ is a sequence of monotonically non-decreasing real numbers, which has an upper bound $\dfrac{K_1(n+3)!}{\beta^{n+4}}$ where K_1 is the constant given in (39). Hence, this sequence is convergent and the proof is complete.

In view of Theorem 1, we can easily obtain the optimal feedback law for the production at time $t = 0$ by solving the problem $(P(T_f))$ instead of (P) if we choose a sufficient large number T_f.

Note that this problem $(P(T_f))$ belongs to a special class of time-delayed control problems, where the initial condition of the state $p(t)$ is a function of the controls at time zero (i.e., $\alpha^i(0)$ and $\alpha^{WIP}(0)$). This problem can be solved by the control parameterization method. (Refer to Kaji & Wong, 1994; Teo et al., 1991; Teo et al., 1984; Wong et al., 1985; Wong et al., 2001; Wong et al., 2001, for details.)

Smoothing the Objective Function

The terms $c_i \max[i(t), 0]$ and $c_D \max[-i(t), 0]$ inside the integral of the objective function $J^{T_f}(\alpha^i(t), \alpha^{WIP}(t))$ are non-smooth. Thus, in order to obtain a smooth objective function, these terms should be replaced by $c_i S_\rho(i(t))$ and $c_D S_\rho(-i(t))$ respectively, where $\rho > 0$ is a very small number and

$$S_\rho(x) = \frac{x^2}{4\rho} + \frac{x}{2} + \frac{\rho}{4}. \tag{44}$$

Thus, the new objective function of the approximated problem becomes

$$J_\rho^{T_f}(\alpha^i(t), \alpha^{WIP}(t)) = \int_0^{T_f} e^{-\beta t}\{c_p p(t) + c_i S_\rho(i(t)) + c_D S_\rho(-i(t))\}dt.\qquad(45)$$

The problem obtained by replacing $J^{T_f}(\alpha^i(t), \alpha^{WIP}(t))$ by $J_\rho^{T_f}(\alpha^i(t), \alpha^{WIP}(t))$ in $P(T_f)$ will be denoted by $(P_\rho(T_f))$.

Gradient Calculation

In order to solve the problem $(P_\rho(T_f))$ by the control parameterization method, we need to calculate the gradient of the objective function $J_\rho^{T_f}(\alpha^i(t), \alpha^{WIP}(t))$ with respect to the controls $\alpha^i(t)$ and $\alpha^{WIP}(t)$.

First, we define the adjoint system for the problem $(P_\rho(T_f))$ as follow:

$$\frac{d\lambda_1(t)}{dt} = \alpha^{WIP}(t)\lambda_1(t) - \alpha^{WIP}(t)\lambda_1(t+h) + \alpha^i(t)\lambda_1(t+h),$$
$$-\lambda_2(t+h) - e^{-\beta t}c_p, \qquad t \in [0,T] \qquad (46)$$

$$\frac{d\lambda_2(t)}{dt} = e^{-\beta t}\left\{c_i \frac{\partial(S_\rho(i(t)))}{\partial(i(t))} + c_D \frac{\partial(S_\rho(-i(t)))}{\partial(i(t))}\right\}, \qquad t \in [0,T] \qquad (47)$$

$$\lambda_1(T_f) = 0 \qquad (48)$$

$$\lambda_2(T_f) = 0 \qquad (49)$$

$$\lambda_1(t) = 0, \qquad t \in (T_f, T_f + h] \qquad (50)$$

$$\lambda_2(t) = 0, \qquad t \in (T_f, T_f + h]. \qquad (51)$$

Then the gradient of the objective function is given by

$$\frac{\partial J}{\partial(\alpha^{WIP}(t))} = \int_0^{T_f}\left[-p(t)\lambda_1(t) + p(t-h)\lambda_1(t) + \frac{\hat{h}}{T}d(t) - \frac{\hat{h}}{T}D(t-T)\right]D(t)$$
$$+ [\hat{h}\times\bar{D}(0) - h\times p^{WIP}(0)]\times\lambda_1(0)$$

(52)

$$\frac{\partial J}{\partial(\alpha^i(t))} = \int_0^{T_f}[-p(t-h) + D(t)]\lambda_1(t)dt - i_0\times\lambda_1(0).$$

(53)

Remark 3. Theoretically speaking, in order to solve the problem $(P_\rho(T_f))$ by the control parameterization method, we also need to convert the constraint (6) into canonical form and then calculate the gradient of this constraint with respect to the controls $\alpha^i(t)$ and $\alpha^{WIP}(t)$. However, if the assumption imposed on $D(t)$ by Lemma 2 holds, then the problem $(P_\rho(T_f))$ becomes simply an unconstrained, time-delayed problem, where the constraint (6) is automatically satisfied.

Numerical Results

The problem $(P_\rho(T_f))$ has been solved by using $T_f = 100$ months, $T = h = \hat{p} = 1$ month, $i_0 = 100$, $\omega_0 = 100.0$, $t\in[-h,0)$, $\gamma(t) = 300.0$, $t\in[-h,0)$, $c_i = 100$, $c_D = 200$, $c_p = 40$, $\beta = 2.7\times10^{-4}$ together with two different functions for $D(t)$. The two different functions for $D(t)$ are:

(i) $D(t) = 300 - t$
(ii) $D(t) = 300 + t$.

From the graphs of the optimal trajectory $p^*(t)$ and $i^*(t)$ given in Figure 1 (for Case (i)) and Figure 2 (for Case (ii)), we observe the following important result:

Suppose $c_p < c_i$ and $c_p < c_D$. Let $p^*(t)$, $i^*(t)$ be the optimal trajectories of the problem $(P_\rho(T_f))$. When T_f is sufficiently large, there exists $\hat{\tau} < T_f$ such that

$$p^*(t-h) = D(t) \quad \text{and} \quad i^*(t) = 0 \text{ for all } t \in [\hat{\tau}, T_f].$$

The optimal objective function value for Case (i) and Case (ii) are 10685.81 and 21161.76 respectively.

Conclusions

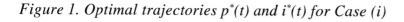

We have successfully modeled the dynamics of a supply chain considered by several authors. A method has been developed to solve this supply chain problem. Numerical results clearly demonstrated the efficiency of our method.

Figure 1. Optimal trajectories $p^*(t)$ and $i^*(t)$ for Case (i)

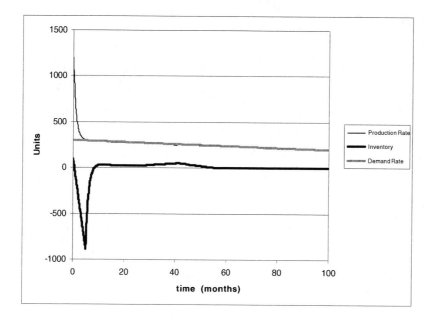

64 Wong, Lee and Chan

Figure 2. Optimal trajectories p(t) and i*(t) for Case (ii)*

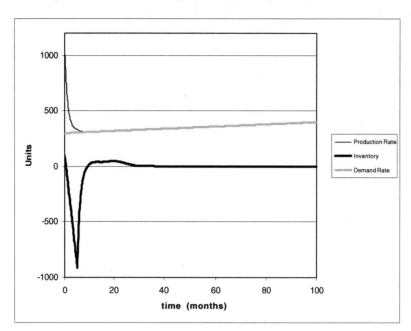

References

Bellman, R., & Cooke, K.L. (1963). *Differential-difference equations.* New York: Academic Press.

Forrester, J.W. (1961). *Industrial dynamics.* Cambridge, MA: MIT Press.

Forrester, J.W. (1973). *World dynamics.* Cambridge, MA: MIT Press.

Hafrez, K., Griffiths, M., Griffiths, J., & Naim, M.M. (1996). Systems design of two-echelon steel industry supply chain. *International Journal of Production Economics, 45,* 121-130.

Jennings, L.S., Fisher, M.E., Teo, K.L., & Goh, C.J. (1990). *"MISER 3" optimal control software: Theory and user manual.* EMCOSS Pte Ltd.

Kaji, K., & Wong, K.H. (1994). Nonlinearly constrained time-delayed optimal control problems. *Journal of Optimization Theory & Applications, 82*(2), 295-313.

Macdonald, N. (1978). *Time lags in biological models.* New York: Springer-Verlag.

Copyright © 2005, Idea Group Inc. Copying or distributing in print or electronic forms without written permission of Idea Group Inc. is prohibited.

Marshall, J.E. (1979). *Control of time delay systems.* Stevenage, UK: Peter Peregrinus.

Niculescc, S.L., Verriest, E.L., Dugard, L., & Dion, J.M. (1997). Stability and robust stability of time-delay system a guided tour. In L. Dugard & E.L. Verriest (Eds.), *Stability and control of time delay systems*, 1-71. LNCIS 228. London: Springer-Verlag.

Riddals, C.E., & Bennet, S. (2000). Modeling the dynamics of supply chains. *International Journal of Systems Science, 31*(8), 969-976.

Riddals, C.E., & Bennet, S. (2002). The stability of supply chains. *International Journal of Systems Science, 40*(2), 459-475.

Simon, H.A. (1952). On the application of servomechanism theory in the study of production control. *Econometrica, 20,* 247-268.

Sterman, J.D. (1987). Testing behavioral simulation models by direct experiment. *Management Science, 33*(12), 1572-1592.

Sterman, J.D. (1989). Modeling managerial behaviour: Misinterpretations of feedback in a dynamic decision-making experiment. *Management Science, 35*(3), 321-339.

Teo, K.L., Goh, C.J., & Wong, K.H. (1991). *A unified computational approach to optimal control problems.* Longman Scientific and Technical.

Teo, K.L., Wong, K.H., & Clements, D.J. (1984). Optimal control computation for linear time-lag systems with linear terminal constraints. *Journal of Optimization Theory and Applications, 44*(3), 509-526.

Towill, D.R. (1991). Supply chain dynamics. *International Journal of Computer Integrated Manufacturing, 4*(4), 197-208.

Towill, D.R. (1992). Supply chain dynamics the change engineering challenge of the mid 1990's. *Proceedings of the Institution of Mechanical Engineers*, 206, 233-245.

Towill, D.R., & Del Vecchio, A. (1994). The application of filter theory to the study of supply chain dynamics. *Production, Planning & Control, 5*(1), 82-96.

Wikner, J., Towill, D.R., & Naim, M.M. (1991). Smoothing supply chain dynamics. *International Journal of Production Economics, 22,* 231-248.

Wong, K.H., Clements, D.J., & Teo, K.L. (1985). Optimal control computation for nonlinear systems. *Journal of Optimization Theory and Applications, 47*(1), 91-107.

Wong, K.H., Jennings, L.S., & Benyah, F. (2001). Control parametrization method for free planning time optimal control problems with time-delayed arguments. *Journal of Nonlinear Analysis*, Series A, 47, 5679-5689.

Chapter IV

Life Cycle Considerations for Supply Chain Strategy

Toru Higuchi, Sakushin Gakuin University, Japan

Marvin D. Troutt, Kent State University, USA

Brian A. Polin, Jerusalem College of Technology, Israel

Abstract

The goal of this chapter is to propose a framework for the dynamics of supply chains from a life cycles point of view. It is inevitable for supply chains to be affected by the life cycles of the product. There are three important interrelated life cycles that have effects on the dynamics of supply chains and are associated with the product. These are: (i) the innovation (Abernathy & Clark, 1983), (ii) the market (Kotler, 1999), and (iii) the location (Vernon, 1966). The first life cycle related to the innovation illustrates how the product and production process progress. It gives us a hint to consider the feasibility of the location dependent on the degree of innovativeness of the product. The second one related to the market clarifies the marketing objectives in each stage. It suggests the reasonable location strategy. The last one related to the location proposes the relation between the product and the reasonable location of the manufacturing facilities. It is operational because it considers the timing and the reason to shift the manufacturing facilities. In this chapter, we discuss the mission and structure of the supply chain in the different stages of these life cycles. We illustrate the proposed framework using the case of the VCR.

Innovation and Productivity Dilemma

From the viewpoint of innovation, Abernathy (1978) and Abernathy et al. (1983) introduced the concepts of *maturity* and *de-maturity*. They explained the development of a product in terms of radical and incremental innovations. A new category of products usually begins with a radical innovation. At the beginning, companies compete with each other based on their own unique approaches and take the very substantial risk that their technology and design might be out of use in the event that another company succeeds in establishing the dominant design, which then becomes the *de facto* standard. The dominant design sets the specifications for the product and causes competition to cool down. Once the dominant design has been established, the focus of innovation shifts from product *category* to the product *itself*. The manufacturers start automating factories to make products efficiently. At the same time, the opportunities for improvements and innovations of the product diminish gradually. Abernathy called this phenomenon the *productivity dilemma*. To be successful in this situation, the companies need a brand-new technology, usage, material, or design. After that, the status of competition becomes fluid again. This is called the *de-maturity* stage or phase. Once de-maturity starts, existing technologies and products rapidly become obsolete, and competition broadens to include alternate designs competing for dominance in an entire product category. Hence, de-maturity is destructive.

In Figure 1, the vertical axis requires additional explanation. Abernathy (1978) used the terms, Innovation and Stage of Development (Rate of Major Innovations). He counted technical changes related to the product and classified them as major (radical) or minor (incremental) changes. However, unambiguous criteria for deciding these classifications were not advanced. To reflect this caution, we have labeled the vertical axis as "Total Impact of the Innovation." Innovations are divided into product innovations and process innovations.

Figure 1. Normal direction of development transition

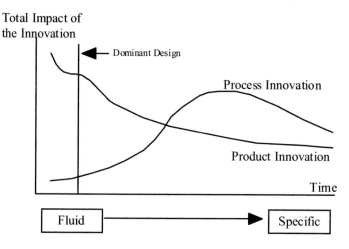

Based on Abernathy (1978, p.72)

Although innovations may be countable, the impact of each one differs. So we use Total Impact of the Innovation. Product innovations have a large effect on the product's performance (development) while process innovations tend to affect cost and quality. At the beginning (upon the emergence of a dominant design), product innovation plays a very important role in product development. Later, process innovations have bigger effects on product development than product innovations because the number of product innovations tends to decrease. Finally, in the last stage, the opportunities decline for both product and process innovations.

Nowadays, supply chains seek to actively manage innovations. In the modern business environment, it is increasingly difficult or inefficient for a single company to cover and lead all links in the supply chain because of technical and market factors. Most products, especially high-tech ones, have become too complex and risky for a single company to create complete products from the materials by themselves. Auto and electric industries are good examples. In both industries, a company called the integrator, or set maker, exists and is surrounded by the sub-integrators, or key suppliers. The customer needs are so advanced that the distribution channel becomes complex, ranging from various types of retailers to mail-order selling through the Internet. Supply chains have to deal with developing new products and spreading them to the market simultaneously.

Figure 1 shows the shift in type of innovation depending on the degree of the maturity of the product. At the beginning, when the product innovations become initially popular, supply chains face two kinds of competition. The first one is how fast a product can be developed. It is the collaboration in R&D among the supply chain that affects the feasibility and the speed of developing a brand-new product. As time goes by, the brand-new products become complicated, highly specialized and combine different technologies. It becomes more difficult to make a new product based on a simple idea or a new technology than before. Hence, first, supply chains should find seeds of future success in the market, which include new technologies, materials, and usages. Then, they identify the related technologies and construct appropriate partnerships, and coordinate operations to commercialize it quickly.

The second kind of competition is how best to bring the popular, de-facto standard, to the market. This depends on the excellence of the design and the strength of the distribution channel. Latent customer needs must be articulated appropriately for success with a brand-new market. Even if a new product is technically excellent, it cannot be popular unless harmony with customer needs is achieved. To be a de-facto standard, the supply chain sells a brand-new product worldwide though various distribution channels. Recently, different *de jure* standards compete with each other as in the present cell phone and DVD environments. Hence, supply chains make strategic alliances for global promotion of the de-facto standard.

The dominant design is the first to satisfy latent customer needs and then is adopted widely, if not in fact, globally. The Model T was an early example of a dominant design in the auto industry. It was introduced by Ford in 1908 at a price less than $1,000, and was a great success. It established the production framework of the automobile as a high level of component aggregation. Although Ford added only a few innovations to the Model T throughout the lifetime of the car, it synthesized the existing technologies and became a dominant design (Abernathy, 1978, p. 13). In the fluid, early stage of the product, supply chains must struggle for the dominant design.

In the next stage, supply chains and individual companies advance the product based on the dominant design. After this design evolves, standardization and modularization processes begin to advance. These play a very important role in this stage. Abernathy (1978) points out two significant effects of standardization and modularization. One is the localization of the impact of changes and the other is the guarantee of compatibility with other suppliers in the chain. The former means that when some parts change, supply chains can absorb them

Figure 2. De-maturity

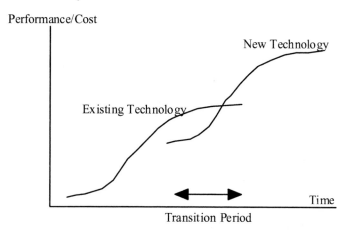

Source: Shintaku (1994, p.16)

without change or cope with them by only minor changes. The product can be developed incrementally and process innovations become routine or more mainstream. Modularity also has great significance to the supply chain by increasing the compatibility among suppliers, enabling a wider range of products, and keeping the level of inventories low. Compatibility makes it easy for companies to collaborate together beyond the borders of supply chains, company groups, nations and regions. This intensifies the competition within the supply chain and accelerates the development of what might be called the *performance/cost* orientation as in Figure 2.

The *productivity dilemma* becomes evident after the advance of each stage. The quality of the product becomes higher and the price goes down. Thus, the performance/cost ratio rises rapidly, but then plateaus. This is because enough units have been produced so that manufacturers have the benefit of the learning curve and will have largely recovered investments. The supply chains, however, have fewer opportunities for innovations and improvements day by day. Customers will have become satiated with the products and want a novel design. Some supply chains might initiate the *de-maturity* stage by introducing new technologies and usages for a brand-new market. Figure 2 makes a comparison with the performance/cost on existing and a new technology. In the transition period, the performance/cost of the new one is usually less than that of the existing one. But possibly it may have a big potential that might be far beyond the limit of the existing one. There is a major risk that another supply chain might breakthrough the *productivity dilemma* earlier. This could make

Table 1. Mission and activities of the supply chain based on the innovation

Stage	Mission	Activities
Before Dominant Design	Establishment of the Dominant Design	- Search for "Seeds" - Articulation of Customer Needs - Matching Seeds and Needs (Simulation of the Product) - Formation of the Supply Chain - Sharing Information within the Supply Chain - Flexible Manufacturing System - Diffusion of the Product
Immature	Development of the Product	- Maximization of Product Performance - Improvement of Product Quality - Addition of New Functions - Localization of the Impact of Changes by the Modular System - Automation of the Manufacturing Process - Providing with the Variety of the Product - Finding and Removing Bottlenecks - Diffusion of the Product
Mature	Reduction of the Cost	- Development of the Efficient Manufacturing System - Advancement of the Automation of the Manufacturing - Global Allocation of the Manufacturing Facility - Outsourcing the Standard Parts - Improvement of the Forecasting Techniques - Rationalization of Distribution System - Sharing the Information on Time - Shortening the Cycle Time - Reduction of the Inventory - Use of Original Equipment Manufacturing (OEM) - Decision Making Whether Withdraw from the Product or Not
De-Mature	Creation of the Next Generation Product	- Search for the New Materials and Usage - Radical Change of the Dominant Design - Destruction of the Existing Supply Chain - Reorganization of the Supply Chain

the existing manufacturing facilities and technologies obsolete. For example, in the auto industry, new struggles for the dominant design of hybrid vehicles and Intelligent Transportation Systems (ITS) are presently becoming more and more fervent.

Table 1 summarizes the mission and activities of the supply chain from the viewpoint of product innovation. Before the dominant design occurs, the supply chain's mission is to compete for establishment of that dominant design. In this stage, the leader (or integrator) plays an important role as a director and coordinator to incubate the product. After the dominant design emerges, then maturity proceeds. In the immature stage, each supply chain member contributes to develop the product. Achievement of the dominant design then enables modular manufacturing. As a result, the impacts of changes become isolated or localized and components that each supply chain member provides can be incorporated into the product easily. In the mature stage, the specifications and manufacturing process become stable. On the other hand, supply chains then become under increased pressure to cut costs. Supply chains must review their logistics costs and manufacturing system to provide the product more efficiently. When the maturity advances to some extent, technological advantage would disappear. Supply chains should make a decision whether to withdraw or to survive in the market. Survivors can be divided into two types, the last one or innovator. The latter overcomes the productivity dilemma and induces the next new cycle.

The rest of the chapter is organized as follows. In the second section, we review the classical product life cycle and its implications for the supply chain. The next section covers Vernon's Product Cycle theory, which provides insight and guidance on physical/geographic production facilities' location decisions. This is followed with a section in which we develop a case study of the VCR in light of these life cycles issues. While the VCR case illustrates many of the general principles, it also deviates from Vernon's theory in some respects. The chapter then concludes.

Product Life Cycle

The second life cycle of interest is the well-known Product Life Cycle (PLC). PLC is composed of the introduction, growth, maturity and decline stages (Kotler, 1999). As noted in Chopra and Meindl (2003), the PLC is another consideration in achieving strategic fit of the supply chain. They observe that as product maturity occurs, supply and demand become more predictable, and the competitive pressures usually increase, which in turn leads to lower margins. Also the price becomes a more significant factor in customer choices. Strategic fit, then, requires that the supply chain move from responsiveness to efficiency. These issues can be especially critical in dynamic or high-tech industries such as consumer electronics and pharmaceuticals. Beyond these particular industries, there is a general trend toward shorter product life cycles. In a 1981 study measuring the duration of the growth stages of various household appliances over three time periods (1922-1942, 1945-1964 and 1965-1979), Qualls et al. observed a five-fold decrease from 33.8 years in period I to 19.5 years in period II and 6.8 years in period III. Additionally, environments of multiple products and consumer segments can exacerbate supply chain complications resulting from product life cycle issues. Also, as noted in Higuchi and Troutt (2004), a very short life cycle can also interact disastrously with the Bullwhip effect, boom and bust, and phantom demands.

PLC and SCM are greatly influenced by each other in the same way as are PLC and Business Logistics (Bowersox & Closs 1996). PLC directs the supply chain to the appropriate market strategy, such as pricing, promotions, model changes, distribution channels, service level, etc. On the other hand, SCM has impacts on the durations of each stage in the PLC and deforms or shifts the pattern of profits proposed by PLC. For example, advertisement through the mass media and sales promotions through huge distribution channels have speeded up the diffusion of new products and may shorten and/or lengthen the duration of the stage. The Bullwhip effect, from multi-echelon decisions, and phantom demand, from boom effects, are well-known phenomena, which enlarge the variance of demand and rob the supply chain of profits and stability. In this section, we consider the PLC in more detail from the viewpoint of SCM. Table 2 below summarizes the discussion in this chapter.

The first or introduction stage starts upon release of the brand-new product to the market. In this period, sales growth is slow because of the mixed effect of the expensiveness of the product, low awareness in the market, customers' reluctance to change their behaviors, under-formation of the distribution channel, and so on. A large cost is incurred to promote the new product and to attract distributors, so that the profit may be low or even negative. The typical launch strategy is a combination of pricing and sales-promotion approaches. The price strategy can be divided into the skimming and penetration strategies (Kotler, 1999)[3]. In this introduction stage, the price strategy is mainly adopted to skim the margin of the product or to penetrate widely in the market. In the skimming strategy, the price and margin is set at a high level to capitalize on the first mover advantage. In the penetration strategy, the number of potential customers is emphasized much more than the margin for attaining commercial success and benefits of the learning curve effect. The results are then observed and permit determination of the profit per unit and the range of potential customers. The sales promotion functions as a catalyst that controls the diffusion speed. A large expenditure on advertising makes the product popular quickly and a smaller one delays the diffusion. Thus, the launch strategy is very important because it can affect the whole life of the product.

This first stage has a significant meaning for the supply chain as a time for circumstantial judgment and preparation for future success. At this time, it will be uncertain whether the new product succeeds and to what degree and how fast it diffuses. The supply chain should make a launch strategy and plan the timing to expand the manufacturing ability. Usually, downstream players (retailers and wholesalers) can respond more quickly to customer needs than upstream players (set-maker and suppliers) because of the characteristics of the processes and the degree of flexibility of equipment. Upstream players need a longer time to expand their capacity and take much more risk than downstream players. Upstream players have strong constraints in the use and duration of equipment and the rearrangement of the resources (labor, equipment, capital) related to existing products. In addition, the supply chain has a path dependency in that a process starts after all the previous processes finish as the Theory of Constraints (TOC) illustrates (Goldratt, 1990). For example, the lack of a part may become an obstacle to produce and sell the product. Hence, it also important to estimate and identify the future bottlenecks.

The second stage is the growth stage in which the sales volume increases rapidly because the majority of consumers start buying the product. This contributes to reducing the production costs and increasing profits due to large-scale production and the experience curve effect. At the same time, the expansion of the market attracts new competitors into the market. Companies must adopt the various market-expansion strategies by improving the product quality and style, adding new models with new functions, creating new market segments and distribution channels, lowering the price, and so on.

In this stage, the competition, supply chain vs. supply chain, intensifies as the number of competitors increases. The supply chain also takes on market-expansion strategies. Sometimes, the supply chain faces bottlenecks in the production process and incurs opportunity loss because upstream players (manufacturers) take a much longer time to respond to the market expansion than downstream players (wholesalers and retailers). At the worst, this creates internal problems, such as the Bullwhip effect and phantom demand, and gives competitors the chance to enter the market. It is essential for the supply chain to minimize the gap between the demand and supply by improving the production and information system and controlling the diffusion speed. The improvement of the production system includes the expansion of the flexibility with respect to variety and quantity of products, the use of outsourcing, and the appropriate policy and timing to expand the production facility. The information system helps the supply chain to shorten the cycle time to the market and to forecast future demand. In the short term, there is an upper limit for the supply chain to produce. On the other hand, in the long term, there is an appropriate level of production facility in consideration of the shrinkage after the peak demand. Hence, it is a critical factor for supply chains to estimate the trend of the demand correctly and to adjust the manufacturing capability to a reasonable level.

The third stage is the maturity stage in which the sales growth slows down. This stage is divided into three phases: growth maturity (the growth rate starts declining), stable maturity (the sales volume flattens), and decaying maturity (the sales volume starts declining). The slowdown of growth makes overcapacity tangible and induces severe competition. Competitors can be classified into two types: the volume leader (a few giant firms) and the "nichers" (others). The volume leaders pursue maximum profit through economy of scale, while nichers pursue high margins in small target markets. Companies tend to concentrate their resources on profitable and new products and abandon others.

In this stage, supply chains are eager to defend their market shares and to maximize their profits. There are few possibilities left for the supply chains to increase their sales (except the foreign market) because the market has segmented and becomes surrounded by strong barriers and because severe competition tends to induce price competition. So the best way to maximize the supply chain profit is to reduce the cost by the rearrangement of the manufacturing facility and the pursuit of efficient operations. The major rearrangement methods are the standardization of the parts and global outsourcing. These contribute to further cost reduction by enhancing open transactions. Efficient operations can be achieved relatively quickly and easily by strategic alliances for the sales promotion in the foreign market and for the economy of scale by Original Equipment Manufacturing (OEM).

In the last or declining stage, sales decline because of technological and commercial obsolescence. These lead to overcapacity, price competition and profit erosion. Some competitors withdraw from the market. Even the remainders tend to abandon some weak or small segments and harvest their investments quickly.

In this stage, supply chains are forced to make a decision whether to be a survivor or to withdraw form the market. Either way, they must identify weak products and segments and then abandon them. If they decide to be a survivor, however, SCM plays a very important role because SCM contributes to reducing the risk by enhancing the JIT system and outsourcing, and because SCM enables various strategic options. These can be divided into flexible transactions and borderless locations. The flexible transaction includes the use of outsourcing and OEM. The borderless location is suitable for the global sourcing and the economy of scale.

It may be one of the critical factors for supply chains to estimate future demand, taking into account Product Life Cycle considerations. The following case, *Tamagotchi*, illustrates the difficulty and importance of this. *Tamagotchi*, an

Table 2. Product life cycle and SCM

Stage	Marketing Objectives	SCM Implication
Introduction	Creation of Product Awareness and Trial	-Anticipation and Ascertain of the Trend -Linkage of Launch Strategy and Facility Planning -Identifying the Future Bottlenecks

Growth	Maximization of Market Share	-Adoption of Market-expansion Strategy
		-Minimization of the Gap Between the Demand and Supply
		  -Improvement of Production and Information System
		  -Control of the Diffusion Speed
		-Reasonable Forecast of the Future (Peak and After-peak) Demand

Maturity	Maximization of Profit While Defending Market Share	-Rearrangement of Manufacturing System
		  -Standardization of Most Parts
		  -Use of Outsourcing (Formation of Global Supply Chain)
		-Formation of Strategic Alliances for the Sales Promotion
		  -Sales Promotion in the Foreign Markets
		  -OEM

Decline	Reduction of Expenditure and Milk the Brand	-Decision Making on Whether Survival or Evacuation
		If Survival,
		  -Withdrawal from the Weak Products and Segments
		  -Thoroughgoing Rationalization of the Manufacturing Facility

egg-shaped computer game and the first virtual pet game, was launched into the market by Bandai Co., a Japanese toy manufacturer, at the end of November, 1996. It was so brand-new that nothing was comparable. Bandai Co. set the initial target sales volume at 300,000 by the end of 1996 without using mass media advertisement. However, the effect of word of mouth advanced the popularity of the product at such a tremendous speed that they actually sold 4,000,000 units by the end of March 1997. In this case, the introduction stage was over almost immediately and the growth stage started very early. A very severe gap between the demand and supply had occurred. When they enlarged the manufacturing facility in July 1997, the stage of the product had already entered into the decline stage. As a result, although they sold over 2,400,000 units worldwide by the end of October 1997, they announced 16 billion yen (US$136 million at US$1=118 yen) in after-tax losses in fiscal 1998 ending March 1999, mainly because of huge numbers of unsold *Tamagotchi* (Higuchi & Troutt, 2004).

Vernon's Product Cycle Theory

Vernon's (1966) product cycle theory, also called the *product-cycle model* by Dunning (1988), differs from the classical PLC model. The product cycle is oriented toward the production process. By contrast, the PLC focuses on the market and consumer behavior. Vernon concentrated on explaining the relationship between the state of product innovation and the geographical location of manufacturing facilities, from the viewpoint of international trade and economies of scale. While this relationship should certainly be taken into account in the allocation of manufacturing facilities, the economic environment has changed dramatically for several reasons:

(1)   The supply chain has become the basic unit for competition in the market.

(2)   Accessibility and telecommunications have now advanced to the degree that "tele-collaboration" can be executed smoothly.

(3)   The gaps in the standard of living between countries narrows and the differences in labor costs and skill levels diminishes.

(4)   Modularity of product design has progressed so that a single part can improve the product specifications and standardized parts or components can easily be outsourced.

(6)   Developing countries accumulate manufacturing know-how and increase their ability to respond to the innovations quickly.

(7)   Capital markets advance so that difficulties for the international investment diminish.

(8)   Uniqueness of the market becomes very important in creating new products.

National borders are becoming a smaller problem and the uniqueness of countries and regions become more important. In this section, we review the product cycle from the individual process and product innovation stages in the terms of the global supply chain.

In the time period before the decision on where the new product is born and manufacturing facilities are to be located, Vernon assumed that enterprises in any one of the advanced countries are not appreciably different from those in any other advanced countries. However, he mentioned that equal access to the latest technology does not mean equal probability of the application of them in the generation of new products. This is because of possible large gaps between the knowledge of such technologies and their application to the product.

At the early innovation stage, the supply chain should emphasize effective and efficient communication among the customers, R&D departments, and manufactures (including suppliers). R&D departments will locate in the most advanced country available because of the existence of more innovative or sophisticated customers and the merits of aggregation of technologies. For most effective use of communication, not only R&D departments, but also the manufacturing facilities tend to locate in the most advanced country. In this stage, the supply chain concentrates on the linkage within the supply chain and rapid response to the customer demands.

The propensity of multinational enterprises to use their home markets to develop and introduce new products stems from a series of powerful forces. It has been confirmed again and again in empirical studies of various sorts that successful innovations tend to be those that respond to the market conditions surrounding the innovation. The original idea may be developed almost anywhere, but successful innovation depends strongly on the compelling character of the demand. (Vernon, 1977, p.40)

The second stage is the maturity of the product in which the manufacturing process progresses significantly. Demand for the product expands because of global sales growth and the price declines. In order to achieve economies of scale through mass production, the manufacturer wants to use capital-intensive facilities for as long a time as possible. On the other hand, the variety of products will be proliferated by competitors, in part to avoid full price competition. As the product becomes popular in other advanced countries, the barriers to maintaining manufacturing facilities in the most advanced country abate and the pressure to reduce costs begins to predominate.

At this stage, the supply chain seeks to improve the effectiveness of its structure in order to respond to foreign markets. The degrees of maturity of the parts and processes may differ widely, so that it becomes feasible and efficient to shift some processes to foreign countries. For example, it is often easier and less costly to source standardized parts from other countries than to use domestic parts. The setup process also tends to shift to other countries, often immediately accompanied by a large number of new customers. In addition, the local government's regulations often encourage the shift to other countries. Some supply chains shift their new manufacturing facilities to other countries and others make strategic alliances with foreign partners.

In the final stage, the product and processes become so standardized that few processes can create competitive advantages by purely technical improvements. Most processes will have been standardized to the extent that little room is left for differentiation in quality and manufacturing cost, with the exceptions of labor and rent costs. Finally, the country that originated the product becomes an importer from a foreign exporter.

Globalization of the supply chain makes its management still more difficult. Due to economy of scale effects, it is often efficient for some processes to concentrate in a single country. The division of labor in the supply chain becomes global and complex. After that, the pressure increases to reduce logistics costs. The supply chain must then try to achieve efficient and effective flow and storage of the parts and products from the point of origin to the consumer.

Multinationals that have developed a global network commonly see the world as a chessboard on which they are conducting a wide-range of campaigns. The chessboard's squares are nation-states, and an enterprise can consider entering any one of them by a number of different means — by trading with dependent firms in the country, by developing alliances with enterprises already operating in the country, or establishing a subsidiary of its own in the country. (Vernon, 1998, p.22)

Table 3 summarizes the production theory in terms of location. Each stage has its own mission and sources of competitive advantages. In the first stage when the product is new, the supply chain should build a strong linkage between the latent customers in order to incubate the new market. Before information technology (IT) and management technologies advanced, location near to the customers was essential. Now, supply chains can use IT effectively to communicate with customers and to collaborate beyond national borders and without regard to distance. In the second stage, when the product is maturing, supply chains should respond to the expansion of the market and the intensification of competition. Overseas investment and international strategic alliances become inevitable. In the third stage, when the product is more standardized, supply chains need to pursue efficiency in global logistics. To achieve this, it becomes critical to allocate supply chain functions globally and to improve coordination among them.

The development of the home VCR illustrates Vernon's Product Cycle Theory. To commercialize the home VCR, there were some requirements from the customers: the size, price, quality and specifications (for example, recording time). Japanese consumer electronics companies had advantages in that they

Table 3. Stages of the product development and production location

Stage	Mission	Source of Advantage	Location Implication
New (Innovative)	Interaction with a Latent Market Need	Linkage Between the Supply Chain and the Innovative Customers	-Flexibility in Location at the Beginning -Differentiation of Production -The Need for Efficient and Effective Communication among Concerns
Maturing	Building an Effective Supply Chain	Overseas Investment and Strategic Alliances	-Standardizing the Production Process -Access to the Foreign Markets -Economy of Scale (Cost Reduction)
Standardized	Achievement of an Efficient Supply Chain	Global Supply Chain Coordination	-Expansion of the Markets to less- developed countries -Global Division of Labor -Reduction of Global Logistics Costs

already had TV and cassette tape recorder departments that could respond to the consumer feedback quickly. The technologies used in these departments were critical to the commercialization of the home VCR. Between 1976 and 1985, Japanese companies monopolized the production of VCRs. After 1985, Japanese companies started offshore production for sales promotions in the other advanced countries and costs were cut to win the price competition. Up to now, Japanese companies are losing room for further differentiation and new competitors from Asian countries are increasing their shares all over the world in the industry (see further details in the next section).

VCR Case Study

To demonstrate the three life cycles, we examine the development of the home VCR industry. JAPAN VICTOR0(JVC) developed VHS technology and succeeded in creating the market in 1976. After that, other companies, for example, MATSUSHITA, HITACHI, MITSHUBISHI Electric, SANYO, SHARP, AKAI Electric, AIWA, and FUNAI, started selling VHS products. VHS products became popular in Japan and the United States first, and later became the global standard. In the first decade (1976-1985), most of these products were produced in Japan and exported to other countries. In the next decade (1985-1994), some manufacturing facilities and/or processes started shifting to other countries. Finally, in the latest decade, Japan imported many more than they exported in terms of quantity. Now at the beginning of this century, a similar transition period appears to be underway from the video cassette to the DVD formats of home video entertainment.

The VCR industry started after AMPEX VRX-1000 (Mark IV) was introduced for industry use in 1956. It was inevitable that this industry-use VCR technology would be miniaturized and made less expensive for home use. SONY was the leader in the development of the home-use VCR market[1]. In 1974, SONY developed the prominent home use VCR, "Betamax," and started selling it at 229,800 Yen (about US$771 at US$1= 298 Yen) in August 1975. However, it was still rather large and expensive to be ideally suited to the home-use market. In 1969, SONY introduced the "Color Videoplayer." In 1970, SONY developed the "U Format" and requested other competitors to adopt it. Several did in fact adopt it and developed the product based on it. Thus, it was believed that Betamax would become the dominant design in the home-use VCR.

JVC had meanwhile been outdone by SONY in popularity and technically. However, in 1975, JVC developed VHS and introduced the HR-3300 model with VHS format at 256,000 Yen (about US$892 at US$1 = 287 Yen) in September 1976. VHS and Betamax units are similar, but they require cassettes of different sizes. Hence, these formats are incompatible. It is debatable whether VHS or Betamax was technically superior. VHS emphasized lower weight and a longer recording time capacity. The HR-3300 model was lighter than Betamax by 5 kg and HR-3300 could record for two hours while Betamax could record for only one hour at that time[2]. These features appealed to the customers in the United States, Europe and Japan. Then the struggle for the de-facto standard became heated.

In the mid 1970's, JVC effectively made strategic alliances with competitors. In response to JVC's call, MATSUSHITA, HITACHI, MITSUBISHI, SHARP and AKAI all accepted the VHS format. This alliance was quite effective for recovering from the technical confusion and inefficiency, and also promoted recognition of the product in the market. SHARP contributed the front-loading technique, MITSUBISHI the fast forward technique, HITACHI the IC techniques, and MATSUSHITA HiFi techniques. At that time, MATSUSHITA had the largest distribution channel in Japan. In addition, VHS expanded to the United States and Europe by OEM (Original Equipment Manufacturing). Finally, VHS overtook the Betamax and became the global standard, the dominant design, in the home use VCR (NHK, 2000).

Figure 3 shows the shift in the numbers of output and the average production cost of home use VCRs in Japan. The average cost declined rapidly in the late 1970s and more stably in the 1980s and 1990s. The diffusion rate reached 5% in 1981. Fifteen years after SONY introduced the first home use VCR, the CV-

Figure 3. Number of output and production cost

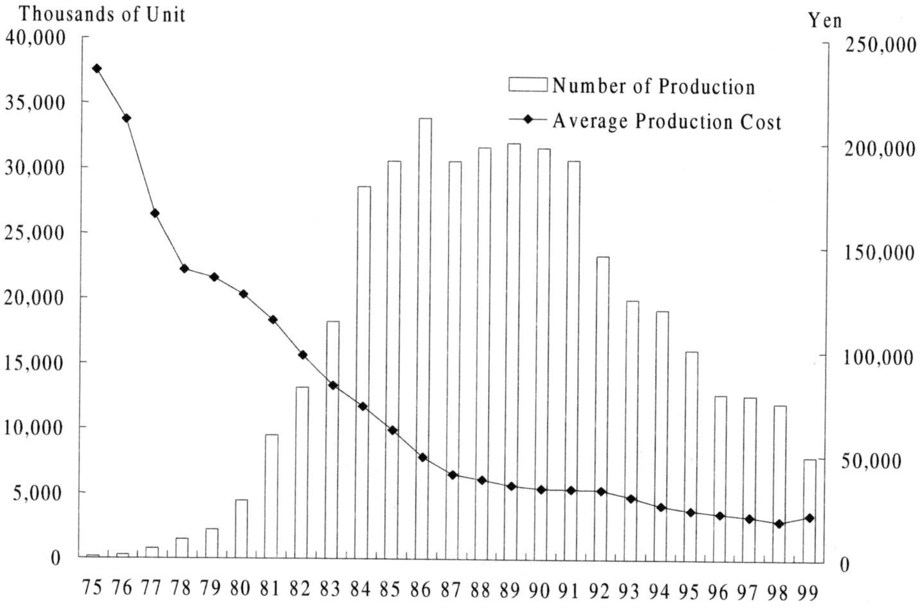

Source: http://www.jeita.or.jp/english/index.htm

2000, its market grew rapidly to 63% in 1980s. In the 1990s, the speed of diffusion slowed down and the level rose to 78%. The reduction of costs enlarged the market, and at the same time, the expansion of the market induced further cost reduction by economy of scale effects, the learning curve, and competition.

Product innovations also contributed to the diffusion of the VCR. VHS continued to develop with new functions, such as tripled recording time (1979), HiFi sound (1983), Super-VHS (1987), W-VHS (1993) and the dynamic drum system (1995). As Abernathy (1978) pointed out, new features tend to have less impact at the later end of the cycle than at the beginning. However, these are critical factors for the location of supply chain functions. JVC has been the leader and introduced new products with new functions. Their manufacturing facilities tended to locate in the advanced countries, while less innovative manufacturers tended to locate in developing countries.

Almost all VCRs have been produced in Japan. Figures 4 and 5 show the shifts in the import and export numbers in Japan and the shifts of domestic and

Figure 4. Shift of export and import

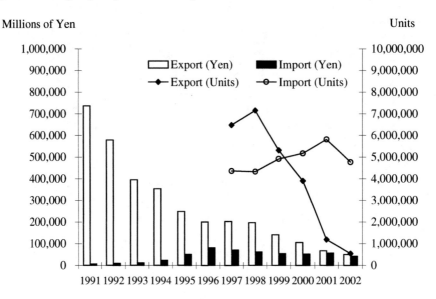

http://www.jeita.or.jp/english/index.htm

Figure 5. Domestic and offshore production

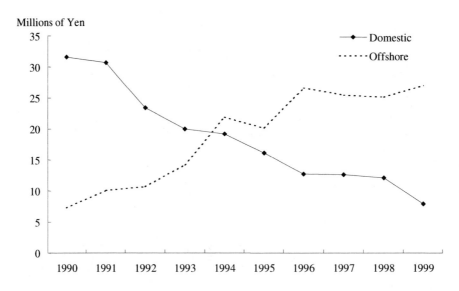

http://www.jeita.or.jp/english/index.htm

Figure 6. Lowest prices in each category by companies

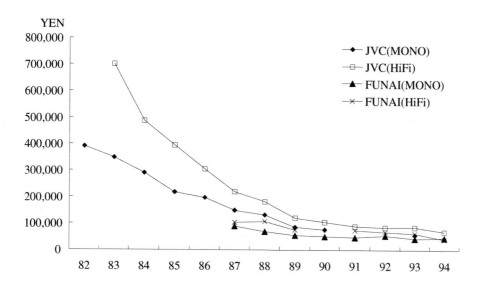

Note: Prices have been adjusted by the GNP deflator (1994:100%)

Figure 7. Price zone in 1993-1994

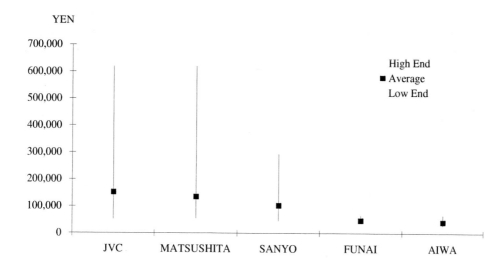

offshore production by Japanese companies. In the early 1990s, some Japanese companies started producing VCRs in foreign countries. In 1994, the offshore production surpassed the domestic production. Finally, overseas production tripled, and by 1999, imports to Japan exceeded exports.

At the present time, the de-maturity process is likely underway. The DVD is rapidly catching up with VHS. Although the DVD recorder is more expensive than the VCR, the DVD appears to have a greater potential. The DVD is much smaller and more durable than the VHS cassette and can record much longer at a higher quality than the VHS. DVD also has attractive interactive features. In Japan, the sales volume of DVD software exceeded that of the VHS in 2003.

It is important to note that by way of this case study, we obtained a result inconsistent with Vernon's Product Cycle Theory. Although the VCR industry must have reached the third stage when the product became highly standardized, Japan still exports more than it imports in monetary terms. This is because some Japanese supply chains have delayed the onset of the maturity stage by adding new functions. Figure 6 illustrates the lowest fixed prices in each category, monaural and HiFi sound, by the companies JVC and FUNAI. While JVC is a leading innovator, FUNAI is a specialist in cost cutting. JVC tried to avoid the price competition by adding new functions. From Figure 7, it is clear that JVC had a wider range of products than FUNAI. Thus, the differing strategies had profound effects on the structure of the supply chain, the degree of maturity of the product, and so on. Hence, we need further research on the relationship between supply chain strategy and dynamics.

Conclusions

The three life cycles of the product innovation, market and facilities location provide useful landmarks for supply chain planners and managers. Table 4 describes the stages of these three life cycles. In Table 4, "location" refers to geographic location of factories. In Vernon's product cycle theory, the location of factories has a close relationship to the degree of maturity of the product. When the product is new (the innovative stage), companies tend to locate factories in the most advanced countries. After maturing of the product, they tend to spread production facilities to other advanced countries. Once the product becomes standardized, it becomes efficient to locate production in developing countries.

Table 4. Stages of the three life cycles

		Innovation	Customer	Location
	0	Before Dominant Design	Introduction	New (Innovative)
		Immature	Growth	
T				Maturing
I		Mature	Maturity	
M				Standardized
E			Decline	
		De-mature		
	t			

By focusing on where the chain is in terms of these cycles, guidance is provided about globalization and location decisions, activities to emphasize, and R&D priorities. A case study of the VCR supply chain illustrated many of the general principles. However, it also illustrated how some stages could be manipulated by emphasis on developing new features and functionalities. This point also illustrates an important point in evaluating new seed innovative products. Other things being equal, those innovations that promise a larger variety of potential variations and feature innovations should be of special interest.

References

Abernathy, W. J. (1978). *The productivity dilemma.* Baltimore, MD: The John Hopkins University Press.

Abernathy, W. J., Clark, K. B., & Kantrow, A.M. (1983). *Industrial renaissance.* New York: Basic Books.

Ampex Corporation. (2003). Retrieved September 10, 2003 from the WWW: *http://www.ampex.com/*

Bowersox, D. J., & Closs, D. J. (1996). *Logistical management: The integrated supply chain process.* New York: McGraw-Hill.

Bradley, P.J., Thomas, T.G., & Cooke J. (1999). Future competition: Supply chain vs. supply chain. *Logistics Management and Distribution Report, 39*(3), 20-21.

Chopra, S., & Meindl, P. (2003). *Supply chain management: Strategy, planning and operation (2ⁿᵈ ed.).* Upper Saddle River, NJ: Pearson Prentice Hall.

Dunning, J. H. (1988). *Explaining international production.* London: Unwin Hyman.

Electronics Industries Association of Japan. (2000). Retrieved September 10, 2003 from the WWW: *http://www.jeita.or.jp/eiaj/english/index.htm*

Goldratt E. (1990). *The theory of constraints.* Croton-on-Hudson, NY: North River Press.

Higuchi, T., & Troutt, M. D. (2004). Dynamic simulation of the supply chain for a short life cycle product - Lessons from the Tamagotchi case. *Computers & Operations Research* (forthcoming).

Japan Electronics and Information Technology Industries Association. (2003). Retrieved September 10, 2003 from the WWW: *http://www.jeita.or.jp/english/index.htm*

Kotler, P. (1999). *Marketing management (Millennium ed.).* NJ: Prentice Hall.

NHK (Japan Broadcasting Corporation). (2000). *Project X: Challengers 1.* Tokyo: Japan Broadcast Publishing.

Qualls, W., Olshavsky, R. W., & Michaels, R. E. (1981). Shortening of the PLC—An empirical test. *Journal of Marketing, 45*(4), 76-80.

Rosenbloom, R. S., & Abernathy, W. J. (1982, November). The climate for innovation in industry. *Research Policy, 11*(4), 209-225.

Shintaku, J. (1990). *Nihon Kigyou no Kyousou Sennryaku* (Competitive Strategies of Japanese Firms). Tokyo: Yuhikaku.

Sony Corporation. (2003). *Sony history.* Retrieved September 10, 2003 from the WWW: *http://www.sony.net/Fun/SH/*

Stanley, E. F. & Birou, L. M. (1992). Exploring the logistics interface between global and JIT sourcing. *International Journal of Physical Distribution & Logistics Management, 22*(1), 3-14.

Vernon, R. (1966). International investment and international trade in the product cycle. *Quarterly Journal of Economics, 80*, 190-207.

Vernon, R. (1977). *Storm over the multinationals.* MA: Harvard University Press.

Vernon, R. (1998). *In the hurricane's eye.* MA: Harvard University Press.

Victor Company of Japan. (2003). Retrieved September 10, 2003 from the WWW: *http://www.jvc-victor.co.jp/english/global-e.html*

Endnotes

[1] To develop the home use VCR market, Japanese consumer electronics companies had advantages. First, they incorporated the tape recorder industry and TV department within a company. VCRs use "mechatronics," which is the combination of mechanics and electronics. To develop the VCR, the mechanics (such as in a tape recorder) and the electronics (such as in TVs) were necessary. At that time, collaboration with other companies was an unexplored area. Hence, Japanese companies, which possessed both technologies, managed to develop the home use VCR in the commercial market. Secondly, they had excellent competitors and suppliers indispensable for the home use VCR. Finally, they had established expertise in miniaturization, which was a critical factor for succeeding in the design of the home use VCR.

[2] Customers mainly record movies from TV. This requires a recording time capacity of at least two hours in general.

[3] Kotler (1999) originally combined the price and promotion strategies, and thereby proposed four strategies: fast and slow skimming and fast and slow penetration.

Chapter V

The Effect of Different Payment Terms on Order Variability in a Supply Chain

I Nyoman Pujawan, The University of Manchester, UK

Abstract

Literature on supply chain management has acknowledged the effects of forecasting techniques, lot sizing rules, centralising information system, vendor managed inventory, and various biases and noises on order variability or bullwhip effect. We will show in this chapter that order variability from a buyer is also affected by the payment terms offered by the supplier. We develop mathematical models to accommodate different payment terms into the lot sizing techniques. The models are then simulated under uncertain demand situations over a range of parameter values. The results suggest that payment terms have substantial impacts on order variability passed by a supply chain channel onto its upstream channel.

Introduction

The difficulty in managing supply chain operations is much attributable to the degree of variability of orders or demands flowing from a downstream to the upstream channels in the supply chain. It is believed that order variability could be disruptive to achieving efficient supply chain operations: it results in higher inventories, lower service levels, and more difficulties in managing capacities. Authors on supply chain management have discovered that order variability could be a result of various processes in a supply chain such as forecasting, rationing and gaming, order batching, quantity discount policy, etc. (see, for example, Lee et al., 1997; Fransoo and Wouter, 2000; Disney and Towill, 2003). Several of those processes are rational responses for dealing with uncertainty while others, such as order batching and quantity discount, are processes to exploit economies of scale in a supply chain. Mason-Jones and Towill (2000) asserted that at each supply chain channel, order information is subject to delay, bias, and noise before it is transferred to the immediate supplier. In other words, the demand information from a downstream channel is distorted, and as a result, the further away a channel is from the end customer, the larger is the distortion of the demand of the end customer he or she receives. Such a phenomenon creates difficulty in managing a supply chain and is disruptive to achieving effective and efficient supply chain operations.

Amplification of order variability in a supply chain has been a subject of interest for academics. Forrester (1960) is probably the first scholar to present the amplification of demand from a downstream to an upstream channel in a supply chain. More recent literature has termed this phenomenon as a Bullwhip Effect (Lee et al., 1997; Dejonckheere et al., 2002; Pujawan, 2004; Disney and Towill, 2003; Zhang, 2004). Various issues have been addressed in relation to the bullwhip effect in the recent literature. Metters (1997) presented experimental results that show the impact of the bullwhip effect on supply chain profitability. Chen et al. (1998) provided quantitative models that measure the impact of forecasting techniques and information centralisation policy on the bullwhip effect. With respect to the forecasting techniques, for example, the authors showed that the exponential smoothing technique led to a higher bullwhip effect compared to the moving average. Disney and Towill (2003) evaluated the effect of using a Vendor Managed Inventory system on the bullwhip effect. They showed that VMI could reduce demand amplification up the supply chain and, hence, provides better supply chain stability. Zhang (2004) modeled and evaluated the impact of forecasting methods on the bullwhip effect and suggested that different forecasting methods could have a different impact on the bullwhip effect, but their impact is affected by other factors, i.e., the lead time and the demand autocorrelation. Kelle and Milne (1999) studied the effect of (s,S) ordering policy on the order variability. They revealed that the variance of orders produced relative to the variance of demand received is proportional to the periods between the successive orders. In a recent paper, Pujawan (2004) presented a model on the effect of lot sizing rules on order variability created by a buyer. The author suggested that different lot sizing rules could have an effect on the order variability passed by a supply chain channel to its supplier.

In this chapter, we will show that payment terms could also have an impact on order variability. We will observe order variability from the pattern of an order that a buyer sends to the supplier. Different payment terms agreed on by the buyer and the supplier might finally create different ordering patterns from the buyer. Previous publications addressing the bullwhip effect have neglected the potential impact of different payment terms offered by a supplier on the variability of orders passed on by its buyer. In a practical environment, it is logical that the buyer would adjust its ordering policy if different payment terms were offered by the supplier in an attempt to maximise the financial benefits of the payment terms. Pujawan and Kingsman (2003) asserted that payment terms could have an impact on the ordering patterns from the buyer, i.e., one payment term could result in more lumpiness in the buyer's order than the other. This has raised a suspicion that different payment terms could have a significant impact on the variability of orders received by an upstream supply chain channel.

In the literature, payment terms have been analysed under a constant demand setting. When demand is assumed constant, the optimal order quantity would certainly be the same from time to time. In this chapter, uncertain time varying demand will be analysed. Two traditional dynamic lot sizing methods will be modified to accommodate different payment terms, i.e., the Silver Meal (SM) rule and the least unit cost (LUC) rule.

Literature on Payment Terms

In practice, immediate payment on the receipt of the goods ordered by the buying company rarely happens. The suppliers usually provide certain credit terms to the buyer. Thus, the buyer is allowed to delay payments for a certain period. Most inventory control models presented in the literature have neglected this phenomenon and assumed that payments took place immediately on the receipt of the items by the buyer. However, there have been efforts spent by researchers to investigate the effect of payment terms on the inventory control models. Kingsman (1983) and Carlson and Rousseau (1989) pointed out that there are two payment terms commonly applied in practice. The first is a so called day-terms contract where payments are due a fixed period after the receipt of the items. The second is a date-terms payment contract, where the buyer is allowed to delay payment of all items received in month t to a specified date in month $t+1$. In contrast to the day-terms case, the length of the credit periods in date-terms vary according to the date the items are received by the buyer.

Several variations of these credit payment systems have been studied by researchers. Chapman et al. (1984), for example, presented four situations of credit terms. They showed that the economic order quantity is determined by the relative length of credit periods to the order cycle and whether or not the credit periods are based on the units remaining in stock. Later, Chung (1989) also considered the same four situations and derived expressions for the economic order quantity based on a discounted cost approach applying a continuously compounded interest rate. The paper by Wilson (1991) presents a payment system that can be considered as one case of those studied by Chapman et al. (1984), that is, when the credit period is less than the order cycle.

Another assumption can also be made in conjunction with the cash inflow from sales. In some cases, the delayed payment enables the firm to earn interest from the revenue obtained before the payment is due. This is particularly true if the firm sells the items for immediate payment, such as in the case for retailers. Halley and Higgins (1973), Goyal (1985), and Chung (1998) consider this situation and differentiate between the borrowing and lending interest rates in their models. Teng (2002) amended Goyal's models by considering the difference between the unit price and the unit cost. Huang (2003) extended the previous models, taking into consideration that the retailer who receives a payment delay from the supplier also offers a similar trade credit policy to its customers.

The date-terms payment contract has received very little attention in recent studies. There are very few papers dealing with modeling economic order quantity under date-terms payment contract, for example, Kingsman (1983,

1991), Carlson and Rousseau (1989), Carlson et al. (1996), and Luo and Huang (2002). The papers by Carlson et al. (1989) and Carlson et al. (1996) suggest that the optimal order quantity can only be obtained by using a search procedure. Its complexity may explain why little attention has been devoted to this payment term.

Modeling Lot Sizing Decisions with Different Payment Terms

Assumptions and Notations

The underlying principle in modeling the lot sizing problems under different payment terms is the separation of inventory holding costs into two parts. The first part, which will be referred to as the physical holding costs, includes those holding costs which are associated with the flow of items such as storage cost, tax, insurance, and obsolescence. We use the usual assumption that the physical holding cost is charged based on inventory values at the end of each period. The second part covers the holding cost which depends on the flow of funds, i.e., the cost of capital. According to Bowersox and Closs (1996), the average annual cost of capital for various enterprises is about 15%, while the physical holding cost forms only about 4.5%.

Three payment terms will be considered in this section, namely, immediate payment, day-terms, and date-terms. For modeling purposes, time is divided into discrete periods of uniform length. Ordering decisions can only be made at the start of a period. It will be assumed that the permitted payment delay is always an integer number of time periods. In modeling date-terms payment system, the payment cycle is defined as the period between successive payment dates. For example, if it is assumed that one month is equal to four periods and payment is due at the start of the second period of the following month, then there is a four-period payment cycle and a one period permitted payment delay after the cycle ends.

In the models that follow, A is defined as the ordering cost, c is unit price of the item, h is physical holding cost per period as a fraction of unit price, r is cost of capital which is assumed equal to the interest rate, and d_k is demand in period k. The following are further notations that will be used in the models:

δ	= allowed payment delay in day-terms, stated in periods.
m	= payment cycle in date-terms.
γ	= allowed payment delay in date-terms after the corresponding payment cycle ends.
φ	= integer numbers, started from zero, indicating the order of payment cycle in date-terms.
$i(k)$	= the increase of inventory holding costs if order quantity is increased from covering demand for k-1 periods to k periods.
$f(k)$	= the sum of inventory holding cost for an order covering k periods of demand.
$PWC(k)$	= present worth of cost for an order covering k periods of demand.
$ARC(k)$	= average cost per period for an order covering k periods of demand.
$AUC(k)$	= average unit cost for an order covering k periods of demand.

Heuristic Rules to Determine Order Quantity

The optimal policy in deterministic lot sizing problems is to place an order covering demand for an integer number of periods. Based on this property, the principle of lot sizing heuristic is to increase incrementally the number of periods to cover in one order until a certain condition is met. In the Silver Meal rule, the condition is based on the incurred average cost per period. The number of periods covered in one order is the one which first gives the local minimum cost per period. In the LUC rule, on the other hand, the number of periods covered in one order is that which gives the minimum cost per unit.

When comparing policies that have cash inflows and outflows at different times, it is generally considered that discounting the costs and comparing policies on their net present worth at the start of time one is more accurate than the use of the average costs approach, although it might lead to a more complicated mathematical analysis. In some situations, including delayed payment terms, the cost functions are more easily represented using discounted cash flow analysis. If a sum invested earns interest continuously at a rate r per period, then after t periods, £1 has increased to £e^{rt}. Thus £1 paid out at time t is equivalent to £e^{-rt} at the start of time one. If the demand d_t is bought at a cost c per unit at the start of period t, then the discounted cost would be $cd_t e^{-r(t-1)}$, since it is discounted back over the t-1 periods to the start of period 1. If this demand were bought as part of a lot at time one then it would cost cd_t. Thus the extra financing due to making d_t part of the lot bought at time one is the difference between these two values, that is, $cd_t(1\text{-}e^{-r(t-1)})$. Assuming that the period an order to be placed is always referred to as period one, present worth of cost for an order covering k periods of demand under the assumption of immediate payment is given by:

$$PWC(k) = A + hc\sum_{t=1}^{k-1}\left(\sum_{j=t+1}^{k}d_j\right)e^{-rt} + c\sum_{t=2}^{k}d_t\left(1-e^{-r(t-1)}\right) \qquad (1)$$

Where the last two terms represent respectively the physical holding cost and cost of capital. Similarly, when the number of periods covered is k-1, the present worth of cost is:

$$PWC(k-1) = A + hc\sum_{t=1}^{k-2}\left(\sum_{j=t+1}^{k-1}d_j\right)e^{-rt} + c\sum_{t=2}^{k-1}d_t\left(1-e^{-r(t-1)}\right) \qquad (2)$$

Subtracting $PWC(k\text{-}1)$ from $PWC(k)$ gives the increase in the present worth of cost when the number of periods to cover is increased from k-1 to k. This cost will be referred to as incremental cost of period k which is given by:

$$i(k) = PWC(k) - PWC(k-1) \quad = hcd_k\sum_{t=1}^{k-1}e^{-rt} + cd_k\left(1-e^{-r(k-1)}\right) \qquad (3)$$

If payments follow a day-terms contract, then the financing cost of the capital invested in stock will be lower than that in the immediate payment case because the supplier allows the payment to be delayed for δ periods. The financing cost will be the difference between paying for the demand d_t in period one and paying in period $t+\delta$, but the physical holding cost will remains the same since it is not affected by the payment terms. Following the logic for the immediate payment, the incremental cost of increasing the order to cover k periods rather than k-1 periods' demand for the day terms case is given by:

$$i(k) = hcd_k \sum_{t=1}^{k-1} e^{-rt} + cd_k e^{-r\delta} \left(1 - e^{-r(k-1)}\right)$$ (4)

A more complicated expression is required to model the lot sizing decisions in date-terms payment contract. When an order is placed at the beginning of a payment cycle and the order quantity covers less than or equal to one payment cycle (m), there is no cost of capital incurred. For in this case the payment for the whole order takes place at exactly the same time as would be the case for the payments if individual orders were placed for each successive period. For example, if the payment cycle is four periods and the permitted payment delay is γ period in the next payment cycle, then orders placed at the start of period 1, 2, 3 or 4 will all be paid for at the same time. Thus an order in period one will not incur any financing cost if the order quantity covers four periods or less. However, once an order covers periods belonging to two or more payment cycles, a considerably larger cost of capital will be encountered. The present worth of the costs incurred if an order at the beginning of a payment cycle covers the demand for k periods in the date-terms contract can be expressed as follows:

$$PWC(k) = A + hc \sum_{t=1}^{k-1} \left(\sum_{j=t+1}^{k} d_j \right) e^{-rt} + ce^{-r(\gamma-1)} \sum_{t=2}^{k} d_t \left(e^{-rm} - e^{-rm(\varphi+1)}\right)$$ (5)

Payment of the purchase cost for the demand d_t is made in period $m + \gamma$ if it is included in the lot bought at the start of period 1. If it were bought at the start of period t, then payment would be made at time $m(\varphi+1)+\gamma$, where φ is the largest integer less than or equal to $(t-1)/m$. The period t occurs in the $(\varphi+1)^{th}$ payment cycle, so the payment would take place γ periods into the next payment cycle. Consider a payment cycle of four periods, so $m = 4$, and a permitted payment delay after the payment cycle terminated of one period, so $\gamma = 1$. Hence, the payment for an order placed in any time between period 1 to period 4 is due in period 5 and the payment for an order placed any time between period 5 and period 8 is due in period 9. If the order in period 1 is to cover demand up to period 4, there is no cost of capital incurred. (In this case, the value of φ in equation (5) is zero.) When demand in period 5 is included in the order placed in period 1, there is a cost of capital. Instead of paying in period 9 for placing the order in period 5, the buyer has to pay for the demand of period 5 in period 5, since it was ordered in period 1. The value of φ in this case is one.

A similar expression can be derived for PWC(k-1). The incremental cost is then given by the following formulation:

$$i(k) = hcd_k \sum_{t=1}^{k-1} e^{-rt} + ce^{-r(\gamma-1)} d_k \left(e^{-rm} - e^{-rm(\varphi+1)} \right) \tag{6}$$

The number of steps in determining the order quantity can be substantially reduced since the present worth can be expressed in term of a recursive function as follows:

$$PWC(k) = PWC(k-1) + i(k) \tag{7}$$

Where PWC(1) = A and $i(k)$ is as defined in (3), (4), or (6) for immediate payment, day-terms, and date-terms respectively. Since $f(k)$ is the total inventory holding cost for an order covering demand for k periods, the present worth can also be written as:

$$PWC(k) = A + f(k) \tag{8}$$

In the Silver Meal rule, the cost per period is then obtained from dividing $PWC(k)$ by k, the number of periods to cover. In other words, $ARC(k) = PWC(k)/k$. Similarly, when $PWC(k)$ is divided by D_k, the total demand for k periods covered in an order, the cost per unit, $AUC(k)$, is obtained. This is done when the LUC rule is applied. More analyses on the above models can be found in Pujawan (2000) and Pujawan and Kingsman (1999).

Effect on Order Variability

System Description and Experimental Design

To evaluate the impact of different payment terms on the order variability passed by a buyer to its upstream channel under uncertain demand situations, a simulation study has been conducted. The variability of order is measured in terms of quantity variability as well as interval variability. Quantity variability, which represents fluctuation in the quantities ordered by the buying firm to its supplier, is measured based on the coefficient of variation of the positive order quantities, notated as $CV(Q)$. The variability of order interval, $CV(I)$, is measured based on the coefficient of variation of the interval between orders. Demand coming from the end customers to the buying firm is assumed to follow a normal distribution with mean μ and standard deviation σ. Figure 1 illustrates the system where demand from the end customer, the lot sizing rules, and the payment terms are inputs to the system. Orders to the supplier are the output under which the two types of variability will be measured.

The system works in the situation where demands from the end customers are uncertain, but the buying firm is assumed to obtain exact information of the demand for the current period at the beginning of each period. Demand information for the succeeding periods is available in the form of forecasts which are subject to errors. Forecasts are made at the beginning of a period after the information on the exact demand for the current period is obtained. The following exponential smoothing technique is used to generate the forecast:

Figure 1. Illustration of the system

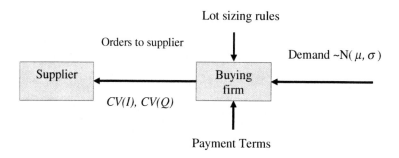

$$F_{t,j} = \vartheta + \alpha d_t \qquad\qquad \forall j \in \{t+1, t+2, \dots t+R-1\} \qquad (9)$$

and the actual demand in a period is generated by using a random process as follows:

$$d_t = F_{t-1,t} + e_t \qquad\qquad (10)$$

where

$F_{t,j}$ = forecast made at the beginning of period t for period j in the planning horizon after demand of the current period (t) is known.

ϑ = the constant level of the forecast

α = the weight of the current demand to the forecast

d_t = demand in period t

R = the length of the planning horizon

e_t = forecast error in period t, assumed to follow a normal distribution with mean 0 and standard deviation σ.

Demand uncertainty is reflected by the ratio of the standard deviation of forecast error to the mean demand, i.e., σ/μ. In the experiments, two different degrees of demand uncertainty have been used, i.e., 10% and 40%. In addition, four cost structures leading to time between order (TBO) of 2 to 5 periods have also been included in the experiments, where TBO is defined as the number of periods to cover in one order under a constant demand situation. The payment terms have been simplified into two, immediate payment (IP) and date-terms (DT). The day-terms payment has been excluded because it has almost the same ordering decisions as the immediate payment for virtually all reasonable parameters tested. In the case of date-terms payment, it is assumed that the payment for all orders received in month t is due at the end of the first week of month $t+1$. It is assumed that one month is consisted of four weeks. Furthermore, the physical holding cost rate is assumed to be one forth of the cost of capital. Two lot sizing rules, SM and LUC, have been used to determine the lot sizing decisions. The two lot sizing rules have been modified to accommodate different payment terms as presented previously.

Table 1. Experimental factors

Experimental factor	Levels	Number of levels
Payment terms	IP, DT	2
CV demand	10%, 40%	2
TBO	2, 3, 4, 5	4
Lot sizing rule	SM, LUC	2
Experimental cells		32
Total experiments		32 x 5 = 160

The simulation program was coded using Pacal © programming language. The code was previously verified by comparing the results of the simulation for several periods with manually calculated examples. The experiments were run after the simulation program had been verified. Table 1 summarises that there are four experimental factors and each factor has either two or four levels. The total number of experimental cells is 32 and each cell is replicated five times leading to a total of 160 experiments. Each experiment is run for 300 periods and to mitigate the impact of the initial period, the statistics for the first 27 periods have been discarded. The results of five replications in each experimental cell were then averaged.

The Results

The results of the experiments are summarised in Tables 2 and 3. The most evident finding from the experimental results is that different payment terms could result in significantly different order variability. More specifically, the date-terms payment system results in more fluctuated order quantity as well as more fluctuated order interval in almost all situations evaluated in the experiments, irrespective of the lot sizing rules, the cost structure, and the degree of demand uncertainty. The results are sensible. With the supplier offering a date-terms payment system, where the payment of orders only takes place once in a month, the buyer would have more incentive for ordering as far from the payment due date as possible. However, this is not always possible when demand from the end customer is uncertain. Under demand uncertainty, it would often be the case that a shortage happens just a few days before the payment date. If this is the case, the optimal order quantity would be much smaller than if the order were to be made just a few days after the payment date for the orders of the previous month. This explains why the date-terms payment results in higher fluctuation in both the quantity of and the interval between orders created by the buyer.

The results confirm our initial thought that payment terms could have a role in amplifying demand variability from a downstream to an upstream channel. Clearly, as orders from a downstream channel are more fluctuated, the upstream channel will face more difficulties in satisfying those orders in an efficient way. Variability in both order interval and order quantity from a buyer will inevitably increase inventory level to be kept by the supplier while at the same time also lower service level to the buyer. This suggests that in order to have an effective supply chain relationship, there should be a careful design on how the buyer should pay for the orders. Immediate payment or day-terms payment would certainly be more desirable in terms of achieving better order stability from the buyer.

The results also show that demand uncertainty has substantial impact on the variability of orders from the buyer, that is, higher demand uncertainty leads to higher order variability. The result is obviously logical. Since the demand forecast is made based on the exponential smoothing technique, larger forecast error translates into more fluctuated forecasts. The lot sizing rules, which determine the order sizes based on the forecasts, will then produce more fluctuated orders both in terms of quantity as well as in terms of order interval. Moreover, as demand becomes less predictable, it is often the case that the same amount of inventory could last for much longer or much shorter time in the planning horizon, resulting in a more fluctuated time between orders.

The lot sizing techniques also have impacts on order variability. Under the immediate payment system, SM produces higher variability in order quantity but lower variability in order interval, compared to the LUC rule. Pujawan (2004) developed mathematical models to investigate the impacts of these two lot sizing rules on order variability under an implicit assumption of immediate payment. The models explain why the above behaviour happens. However, as the date-terms payment system is in place, the differences in the variability of orders produced by the two rules diminish significantly. Figures 2 (a) and (b) present, respectively, the graphs of the effect of payment terms and lot sizing rules on the variability of order quantity and order interval.

The results presented in Tables 2 and 3 also clearly show that the cost structure, which governs the time between orders (TBO), has a significant impact on order variability. Longer time between orders, which is a result of larger order cost relative to the inventory holding costs, leads to lower order variability. This is due to a pooling effect. Longer TBO means that demands from more periods

Table 2. Order quantity variability

TBO	CVD =10%				CVD = 40%			
	IP		DT		IP		DT	
	SM	**LUC**	**SM**	**LUC**	**SM**	**LUC**	**SM**	**LUC**
2	0.276	0.086	0.426	0.425	0.264	0.146	0.381	0.386
3	0.157	0.074	0.408	0.265	0.183	0.104	0.376	0.331
4	0.104	0.063	0.211	0.223	0.148	0.077	0.239	0.235
5	0.079	0.051	0.070	0.128	0.142	0.069	0.194	0.188
Average	**0.154**	**0.069**	**0.279**	**0.260**	**0.185**	**0.099**	**0.298**	**0.285**

Table 3. Order interval variability

TBO	CVD =10%				CVD = 40%			
	IP		DT		IP		DT	
	SM	**LUC**	**SM**	**LUC**	**SM**	**LUC**	**SM**	**LUC**
2	0.330	0.348	0.387	0.381	0.395	0.395	0.434	0.440
3	0.195	0.249	0.369	0.302	0.267	0.308	0.428	0.414
4	0.142	0.174	0.185	0.178	0.241	0.247	0.345	0.338
5	0.110	0.138	0.179	0.207	0.228	0.227	0.284	0.271
Average	**0.194**	**0.227**	**0.280**	**0.267**	**0.283**	**0.294**	**0.373**	**0.366**

are pooled into an order. The central limit theorem, which suggests that the sums of numbers coming from the same distribution will have less variability than the individual numbers, applies in this case. Such an effect, as shown by the above tables, is more evident when demand from the end customer is more predictable. It is interesting to note here that from the perspective of the supplier, which receives the orders, having the buyer ordering less frequently is desirable for it results in more predictable ordering behaviour. On the other hand, the buyer would not be always beneficial from ordering less frequently as he or she will keep more inventories. A buyer would normally prefer small quantity deliveries from the supplier. Fortunately, as the delivery frequency is not necessarily the same as the order frequency, a compromising solution which bridges the above conflicting objectives is possible, i.e., the buyer orders less frequently and hence more predictable, but the supplier is requested to deliver in smaller lots and hence, the buyer does not need to keep large inventories.

Figure 2. Effect of payment terms and lot sizing rules on coefficient of variation of order quantity (a) and order interval (b)

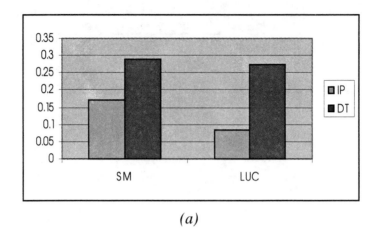

(a)

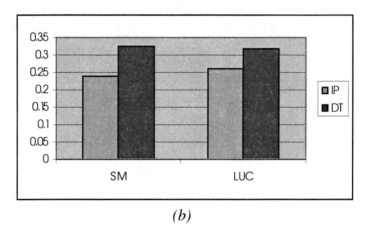

(b)

Concluding Remarks

The effect of different payment terms on order variability has been presented in this chapter. Mathematical models have been developed to accommodate different payment terms into dynamic lot sizing rules and simulation experiments have been conducted to evaluate the models over a range of parameters' values. The study reveals that the payment terms agreed by the buyer and the supplier have much impact on the variability of orders passed by the buyer onto the supplier. More specifically, the date-terms payment where the payment of all orders in a month is due on a given date of the following month results in more fluctuated orders than the immediate payment or the day-terms where the payment for each order takes place in a fixed time interval from the date an order is received. This result contributes to the current literature on order variability or the bullwhip effect where the role of payment terms has never been previously investigated.

The results suggest that it is important for supply chain members to set an appropriate payment system for the benefit of both the buyer and the supplier. Certainly, receiving more fluctuated or irregular orders from the buyer is detrimental to creating effective and efficient supply chain operations. However, it is important to note that order instability is not the only performance measure a supply chain should look at in this regards. Other measures, such as payment simplicity, might also be considered as an important criterion. The date-terms payment might be preferred due to less administrative burden related to payments, but care should be taken as offering it could entice the buyer to order more irregularly in terms of quantity as well as in terms of order interval.

While the study sheds light on the impact of payment terms on supply chain instability, further future developments are necessary. Future studies should attempt to evaluate payment terms from more comprehensive performance measures. An important extension that should be taken into account is the effect of different ordering patterns the buyer sends to the supplier on the inventory and financial performances of the supplier. The recent performance measurement systems applied for a supply chain, such as the SCOR (supply chain operation reference) model promoted by the Supply Chain Council (www.supply-chain.org), included financial performances such as cash-to-cash cycle time, average days of receivables, and average days of payables which are directly affected by the payment terms (Ceccarello, 2002). Certainly it is interesting to observe how different payment terms and the lot sizing decisions affect those performance measures in a supply chain.

Acknowledgment

Part of the research presented in this paper was supervised by Professor Brian Kingsman of Lancaster University. Professor Brian Kingsman recently died unexpectedly and we will miss his excellent supervision and works. The research was also partially done when the author was in the Department of

Industrial Engineering, Sepuluh Nopember Institute of Technology, Surabaya, Indonesia. The author also wishes to thank the referee for providing construc- tive comments on the earlier version of this chapter.

References

Bowersox, D. J., & Closs, D. J. (1996). *Logistical management: The integrated supply chain process*. McGraw Hill.

Carlson, M. L., & Rousseau, J. J. (1989). EOQ under date-terms supplier credit. *Journal of the Operational Research Society, 40*, 451-460.

Carlson, M. L., Miltenburg, G. J., & Rousseau, J. J. (1996). Economic order quantity and quantity discounts under date-terms supplier credit: A discounted cash flow approach. *Journal of the Operational Research Society, 47,* 384-394.

Ceccarello et al. (2002). Financial indicators and supply chain integration: A European study. *Supply Chain Forum: An International Journal, 3*(1), 44–52.

Chapman, C. B., Ward, S. C., Cooper, D. F. & Page, M. J. (1984). Credit policy and inventory control. *Journal of the Operational Research Society, 35*, 1055-1065.

Chen, F., Drezner, Z., Ryan, J. K., & Simchi-Levi, D. (1998). The bullwhip effect: Managerial insights on the impact of forecasting and information on variability in a supply chain. In S. Tayur, R. Ganeshan, & M. Magazine (Eds.), *Quantitative models for supply chain management*, (pp. 418- 439). London: Kluwer.

Chung, K. H. (1989). Inventory control and trade credit revisited. *Journal of the Operational Research Society, 40*, 495-498.

Chung, K. J. (1998). A theorem on the determination of economic order quantity under conditions of permissible delay in payments. *Computers and Operations Research, 25*, 49-52.

Dejonckheere, J., Disney, S. M., Lambrecht, M. R., & Towill, D. R. (2002). Transfer function analysis of forecasting induced bullwhip in supply chains. *International Journal of Production Economics, 78*, 133-144.

Disney, S. M., & Towill, D. R. (2003). The effect of vendor managed inventory (VMI) dynamics on the bullwhip effect in supply chains. *International Journal of Production Economics, 85,* 199-215.

Forrester, J. W. (1960). *Industrial dynamics.* Cambridge, MA: MIT Press.

Fransoo, J. C., & Wouters, M. C. F. (2000). Measuring the bullwhip effect in the supply chain. *Supply Chain Management, 5*(2), 78-89.

Goyal, S. K., (1985). Economic order quantity under conditions of permissible delay in payments. *Journal of the Operational Research Society, 36,* 335-338.

Haley, C. W., & Higgins, R. C. (1973). Inventory policy and trade credit financing. *Management Science, 20,* 464-471.

Huang, Y. F. (2003). Optimal retailer's ordering policies in the EOQ model under trade credit financing. *Journal of the Operational Research Society, 54*(9), 1011-1015.

Kelle, P., & Milne, A. (1999). The effect of (s, S) ordering policy on the supply chain. *International Journal of Production Economics, 59,* 113–122.

Kingsman, B. G. (1983). The effect of payment rules on ordering and stockholding in purchasing. *Journal of the Operational Research Society, 34,* 1085-1098.

Kingsman, B. G. (1991). EOQ under date-terms supplier credit: a near optimal solution. *Journal of the Operational Research Society, 42,* 803-809.

Lee, H. L., Padmanabhan, V., & Whang, S. (1997, Spring). The bullwhip effect in supply chains. *Sloan Management Review,* 93-102.

Luo, J., & Huang, P. (2002), EOQ under date-term supplier credit: a comment on a paper by Carlson and Rousseau. *Journal of the Operational Research Society, 53,* 1150-1154.

Mason-Jones, R., & Towill, D. R. (2000). Coping with uncertainty: Reducing "bullwhip" behaviour in global supply chains. *Supply Chain Forum: An International Journal, 1,* 40-45.

Metters, R. (1997). Quantifying the bullwhip effect in supply chains. *Journal of Operations Management, 15,* 89-100.

Pujawan, I N. (2000). *Buyer and supplier relationships, lot sizing decisions and payment terms in a supply chain.* Ph.D. Thesis, Lancaster University.

Pujawan, I. N. (2004). The effect of lot sizing rules on order variability. *European Journal of Operational Research, 159*(3), 635-717.

Pujawan, I N., & Kingsman, B. G. (1999). Dynamic lot sizing problems under different payment terms. *Proceedings of the Fourth Conference on Industrial Engineering and Production Management,* Glasgow, 233-248.

Pujawan, I N., & Kingsman, B. G. (2003). Properties of lot sizing rules under lumpy demand. *International Journal of Production Economics,* 81-82, 295-307.

Teng, J. T. (2002). On the economic order quantity under conditions of permissible delay in payments. *Journal of the Operational Research Society, 53,* 915-918.

Wilson, J. M. (1991). Supplier credit in the economic order quantity model. *International Journal of Operations and Production Management, 11,* 64-71.

Zhang, X. (2004). The impact of forecasting methods on the bullwhip effect. *International Journal of Production Economics, 88,* 15-27.

Chapter VI

Supply Chain Globalization and the Complexities of Cost-Minimization Strategies

Brian A. Polin, Jerusalem College of Technology, Israel

Marvin D. Troutt, Kent State University, USA

William Acar, Kent State University, USA

Abstract

We review the evolving literature on globalization with three aims in mind. First, we introduce the concept of globalization within the context of supply chain management. Second, with an eye toward information that may be useful for supply chain planners, we detail the motivation for global integration of the supply chain. Our third aim is to address global supply-chain issues that may be at odds with cost-minimizing strategies. Specifically, in this time of political debate regarding trade legislation, these issues involve the consideration of country of origin when sourcing, and the disparate demands of customers when marketing. A country offering inexpensive components may be associated with poor quality. Thus, despite inexpensive inputs, the overall profitability of the supply chain may suffer as perceived quality deteriorates. Similarly, a largely standardized product across multiple markets may present the lowest cost alternative from a production standpoint, but a high degree of standardization may reduce the attractiveness of the product in the eyes of the end consumer, and reduce overall profitability.

What Does Global Actually Mean?

The concept of globalization is undergoing a shift from simply referring to the generic concept of a product to being related to the whole supply chain. To delve into these notions, one has to hark back to the sociological roots of globalization theory. Much of the research on the sociological aspects of global business can be traced back to Howard Perlmutter's (1969) article on the evolution of the multinational corporation. Although his article preceded the wide-scale usage of the term "global" in the field of management, his definition of geocentrism closely parallels the modern use of the term. In his words, *geocentrism* is:

... a worldwide approach in both headquarters and subsidiaries. The firm's subsidiaries are neither satellites nor independent city states, but part of a whole whose focus is on worldwide objectives as well as local objectives, each part making its unique contribution with its unique competence. Geocentrism is expressed by function, product and geography. The question asked in headquarters and the subsidiaries is: "Where in the world shall we raise money, build our plant, conduct R&D [research and development], get and launch new ideas to serve our present and future customers?"

In other words, geocentrism, and by corollary, globalization, goes well beyond a mere presence in a country outside of the firm's home. But this is a subtle difference. Indeed, in the popular press internationalization and globalization are often used interchangeably. Dicken (1998) distinguished between the internationalization, which is a (quantitative) geographic extension of existing economic activities, and globalization, which is a functional integration (qualitative) of economic activities. He provides the spice trade as an example of the former, where the transport of spices from their country of origin to their country of consumption constitutes an international, rather than a global process.

In light of the overuse and misuse of the term "global" in popular business publications, Lussier, Baeder and Corman (1994) offer executives a self-diagnostic test for determining if their firm is indeed global. They utilize six criteria (management teams, strategy, operations and products, technology and R&D, financing and marketing), each of which consists of multiple dimensions. Also, Bartlett and Ghoshal (1989) define multiple dimensions to identify a firm's position on the "multinational to complex global" continuum.

Similarly, Kanter and Dretlet (1998) attempt to define what global really means. Their approach is to identify six pervasive myths and dispel them. Their suggestions were:

1. Global is synonymous with international.
2. Global strategy means doing the same thing everywhere.
3. Globalizing means becoming stateless, with no ties to a home country.
4. Globalizing requires abandoning images and values of a home country.
5. Globalizing involves acquisitions without integration.
6. A firm must engage in sales or operations in a foreign country to be considered global.

After enumerating what globalization is not, Kanter and Dretler conclude that "integrated," and not the more popularly perceived "international" is the word that best defines globalization.

Ramarapu and Lado (1995) state that globalization is most often explained in terms of three factors: the nature of the headquarters-subsidiary relationship, product/market breadth, and geographic scope of business. Just as quality can be used to mean both the epithet "good" and also "the degree of goodness," Ramarapu and Lado argue that global doesn't only mean global, in the colloquial sense, but the degree of globalness as well. Perlmutter (1969) had identified three positions on the globalness spectrum. Geocentrism, as defined earlier, represents the highest degree of integration and the highest degree of globalization. Polycentrism is associated with a worldwide presence, but operations in the multiple locations are largely independent of one another. Ethnocentrism is also associated with a worldwide presence, but in this profile the focus of the organization is the home country. A fourth profile, *regiocentric* (Wind, Douglas and Perlmutter, 1974), was later added to the original three. Regiocentric involves regional operations that serve multiple countries. This is a compromise position that offers some central control, while also offering regional autonomy. More than two decades after the introduction of the original E-P-G profiles, Yip (1989, 1992) identified five *strategy levers* to place a strategy "toward the multilocal end of the continuum or the global end":

1. *Market participation* – the choice of countries in which to conduct business and the market share in those countries.

2. *Products/services* – the degree of sameness of products and services across multiple countries.

3. *Location of value-adding activities* – the choice of locating activities from R&D to post-sales service.

4. *Marketing* – degree of sameness of marketing activities in different countries.

5. *Competitive moves* – the extent to which a firm makes competitive moves in individual countries as part of a global competitive strategy.

And Zou and Cavusgil (1995) identify six major dimensions, which include the five levers of Yip, plus the concentration of value-adding activities.

Until now, this section has dealt largely with the issue of globalization in the abstract, and its applications to supply-chain management (SCM) have been indirect. Dornier et al. (1998) identify four areas in which globalization presents difficulties not found in "ordinary" supply-chain management. They are:

1. Substantial geographic distances.
2. Added forecasting difficulties.
3. Exchange rates and other matters of national economic policies.
4. Infrastructure inadequacies.

Table 1. Role of SCM in globalization

Author(s)	SCM as identified in elements of globalization
Perlmutter (1969)	Each part making its unique contribution with its unique competence
Lusier et al. (1998)	Myth: Globalizing involves acquisitions without integration
Ramarapu & Lado (1995)	The nature of the headquarters-subsidiary relationship involves a degree of globalness in logistics and supply chain management
Yip (1989)	Location of value-adding activities
Zou & Cavusgil (1995)	Concentration of value-adding activities

While all of these factors already present challenges in the management of supply chains contained entirely within one country (perhaps with the exception of exchange rates, duties and other policy issues), they become either greater or more highly variable as the supply chain expands beyond national boundaries.

This section has largely concerned itself with the definition of global strategy, or more generally, globalization. Nevertheless, it bears direct relevance to SCM, as SCM is but one manifestation of the larger process of globalization as shown in Table 1. It will be demonstrated in the chapter that the motivation for globalization stems in large part from the need to manage one's supply chain.

What Are the Drivers of the Globalization of the Supply Chain?

In the previous section we introduced globalization and evoked its intimate association with SCM. While investigating the relationship between globalization and SCM, we did not address the *motivations* for the globalization of the supply chain. The current section addresses the rationale for this phenomenon. Some of these explanations include improving the firm's achievement, economies of efficiency, comparative advantage, competitive advantage, cost reduction, quality improvement and customer satisfaction. The various motivations for globalization may best be understood in the context of the supply chain, as the motivation to globalize one aspect of the supply chain may be substantially different from the motivation to globalize another.

Based on his own literature review, Delfmann (2000) has proposed a list of globalization drivers for supply chains. He cites three sources for these (Bhattacharya, Coleman and Brace, 1996; Cooper and Ellram, 1993; Ellram, 1991). The drivers he cites are: reduction of inventory investment in the chain, general reduction in costs, improved customer service, higher customer satisfaction, and building a competitive advantage. Additionally, he cites ten drivers which enable a firm to gain cost or differentiation advantages. These are all taken from Porter (1985). They are: linkages [among various value-adding activities], economies of scale, learning [from past experience and amassing knowledge], the pattern of capacity utilization, interrelationships [among business units that involve shared logistical systems, shared sales force, etc.], integration [of prior and subsequent value-adding activities], timing, discretionary policies, location and institutional factors.

One need not look only at recent literature to investigate the motivation for supply-chain globalization. International commerce has existed for millennia and the motivations for trade among the ancients may be instructive to us. When we consider familiar products that traverse the globe before they reach us, coffee may be among the first to come to mind. Although the coffee supply chain may provide an example of a supply chain literally spanning the globe, it *fails* to provide a true example of a deliberately globalized supply chain, because the "foreign" involvement in the process is strictly as a supplier of the raw ingredient, rather than an integral partner in the value-adding process. Furthermore, the decision of where to source is merely a function of the availability of the raw product in tropical climates and its unavailability in much of the industrialized world. The British economist David Ricardo studied trade patterns among nations in the early part of the 19th century. He questioned why Britain would import wine when the locals were perfectly capable of making it on their own. Further observing the importation of goods in other countries where domestic substitutes were readily available, he developed the concept of comparative advantage. Comparative advantage states that, while a country may be able to domestically produce all of the products it consumes, it is better off allocating its production capabilities to those it produces more efficiently, while importing those expensive to produce. In Ricardo's time, as today, the cool climate in Great Britain made grape cultivation difficult, so farmers were better off importing grapes (or wine) and producing oats, or other similar goods that thrive under local conditions.

Ramarapu and Lado (1995) cite "the logic of economic efficiencies" as the primary driver in the pursuit of global strategies. Similarly, in a commentary on Perlmutter's geocentrism, Simmonds (1985) states the aim of a global strategy is to "improve the firm's ultimate achievement through a reasoned, competitively oriented adjustment of its efforts in supply, and marketing, across all possible locations." While this only topically states the goals of a global strategy, it brings further detail to the economic-efficiencies argument of Ramarapu and Lado, as it succeeds in addressing the question of why firms globalize from both the input side *and* output side of the supply chain. That is, globalization creates economic efficiencies through both cheaper inputs and larger pools of potential customers.

Kogut (1985a) identifies comparative advantage and competitive advantage as the two principles motivating global strategy. *Comparative* advantage, also referred to as location-specific advantage, guides the decisions of "where to source and market." As discussed earlier, this is a modern interpretation of the Ricardian explanation for the existence of international trade. *Competitive* advantage, also called firm-specific advantage, closely parallels the concentration of value-adding activities, as identified by Zou and Cavusgil (1995). In a subsequent article, Kogut (1985b) distinguishes comparative advantage from competitive advantage as the former being driven by the cost of inputs and the latter by differences in the ability of firms to convert the inputs into goods and services. Yip (1989) identifies four possible benefits to be achieved through the use of a global strategy. These include cost reduction, improved quality of products and programs, enhanced customer preference, and increased competitive leverage.

Three benefits of global strategy considered by Chng and Pangarkar (2000), and not addressed in the aforementioned literature include: (1) extra-national scale-economies in manufacturing, when the needs of a single national market are surpassed; (2) coordination of technology transfer between markets; and (3) leveraging reputation by providing a reliable level of service across multiple geographic markets. These explanations for globalization all resonate with familiarity, as some of the oft-quoted explanations for the institution of supply chains include cost reduction and competitive advantage. Similarly, inventory reduction, improved customer service and higher customer satisfaction closely parallel some of the explanations offered for globalization.

Role of Country of Origin in the Global Supply Chain

The previous section addressed the motivation for globalization in readily quantifiable terms. In this vein the decision to source abroad or seek customers outside of a firm's traditional market are straightforward decisions if they offer lower costs and economies of scale. This section addresses factors in the globalization of the supply chain that, although economic, are far more indirect, and as a result, far more difficult to quantify. The notion of "country of origin" (COO) was once fairly clear. Modern supply chains have done much to muddle this concept. Italian leather products were widely considered of high quality, as were Japanese economy cars. What now might be said of leather good designed in Italy, but crafted in Mexico? Does this differ from Toyota cars manufactured in the U.S.? Is there a perceived difference between a Toyota assembled in the U.S. out of Japanese components and a Toyota assembled in the U.S. out of U.S. components? As the debate on tariffs and trade restrictions rages on between the international protectionists and their attendant politicians and economists, could the concept of COO be tightened for the purpose of analysis?

In 1965, Robert Schooler hypothesized that consumers in Guatemala evaluate nearly identical products differently merely because of the national origin of the products. Several subsequent empirical studies, conducted in different locations indicated COO does indeed influence buyer perceptions (Bilkey and Nes, 1982). Although products of mixed origin have been around for decades, much of the early COO literature addressed the birthplace of the product as singular and unambiguous. With the introduction of the World Trade Organization (WTO), North American Free Trade Agreement (NAFTA) and various other trade agreements to ease the flow of raw ingredients, as well as partially and fully manufactured goods, this phenomenon has become more widespread. For example, much of the U.S. textile industry has moved abroad to benefit from lower labor costs. In many instances, though, U.S. made clothing components may be shipped to Mexico for final assembly only. Chao (2001) reviews much of the relevant literature regarding the labeling of these products.

While the "made in USA" designation required no further explanation just a few decades ago, the American Automobile Labeling Act (AALA) and the U.S. Federal Trade Commission (FTC) have rigidly defined these terms. Despite these strictures, and the label that appears on the finished product, brand names may conjure up associations with countries that are more reflective of their traditional COO than their actual COO. Chao cites Zenith televisions and Sony electronic goods that are "associated" with the U.S. and Japan, respectively, even though they may be sourced and assembled in Mexico and lesser-developed Asian countries. In an effort to define the essence of the "made in" designation, Clarke, Owens and Ford (2000) examine numerous court precedents that define four legal tests (the name, character-and-use test; the essence test; the value-added test; and the article-of-commerce test). In fact, defining COO goes well beyond actual country of manufacture or the "traditional" national home of a particular brand. Jaffe and Nebenzahl (2001) developed a synoptic taxonomy reflecting all six aspects of a product's origin(s):

- *HC – Home Country. Consumer's* country of residence.

- *DC – Designed-in Country*, as in Italian-designed furniture, or Japanese-designed electronics.

- *MC – Made-in Country*, usually the location of the final stages of production.

- *PC – Parts Country* signifies the origin of the components, regardless of where assembly actually takes place.

- *AC – Assembly Country*. As opposed to PC, this designates the location of product assembly and not source location of components.

- *OC – Origin Country*. A symbolic or traditional country of origin, as in the cases of the USA for Zenith and Japan for Sony.

In the context of SCM and globalization, a traditionally North American firm might opt to assemble its athletic shoes in Asia due to the lower labor costs. While this may generate a substantial cost savings, it may not result in enhanced profitability. In this age of overseas standardization, label-conscious U.S. consumers might prefer the "made in USA" label, even at the cost of a major price increase. Whether this preference is based on patriotic sentiments or on real or perceived qualitative differences, firms might best consider the impact of globalization on the "bottom line," rather than pursuing maximal cost minimization.

COO and Buyer Perceptions

Much of the COO literature has dealt with perceptions in the abstract, but has left the actual impact of COO on sales largely unaddressed. While identifying the need to quantify the degree to which COO influences buyer perceptions, Bilkey and Nes (1982) neglected to directly identify an indicator by which to measure this effect. Although it may not directly measure buyer perceptions, actual product sales may provide a reasonable surrogate for this effect. In other words, do products from "desirable" COOs sell better than comparable products from "less desirable" COOs? Studies of car buyers in Germany indicate that COO alone is a leading factor in the choice of car make among 27% of the respondents (Loeffler, 2001). While this finding might appear overwhelming, the weight of COO alone may be less significant in other countries and/or product categories (Cordell, 1992). Verlegh and Steenkamp (1999) would disagree with Cordell's use of sales as a surrogate for buyer perceptions, as they distinguish between cognitive and normative aspects of COO effects. They define cognitive in this context as perceptions of product quality, while they define normative to mean an actual purchase decision. Although they do not actually quantify the COO effect, their meta-analysis of 41 studies revealed the "impact of COO is stronger for perceived quality than for attitudes and purchase likelihood." In other words, COO may very well influence buyer perceptions, but it does not significantly alter purchase likelihood.

Another approach to addressing this issue may be an indirect one. We might assume that, in the absence of other moderating effects, COO is the sole determinant of perception. Under this assumption, we may ask not to what degree COO influences perceptions, but rather what factors mitigate this effect. Zhang (1996) found the role of COO in product perception to be inversely related to need for cognition (NFC). Consumers with a high NFC, or those who have the need to research the product under consideration, will evaluate it on its own merits. Those who are less inclined to take the initiative to evaluate the product will rely on surrogate information cues. In this form of heuristic decision making or stereotyping among individuals with low NFC, "Swiss made" may indeed be the sole determinant in the evaluation of, or the decision to purchase, a watch.

Compensating for a Negative COO Effect

As consumers we may be presented with the choice of brand A from country A or brand B from country B. If country B is generally perceived to produce products that are "less desirable" than those from country A, brand B producers may counter this perception by offering products at a lower price. Lampert and Jaffe (1997) identify a direct relationship between the degree of differentiation in a product class and the market price ratio of goods in that category. In other words, there may be only very narrow price differences among different brands of commodity-like, homogeneous goods such as sugar and salt, while highly differentiated product classes, such as automobiles and watches, may present much larger prices differences on the basis of COO alone. This relationship of degree of product differentiation and range of prices for a product class may be instructive for overcoming a negative COO effect. Between homogenous goods and differentiated goods, Lampert and Jaffe also classify goods as of low differentiation (gasoline, tires, toothpaste, etc.) and medium differentiation (vacuum cleaners, color televisions, etc.)

Automobiles, for example, may indeed be highly differentiated. A broad range of models are available, with an even broader range of prices. Within each of the four classifications of product differentiation identified by Lampert and Jaffe, and indeed within each specific product class, there also exists a range of degrees of differentiation. Thus, automobile prices as a whole may vary widely, but price differences among competing models of economy cars are much smaller than price differences among competing luxury models. Far from implying that developing countries may export only commodity-like products[1], this implies that developing countries may export products in any category, provided they are relatively undifferentiated within their product class. While the export of Yugoslavian-made cars to the U.S. was an unquestionable failure, the relationship observed by Lampert and Jaffe suggests that the likelihood of a Yugoslavian car succeeding in the U.S. market was far greater in the sub-compact category than in the sport or luxury categories.

In the same vein, Lampert and Jaffe observed longitudinal changes in COO effect. With reference to Japan, they comment:

During the 1950s a "made in Japan" label signified a cheap imitation of products made in industrialized countries... Today, the "made in Japan" label stands for high quality, excellent workmanship and innovative products (p. 62).

In keeping with this changing perception, the Japanese auto manufacturers achieved their initial successes in the U.S. with undifferentiated fuel-efficient, sub-compact cars. In recent years they have achieved success with high-priced and highly differentiated luxury cars. Although not stated explicitly, it may be gleaned from Lampert and Jaffe that a negative COO may indeed be overcome, and quite successfully at that. Just as a desirable COO may enable a manufacturer to command higher margins on each unit sold, a non-desirable COO may serve as an impetus for a manufacturer to adopt a low-cost/low-price strategy and capitalize on greater volumes, despite the smaller per-unit margin.

Determinants of COO Biases

Cattin, Jolibert and Lohnes (1982) partially resolve the issue of the determinants of COO. They evaluate perceptions of goods originating in five countries and conclude that COO perceptions vary with country of purchase, or alternatively, according to the Jaffe and Nebenzahl taxonomy, they conclude that COO (or CO in the Jaffe-Nebenzahl nomenclature) perceptions are biased by home country (HC).

Beyond identifying HC as a source of bias in evaluating the COO effect, Mohamad, Ahmed, Honeycutt and Tyebkhan (2000) define four constructs as factors impacting consumer attitudes toward country image. A study of Malaysian consumers found that products from developed countries like the U.S., Japan and Italy were preferred for the perceived innovativeness, design prestige and workmanship. This suggests that a country hoping to upgrade the perception of its products among potential consumers needs to concentrate on issues beyond directly measurable determinants such as tangible quality, price, etc. Although this study may provide valuable insight to countries seeking to export, it fails to offer a causal explanation. Are developed countries "successful" because people elsewhere value their products, or are the products of these countries desired because they originate in developed countries with an image of success, wealth and style? Although a full discussion is beyond the scope of this chapter, it is highly significant, as it addresses the degree to which a country may utilize a policy of "economic development through export."

Kleppe, Iversen and Stensaker (2001) partially address this issue in an empirical study on the creation of COO effect. They conclude that a COO effect may be created when an "image-creating moment" occurs. Such a moment occurs when marketing mix, product-country image and target market characteristics are all in alignment. Contrary to the perception that products are desired because they are associated with the wealth or success of a country, these researchers conclude that a COO effect may be created by a perceived "indigenousness" of a product. Specifically discussed in the context of Norwegian fish exports, this principle may apply as well to products with a reputation for durability from "rugged" countries or "warm-weather" products from tropical countries, even though these exporting countries may not be globally perceived as developed or successful.

COO Inter-Correlations

Samiee (1994) classified more than 60 empirical studies addressing the effects of COO from the perspective of a *single* factor. Not surprisingly, the findings were inconclusive. For example, different studies arrived at diametrically opposite results regarding the relationship between patriotic sentiments among consumers and their choice of a brand. Similarly, studies differed on the preference for domestic products. These contradictory findings may have more to do with the interaction of multiple factors rather than the indeterminate effect of a single factor. The inter-correlations between COO and other traits seems to have attracted the least research interest. It appears that this lack of attention stems not from the lack of relevance or lack of interest, but rather from the sheer complexity of the problem.

As mentioned above, Samiee found contradictory studies regarding the preference for domestically produced products. Is this to say that no general conclusions may be drawn about a preference for (or against) domestic products? Gurhan-Canli and Maheswaran (2000) addressed the issue of preference for domestic products. Rather than viewing this preference (or lack thereof) as monolithic and universal, they addressed it from the perspective of consumers in multiple countries. Indeed, consumers may or may not prefer products from a COO the same as their own nationality, but might this be a function of the nation in question? Gurhan-Canli and Maheswaran found there to be significant differences between Americans and Japanese in their preferences for products from their own countries, with Americans preferring foreign-made "quality" products to U.S.-made products of inferior quality and Japanese placing the made-in-Japan label higher than "quality" on their list of preferences. While not laying the contradictions found by Samiee to rest entirely, Gurhan-Canli and Maheswaran highlight the need for COO research that goes beyond the univariate approach. In fact, Gurhan-Canli and Maheswaran consider three variables (country of evaluation, COO and superior/inferior quality) in their 2x2x2 research design. This seemingly robust experiment may be less than conclusive, even when qualifying the differing effects of COO for Japanese and Americans. Can we draw unequivocal conclusions about one COO effect for the Japanese and an altogether different one for Americans? It may be that their findings hold for the (mountain bike) industry they investigated, but differ for other industries. It may also be that this conclusion applies to some Japanese, while other Japanese behave in a way more similar to Americans. There is evidence to suggest that, even within a country, the COO effect varies with age, experience with the product under review, level of education and political conservatism (Beverland and Lindgreen, 2002).

Fortunately, there seems to be an increasing trend toward a multivariate approach to COO research. Parameswaran and Pisharodi (2002) investigate the role of COO in the evaluation of products. Rather than a single product from a single country, they study two very different products (cameras and blenders) from two very different countries (Germany and South Korea). Also, rather than viewing the subjects as monolithic, they classify them as well. In this instance, however, all subjects are residents of the U.S., but they are segmented by degree of acculturation (immigrant, first generation or subsequent generation), or at least a surrogate for it. Despite this segmentation, the authors acknowledge that one of the weaknesses of the study is the greatly varying degrees of acculturation even within a single group of subjects. A foreign-born participant in the study who has been in the U.S. for 25 years may be far more acculturated than one who stepped of the boat only recently — yet this would not be captured by their classification scheme.

The inclusion of multiple factors in the analysis of the degree (or existence) of impact of COO on product evaluation is a positive development. It may serve to validate and substantiate earlier findings and may have important managerial implications for SCM. On the other hand, the recognition of the need for further classification and sub-classification of dependent variables only serves to complicate an already difficult process. Fortunately though, research suggests that the need for sub-classification of variables may not be monotonically increasing. A recent study (Piron, 2000) suggests that product categories may be classified. In a world in which each product category has to be investigated independently, no amount of modeling would provide an indication as to the magnitude of the COO effect for a product not yet studied. Piron suggests that products as diverse as sports cars, home theaters, sunglasses and toothpaste may be grouped on the basis of location of consumption (public versus private) and product type (luxury versus necessity). He found the COO effect to be stronger in luxury goods than in necessities, and stronger in conspicuously consumed goods than in those consumed in the privacy of the home.

Catering to Diverse Markets at the Consumer End of the Global Supply Chain

Globalization at the consumer end of the supply chain introduces multiple managerial complexities. The literature has dealt at length with the issues of "customization" and "standardization" of products as they are introduced into new markets with differing customer preferences. Global firms such as Coca-Cola and Mercedes Benz provide interesting examples of supply-chain globalization and the differing stages of the chain in which their respective products are adapted to local tastes. McDonalds is another example. Local menus are adapted. For example, the American breakfast biscuit cannot be easily explained in Hong Kong, because the original French word "biscuit" suggests what most consumers worldwide would consider to be a cookie. Also, steamed rice is generally preferred to fries in Hong Kong.

The debate among academicians on the issue of product standardization versus product adaptation in multi-national business is not a new one. Most researchers cite the works of Perlmutter (1969) and Buzzell (1968) as the genesis (Shoham, 1995; Diamantopoulos, Schlegemilch & Du Preez, 1995; Leonidas, 1996). Other authors credit Erik Elinder as the progenitor of the standardize/adapt argument (Medina & Duffy, 1998; Solberg, 2001). By the estimation of these authors, the full-fledged discussion on the matter did not begin with Elinder's 1961 piece, as his prescription for success dealt exclusively with the advertising, and not the totality of the product. In an article reviewing the "40-year debate," Agrawal (1995) cites sources from as far back as 1923 extolling the virtues of standardization. Although the preferred strategy of Honda Motor

Company may have changed since the article was written, the firm's former chairman strongly promoted localization of products, profits, production and management (Sugiura, 1990).

While it is not our purpose to provide a comprehensive review of the literature, a disservice would be done by neglecting the context in which it is presented.[2] As firms increase activities beyond their home country, they become cognizant of the disparate needs and wants of the residents in each of the new regions they enter. One often hears the advice of, "Think globally, act locally." As cited earlier, Perlmutter (1969) classified firms according to their ethnocentric, polycentric and geocentric (E-P-G) profiles. They have been discussed in the context of global presence and integration of global activity, but these profiles have implications for product adaptation and standardization as well. A polycentric firm would adapt its products to the requirements of multiple locales, while the geocentric firm would assume a one-size-fits-all approach, regardless of local preferences. The ethnocentric is similar to the geocentric profile in that it involves a standardized format. But, rather than representing an approximate conglomeration of the needs of all, it reflects the requirements of the home country exclusively. From the adaptation/standardization perspective, the regiocentric profile (Wind et al., 1973) promotes product reformulation on a regional basis. Despite these early compromises, it became fashionable among academics in subsequent years to promote either a strategy of standardization or a strategy of adaptation, with the two being highly discrete and mutually exclusive.

- *Standardization.* The primary advantage of standardization stems from economies of scale (Botschen & Hemetsberger, 1998; Levitt, 1983; Porter, 1980, 1985; Shoham, 1995). While much of this literature deals with advertising and promotion, economies of scale extend to production, logistics, distribution and research and development (Hout, Porter & Rudden, 1982; Porter, 1980, 1985; Shoham, 1995). It may be an undeniable truth that a firm producing standard widgets for all consumers worldwide will incur a lower per-unit cost, but this strategy addresses only the cost side of the commerce equation. This caveat is similar to the point raised in the previous section of this chapter—namely, strategies that succeed in reducing costs are not necessarily associated with greater profitability.

- *Adaptation.* Douglas and Wind (1987) identify three primary flaws with the universal standardization approach. They argue that:

1. Customer needs worldwide are *not* becoming more homogeneous, as evidence suggests increasing diversity of behavior within countries.

2. Many customers do not want to sacrifice features for low price.

3. Economies of scale may not be relevant in all industries.

While the relevance of the third argument is based largely on the nature of the industry in question, arguments one and two are necessarily a function of consumer priorities. To fail to address customer preferences would deny a firm the opportunity to exploit a positioning strategy. Samiee and Roth (1992) suggest that adapted products enable price discrimination that result in greater returns than standardized products, despite their higher costs. As a mirror reflection of standardization, full-adaptation may be an ideal strategy when viewed exclusively through the lens of the demand side of the equation.

- *A compromise.* Although they address the issue from the marketing perspective only, Botschen and Hemetsberg (1998) succinctly identify the determinants of the ideal balance between standardization and adaptation:

   If a company can manage to apply the same marketing-mix activities in several countries, with only a few adaptations (e.g., translation of advertising copy), the average costs of marketing per unit will decline. For organizations that adopt a global perspective, the critical point is not whether the buyers are the same everywhere, but to what extent shared customer needs and expectations exists across different nations. The degree of similarity among a company's market largely determines the degree to which the marketing-mix activities can be standardized.

From the above discussion, it appears that firms *should* standardize; but at the same time, they *must* adapt. Those considerations not withstanding, some researchers still cling to the "standardized" school of thought (Cowan, 1998; O'Donnell and Jeong, 2000; Papavassiliou and Stathakopoulos, 1997; Szymanski, Bharadwaj and Varadajan, 1993).

An obvious compromise between these two extremes involves a degree of customization, while at the same time maintaining a degree of standardization.

As in other instances of mixed strategies, this is called a "contingency approach." The scholars, however, disagree upon what approach is actually contingent. Van Mesdag (1999) states that the overwhelming reality is a "glocal" one, in which both global and local considerations are addressed. However, due to the enormous differences in globalizability between product or service categories, it is of little use to generalize about what aspects should be adapted and to what degree. In the context of an empirical study, Morrison, Ricks and Roth (1991) promote regionalization as the ideal compromise between standardization and adaptation. This appears to be popular among international business practitioners who suggest, "think globally and act locally."

- *Critiquing the debate.* In response to a review of the empirical literature on the standardization/adaptation debate, Leonidou (1996) claims that "most multinational companies offer products to overseas markets that are fairly standardized, and that in those cases where adaptations are made, these were of an obligatory nature in the sense that the management was unable to avoid them, while discretionary adaptations, that is those the company chooses to make itself, were generally minimal." Non-discretionary changes might include linguistic and regulatory issues specific to each country. Commenting on the entire body of literature on the standardize/customize debate, Leonidou finds four fundamental flaws:

  1. Most studies have been conceptual instead of empirical.

  2. Studies focus narrowly on advertising and neglect many of the broader aspects associated with introducing products into foreign countries.

  3. Debate has focused on western MNCs at the expense of non-western MNCs.

  4. Debate has been confined to degree of customization in developed markets, and not *developing* markets.

Strategic Considerations

Even those scholars calling for a compromise between adaptation and standardization display inflexibility. Just as the "purists" call for a single optimal degree of adaptation or standardization, the compromisers, too, recognize *an* optimal degree of compromise between the two. This hallowed position on the standardize/adapt spectrum is thought to be purely a function of product or service category (Van Mesdag, 1999), or regional competitive factors (Morrison, Ricks & Roth, 1991).

Although not developed to provide a framework for entry into new foreign markets *per se*, Porter's generic strategies cast the standardize/adapt debate in a different light. As originally stated, Porter (1980) identifies three generic strategies to outperform competitors in an industry: overall cost leadership, differentiation, and focus. Applying this range of strategic alternatives globally, the "optimal" degree of adaptation may be viewed as a function of a consciously crafted strategy rather than a function of exogenous market or product considerations. A firm promoting its product as a low-cost alternative may elect to standardize and capitalize on high volumes and economies of scale, while an upscale competitor in the same product category and the same global markets may elect to adapt in favor of higher margins on each unit sold. Porter specifically warns of the dangers of a "stuck in the middle" strategy that affords neither the benefits of high-margins, nor the benefits of low-cost. Occasionally some scholars have argued that "stuck in the middle" is indeed tenable.[3] But, Porter's admonition is emphatically supported by Acar and Wilson (1993). They cite several studies that empirically confirm this conclusion (Dess & Davis, 1984; Miller & Friesen, 1986a; Reed, 1991). More importantly, they delve into the theoretical roots of Porter's generic strategies in a world of shifting technology and attendant R&D.

This argument is partly a semantic one revolving around the inclusiveness of "stuck in the middle." Conceiving a product murkily as neither low-cost nor differentiated makes it difficult to design a good research strategy for it, and promoting a product as both low-cost and differentiated may send mixed messages to potential consumers and harm profitability [a view supported by Acar and Wilson]. On the other hand, pursuing one *primary* strategy that incorporates elements of a different *secondary* one may improve profitability [a view supported by Proff]. In fact, even those interpreting Porter's "stuck in the middle" in its broadest sense need not present the globalizing firm with an either/or set of choices. As emphasized by Acar and Wilson (1993), the potential dangers of being "stuck in the middle" refer only to the *simultaneous* adoption of [elements of] more than one generic strategy. A migration from a low-cost strategy to a differentiated one may provide the firm with the full benefits of both of these conflicting strategies.

Although highly unusual in the body of standardization/adaptation literature, two previously published articles consider both a migration of a product from standardized (or low-cost) to an adapted (or differentiated) *and* the time at which this migration occurs vis-à-vis entry into foreign markets, albeit from very different perspectives.

- *Delayed adaptation vs. immediate adaptation.* Cavusgil, Zou and Naidu (1993) distinguish between product adaptation that occurs before-entry and after-entry into new markets. A firm promoting a standardized product upon its entry into new markets and only subsequently adapting it would be wittingly, or unwittingly, following a delayed adaptation strategy. Although not absolute in tone, Cavusgil et al. identify "upon-entry" adaptation as mandated by legal and technical requirements, while "after-entry" adaptation "is likely to be discretionary." The goal of their study was not to determine whether delayed adaptation might be associated with higher profitability, but whether adaptation upon-entry and after-entry might correlate with various attributes of the industry, firm and product under investigation.

While this study may assist in addressing the questions *who adapts when*, and *under what circumstances*, it does little in the way of addressing profitability as a function of time of adaptation. In other words, holding all other variables equal[4], would a product adapted in a stage-wise manner generate greater profitability than a product adapted to the same degree, but achieving its full degree of adaptation immediately upon entering the market?

- *A quantitative approach.* Through "extensive computational experiments," Mallick and Mukhopadhyay (2001) attempt to quantitatively determine the degree to which products should be adapted to multiple different environments to maximize profitability. In the absence of a universally ideal degree of customization, these authors distinguish between premium and standard brands. The analytical results they derive stem from assumptions regarding customer preferences for locally adapted products and their sensitivity to price changes as the products become more adapted. Premium brands, they conclude, experience greater profitability with a higher degree of customization, while standard brands are more profitable when their products are largely generalized. Without specifically citing Porter, the distinction made by Mallick and Mukhopadhyay dovetails with his generic strategies, as discussed earlier.

Unlike Cavusgil et al., who view time of adaptation as an exogenous variable, Mallick and Mukhopadhyay (2001) pursue the issue of standardization and adaptation or "local design vs. global design" from the perspective of strategic business choice. In their view, degree of adaptation is a result of a conscious and deliberate strategy. Though they develop the theoretical underpinnings, they do not empirically test their Proposition 2:

In a mature market, it is initially advantageous to switch from a global strategy to a local strategy if the composite quality level of the local strategy is higher than the global design quality level.

This implies greater profitability for global or standardized products at lower quality levels and greater profitability for local or adapted products at higher quality levels. From the perspective of the manufacturer, locally adapted products become more profitable than globally standardized ones as quality rises. In terms of the central thesis of this section, Proposition 2 of Mallick and Mukhopadhyay supports the hypothesis that superior profitability occurs when the product is adapted subsequent to the introduction of a standardized product in global markets.

An Alternative Approach

Up to this point we have reviewed the works of numerous scholars on the adapt/standardize debate in global markets. One school of thought maintains that optimal profitability occurs when adaptation is kept to a reasonable minimum (that meets local legal, cultural and language requirements). Another school promotes adaptation as a mechanism to increase profitability. A third view compromises between the two. Among the scholars who promote this view, opinions differ on the degree of adaptation and the circumstances that are the determinants of the degree. These determinants may include industry- or product-specific competitive strategy. Although this approach is bounded by the two absolutist approaches, the degree of adaptation with increased global market presence may *tend* toward either direction.

The orthodoxy of the absolutist views suggests an "either/or" dichotomy. Profits are maximized through the vehicle of low costs driven by economies of scale, or through large margins that result from catering to specific customer preferences. Even the compromise view suggests that once an optimal position on the adapt/standardize spectrum has been determined, maximum profitability will be achieved by maintaining that rate of adaptation with respect to geographic presence. Despite the diversity of opinions on the matter, they are all similarly flawed, in that they are static. Mathematically stated, the optimal degree of adaptation, as espoused by the vast majority of academics, is represented by a continuous function with a constant slope. While the [segment-wise] constancy of slope should also be subject to closer scrutiny, it is beyond the scope of this section. We propose that, regardless of the rate of adaptation, an adjustment (or multiple adjustments) to the degree of adaptation may yield improved profitability. This form of delayed adaptation need not be associated with an initial low-cost or adaptation-minimizing strategy. Conceptually, once strict adherence to standardization has enabled a product to penetrate markets and obtain the benefits of economies of scale, a modicum of adaptation may differentiate the product and present an up-scale alternative to the former low-cost model. Indeed, this chapter is not the first to identify a segmented, or stage-wise adaptation that varies in degree with respect to market presence; but by our estimation, this chapter contains the first attempt to coherently propose such a strategy as its central theme.

Mallick and Mukhopadhyay advance a similar proposal, but they retain the distinctness of two products, a standardized one and a differentiated one. Although the degree of adaptation of both of these products may change, they are essentially constrained by a predetermined strategy. By contrast, rather than offering both globally and locally oriented products, as in the case of their Proposition 2, we propose that profitability can be maximized by entering markets with a global, or standardized product, and later adapting that very product

An Example: Although unsupported by empirical findings, Schlie and Yip (2000) develop the rationale and recommend the "counter-intuitive strategy of regional follows global." They suggest that firms tend to adapt products upon their introduction into new markets, but as time and familiarity with the product increase, the firms tend to blend these various adaptations into one standardized product. The counter-intuitive strategy they propose involves the opposite: enter new markets with standardized products and adapt them later on. This unequivocal prescription is perhaps unique in the entire body of strategy, marketing and management literatures. Anecdotally, they cite the case of two Japanese cars that have been largely hassle-free to their owners and huge financial successes to their manufacturers over the last two decades. Both the Toyota Corolla and the Honda Accord were introduced as highly generic, global concept cars aimed at the "lowest common denominator". Flexible-width platforms have enabled these manufacturers to cater later models of these cars to the differing automotive needs of "triad" customers in North America, Europe and Asia. In the opinions of Schlie and Yip, *ex ante* regional strategies do not afford the firm the economies of scale associated with leverage against suppliers and global development and sourcing. On the other hand, a wholly global strategy may fail to satisfy the diverse needs of customers who are widely distributed both geographically and culturally.

Practical Implications for Supply-Chain Strategic Planning

Chopra and Meindl (2003) have discussed the importance of achieving fit of competitive strategy with supply-chain strategy. Thus, we generally assume here that globalization in the integrated geocentric sense is consistent with competitive strategy. At the same time, use of the supply chain as an enabler of globalization should not be ruled out. For example, foreign sourcing or manufacturing can acquaint regional consumers with a product and reveal potential demand or product variations that would have higher regional appeal while still being consistent with competitive strategy. Indeed, an initial positioning as ethnocentric and multi-local may yield opportunities for evolution by reexamining the globalization possibilities for rearticulating the competitive strategy and using opportunities opened up by efficiencies in the supply chain.

Economies of scale are clearly important drivers of globalization, but should not be thought of necessarily applicable to or embracing all aspects of the supply chain. For example, fast food firms such as McDonalds usually need to procure perishable supplies locally but can still realize economies of scale from packaging materials, fixtures, equipment and operating procedures. More generally, cost minimization or "the logic of economic efficiencies" may not necessarily be consistent with profit maximization.

The COO and related effects offer several opportunities and potential liabilities. Many of these have to do with marketing-related image and impression management. Sourcing or manufacturing in a region or country with marketing appeal may be more profitable than choices with lower costs. Assembly of clothing in a third-world country will likely be both cost-efficient and appealing to customers of discount stores. However, for stylish high-priced items, this image would not be attractive and, in fact, could be less than attractive if negative associations to socially undesirable practices (child labor, say) are a possibility. For each activity in the supply chain and for each customer country or region, there is a potential interaction that may be favorable or unfavorable to profitability, or may offer opportunity for exploitation. Again, a conscientious focus on profit maximization should help prevent shortsighted choices based on mere cost minimization.

We have introduced the concept of delayed adaptation. This was supported by the research of Schlie and Yip (2000), and observations of successful instances in the automobile and fast foods industries. The point is essentially that adaptation should be delayed to allow for economy of scale benefits and only then should the product to be adapted. This would allow the firm to exert leverage over suppliers and produce an adapted product at the cost, but not necessarily at the price, of a standardized one.

Figure 1. Quality and profitability under two different adaptation strategies

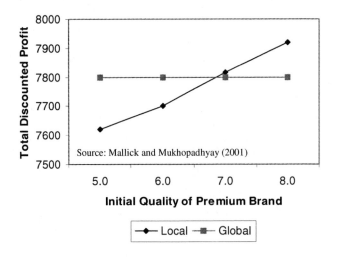

Figure 2. Quality and profitability under a combined local-global, or delayed adaptation strategy

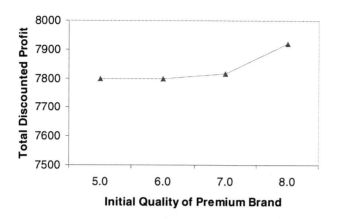

Figure 1 shows that under certain conditions, localized products can be more profitable, while under other conditions, globalized products are more profitable. In light of differing degrees of profitability, a firm may be better off producing a single product, or product line, and varying it, depending on market demands and customer willingness to pay. A firm may create a global product in the low quality range, where it would be more profitable and then transition to a locally adapted product in the higher quality range. In this way, profitability can follow the path of the global line in the < 7.0 range and the local line in the >7.0 range. This type of migration or upgrading is depicted in Figure 2. Whether by design or by accident, this is the type of trajectory that products like the Honda Civic have followed, namely, bland and inexpensive when introduced and fancy and differentiated several years later.

Future Research Needs

Prerequisites for Empirical Testing

Should a binary or a graduated metric be used to quantify the geographic diffusion of the product? Indeed, much has been written on the "degree of internationalization of the firm" (Cavusgil, 1984; Sullivan, 1994), but a measure of the firm itself may not necessarily correlate to the internationalization of the product. In a similar vein, tackling the "degree-of-adaptation" issue may also be a prerequisite for further empirical research. A large and growing body of literature addresses the area of mass customization, but no measure of customization has emerged as dominant. Although they do not fully develop an index of customization, Jiao and Tseng (2000) may well lay the groundwork by classifying degree of customization in terms of both part and process commonality.

To observers of the automotive industry, the successes of the Corolla and the Accord in the 1990s and early 2000s may seem evidence enough of the success of delayed adaptation (i.e., an *ex post* regional strategy), but this is a less than robust conclusion. A more quantitative analysis may shed light on the true competitive implications of this type of strategy. Ideally, this analysis would include indices for identifying the position of a product on both the product and market continua as depicted in Figure 3. The horizontal axis in the figure represents the geographic availability of the product, while the vertical axis represents an as-yet-undefined degree of adaptation. The points indicated with a 't' illustrate a time progression and the response of the product to market and environmental conditions.

Figure 3. Alternative standardization/adaptation strategies

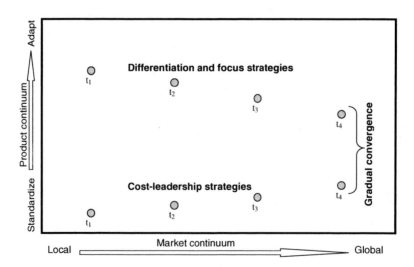

Brand Management

The special influence of brand name in connection with COO appears to have been neglected so far. An example is the Louis Vuitton brand of ladies' handbags and purses, which command prices in excess of $1,000. This brand is sold in high-end shops and advertised in sophisticated magazines by the most popular celebrities. The French-sounding name may bring associations with Paris and its long-standing reputation for fashion leadership, at least in the United States. However, it is doubtful that many customers actually know what, in fact, is the COO associated with this brand. In short, brand name alone may convey whatever COO effects that might be attributed to a product or firm. Moreover, brand name may not bring the same associations in other regions. For example, would this same brand sound very appealing in Montreal? Assuming the company defines its competitive strategy as supplying the most prestigious handbags, different brand names for different regions may prove to be a preferable strategy.

Other Directions

There are several important directions yet to be pursued. It will be useful to explore the nature of the interactions and tradeoffs between covering greater distances versus crossing additional country boundaries. Also, to what degree is globalization pushed by the dictates of supply-chain management and/or pulled by the benefits of large-scale, global marketing? Are there subtle but tangible differences between the management of a supply chain and that of the entire chain of activities of a manufacturing concern?[5] In the complex activity chains of today, does the notion of COO pertain to where most of the dollars are invested, or where most of the creative activities occur?

Conclusions

Although the standardize/adapt debate that raged for decades is now moving to the forefront of international news, neither the scholars nor the practitioners have reached consensus. Without strictly advocating either one of these positions, this chapter has identified the merits of both, and laid the theoretical groundwork for a strategy that captures the advantages of both. As the world becomes an increasingly smaller global-village, delayed adaptation strategies may profitably address the efficiencies required by competition and the product features demanded by increasingly discerning customers.

References

Acar, W., & Wilson, B. (1993). *Out of the segmentation jungle: Reconciling Porter's generic strategies with marketing segmentation.* Unpublished Working Paper.

Agrawal, M. (1995). Review of a 40-year debate in international advertising: Practitioner and academician perspectives to the standardization/adaptation issue. *International Marketing Review, 12*(1), 26-48.

Atac, O. A. (1986). International experience theory and global strategy. *International Marketing Review, 3*(4), 52-61.

Bartlett, C. A., & Ghoshal, S. (1989). *Managing across borders: The transnational solution.* Boston: Harvard Business School Press.

Beverland, M., & Lindgreen, A. (2002). Using country of origin in strategy: The importance of context and strategic action. *Journal of Brand Management, 10,* 147-167.

Bhattacharya, A. K., Coleman, J. L., & Brace, G. (1996). The structure conundrum in supply chain management. *International Journal of Logistics Management, 7*(1), 39-48.

Bilkey, W. J., & Nes, E. (1982). Country-of-origin effects on product evaluations. *Journal of International Business Studies, 13*(1), 89-100.

Botschen, G., & Hemetsberger, A. (1998). Diagnosing means-end structures to determine the degree of potential marketing program. *Journal of Business Research, 42,* 151-159.

Buzzell, R. D. (1968). Can you standardize multinational marketing. *Harvard Business Review, 46*(6), 102-113.

Buzzell, R. D., & Gale, B. T. (1987). *The PIMS principle.* New York: The Free Press.

Cattin, P., Jolibert, A., & Lohnes, C. (1982). A cross-cultural study of "made in" concepts. *Journal of International Business Studies, 13*(3), 131-142.

Cavusgil, T. S. (1984). Differences among exporting firms based on their degree of internationalization. *Journal of Business Research, 12*, 195-208.

Cavusgil, T. S., Zou, S., & Naidu, G. M. (1993). Product and promotion adaptation in export ventures: An empirical investigation. *Journal of International Business Studies, 24*(3), 479-506.

Chan Kim, W., & Hwang, P. (1992). Global strategy and multinationals' entry mode choice. *Journal of International Business Studies, 23*(1), 29-53.

Chao, P. (2001). The moderating effects of country of assembly, country of parts, and country of design on hybrid product evaluations. *Journal of Advertising, 30*(4), 67-81.

Chng, P. L., & Pangarkar, N. (2000). Research on global strategy. *International Journal of Management Reviews, 2*(1), 91-110.

Chopra, S., & Meindl, P. (Ed.). (2003). *Supply chain management: Strategy, planning and operation.* Upper Saddle River. NJ: Pearson Prentice Hall. (Original work published 2001.)

Clarke III, I., Owens, M., & Ford, J. B. (2000). Integrating country of origin into global marketing strategy. *International Marketing Review, 17*(2/3), 114-126.

Cooper, M. C., & Ellram, L. M. (1993). Characteristics of supply chain management and the implications for purchasing and logistics strategy. *International Journal of Logistics Management, 4*(1), 1-14.

Cordell, V. V. (1992). Effects of consumer preferences for foreign sourced products. *Journal of International Business Studies, 23*(2), 251-269.

Cowan, R. J. (1998). Product globalization. *International Business: Strategies for the Global Marketplace, 11*(3), 19-20.

Delffmann, W. (2000). *Supply chain management in the global context.* Working Paper No. 102, Department of General Management, Business Planning and Logistics, The University of Cologne.

Dess, G., & Davis, P. S. (1984). Porter's generic strategies as determinants of strategic group membership and organizational performance. *Academy of Management Journal, 27*, 467-488.

Diamantopoulos, A., Schlegelmilch, B. B., & Du Preez, J. P. (1995). Lessons for pan-European marketing? The role of consumer preferences in fine-tuning the product-market fit. *International Marketing Review*, *12*(2), 38-53.

Dicken, P. (1998). *Global shift: Transforming the world economy*. New York: Guilford Press.

Dornier, P. P., Ernst, R., Fender, M., & Kouvelis, P. (1998). *Global operations and logistics: Text and cases*. New York: Wiley.

Douglas, S., & Wind, Y. (1987). The myth of globalization. *Columbia Journal of World Business*, *22*(4), 19-29.

Elinder, E. (1961, November 27). International advertisers must devise universal ads. *Advertising Age*, p.91.

Ellram, L. M. (1991). Supply chain management. The industrial organisation perspective. *International Journal of Physical Distribution and Logistics Management*, *21*(1), 13-22.

Geren, B. (1989). In pursuit of global strategies: Meeting worldwide competition. *SAM Advanced Management Journal*, *54*(3), 44-48.

Ghoshal, S. (1987). Global strategy: An organizing framework. *Strategic Management Journal, 8*, 425-440.

Guillén, M. F. (2002). What is the best global strategy for the internet. *Business Horizons*, *45*(3), 39-46.

Gurhan-Canli, Z., & Maheswaran, D. (2000). Cultural variations in country of origin effects. *Journal of Marketing Research*, *37*, 309-317.

Hamel, G., & Prahalad, C. K. (1985). Do you really have a global strategy. *Harvard Business Review*, *63*(4), 139-148.

Hout, T., Porter, M. A., & Rudden, E. (1982). How global companies win out. *Harvard Business Review*, *60*(5), 98-108.

Jaffe, E. D., & Nebenzahl, I. D. (2001). *National image and competitive advantage: The theory and practice of country-of-origin effect*. Herndon, VA: Copenhagen Business School Press/Books International.

Jiao, J., & Tseng, M. M. (2000). Understanding product family for mass customization by developing commonality indices. *Journal of Engineering Design*, *11*(3), 225-243.

Kanter, R. M., & Dretler, T. D. (1998). "Global strategy" and its impact on local operations: Lessons from Gillette Singapore. *Academy of Management Executive*, *12*(4), 60-68.

Kim, W. C., & Mauborgne, R. A. (1993). Making global strategies work. *Sloan Management Review, 34*(3), 11-27.

Kleppe, I. A., Iversen, N. M., & Stensaker, I. G. (2002). Country images in marketing strategies: Conceptual issues and an empirical Asian illustration. *Journal of Brand Management, 10*, 61-74.

Kogut, B. (1985). Designing global strategies: Comparative and competitive value-added chains. *Sloan Management Review, 26*(4), 15-28.

Kogut, B. (1985). Designing global strategies: Profiting from operational flexibility. *Sloan Management Review, 27*(1), 27-38.

Lampert, S. I., & Jaffe, E. D. (1998). A dynamic approach to country-of-origin effect. *European Journal of Marketing, 32*, 61-78.

Lei, D., & Slocum, J. W., Jr. (1992). Global strategy, competence-building and strategic alliances. *California Management Review, 35*(1), 81-97.

Lemak, D. J., & Arunthanes, W. (1997). Global business strategy: A contingency approach. *Multinational Business Review, 5*(1), 26-37.

Leonidou, L. C. (1996). Product standardization or adaptation: The Japanese approach. *Journal of Marketing Practice: Applied Marketing Science, 2*(4), 53-71.

Levitt, T. (1983). The globalization of markets. *Harvard Business Review, 61*(3), 92-101.

Lindell, M., & Karagozoglu, N. (1997). Global strategies of US and scandinavian R&D-intensive small- and medium-sized companies. *European Management Journal, 15*, 92-100.

Loeffler, M. (2002). A multinational examination of the '(non-) domestic product' effect. *International Marketing Review, 19*(5), 482-498.

Lovelock, C. H., & Yip, G. S. (1996). Developing global strategies for service business. *California Management Review, 38*(2), 64-86.

Lussier, R. N., Baeder, R. W., & Corman, J. (1994). Measuring global practices: global strategic planning through company situational analysis. *Business Horizons, 37*(5), 56-63.

Mallick, D. N., & Mukhopadhyay, S. K. (2001). Local design vs. global design: A strategic business choice. *European Journal of Operational Research, 131*, 389-399.

McKendrick, D. G. (2001). Global strategy and population-level learning: The case of hard disk drives. *Strategic Management Journal, 22*, 307-337.

Medina, J. F., & Duffy, M. F. (1998). Standardization vs. globalization: a new perspective of brand strategies. *Journal of Product and Brand Management, 7,* 223-243.

Miller, A., & Dess, G. G. (1993). Assessing Porter's model in terms of its generalizability, accuracy and simplicity. *Journal of Management Studies, 30,* 533-585.

Miller, D., & Freisen, P. H. (1986a). Porter's generic strategies and performance: An empirical examination with American data, part I: Testing Porter. *Organizational Studies, 7*(1), 37-55.

Miller, D., & Freisen, P. H. (1986b). Porter's generic strategies and performance: An empirical examination with American data, part II: Performance implications. *Organizational Studies, 7*(3), 255-261.

Mohamad, O., Ahmed, Z. U., Honeycutt Jr., E. D., & Tyebkhan, T. H. (2000). Does "made in…" matter to consumers? A Malaysian study of country of origin effect. *Multinational Business Review, 8*(2), 69-74.

Morrison, A. J., Ricks, D. A., & Roth, K. (1991). Globalization versus regionalization: Which way for the multinational. *Organizational Dynamics, 19*(3), 17-29.

O'Donnell, S., & Jeong, I. (2000). Marketing standardization within global industries: An empirical study of performance implications. *International Marketing Review, 17*(1), 19-33.

Palich, L. E., & Gomez-Mejia, L. R. (1999). A theory of global strategy and firm efficiencies: Considering the effects of cultural diversity. *Journal of Management, 25,* 587-606.

Papavassiliou, N., & Stathakopoulos, V. (1997). Standardization versus adaptation of international advertising strategies: Towards a framework. *European Journal of Marketing, 31,* 504-527.

Parameswaran, R., & Pisharodi, R. M. (2002). Assimilation effects in country image research. *International Marketing Review, 19*(2/3), 259-278.

Perlmutter, H. V. (1969). The tortuous evolution of the multinational corporation. *Columbia Journal of World Business, 4*(1), 9-18.

Peterson, R. A., & Jolibert, A. J. P. (1995). A meta-analysis of country-of-origin effects. *Journal of International Business Studies, 26*(4), 883-901.

Phillips, L. W., Chang, D. R., & Buzzell, R. D. (1983). Product quality, cost position and business performance: A test of some key hypotheses. *Journal of Marketing, 47*(2), 26-43.

Piron, F. (2000). Consumers' perceptions of the country-of-origin effect on purchasing intentions of (in) conspicuous products. *Journal of Consumer Marketing, 17*, 308-321.

Porter, M. E. (1980). *Competitive strategy.* New York: The Free Press.

Porter, M. E. (1985). *Competitive advantage.* New York: The Free Press.

Proff, H. (2000). Hybrid strategies as a strategic challenge—the case of the German automotive industry. *Omega (Oxford), 28*, 541-554.

Proff, H. (2002). Business unit strategies between regionalisation and globalisation. *International Business Review, 11*, 231-250.

Ramarapu, N. K., & Lado, A. A. (1995). Linking information technology to global business strategy to gain competitive advantage: An integrative model. *Journal of Information Technology, 10*, 115-124.

Reed, R. (1991). Bimodality in diversification: An efficiency and effectiveness rationale. *Managerial and Decision Economics, 12*, 57-66.

Rehfeld, D. (2001). Global strategies compared: Firms, markets and regions. *European Planning Studies, 9*, 29-46.

Roth, K., & Morrison, A. J. (1992). Implementing global strategy: Characteristics of global subsidiary mandates. *Journal of International Business Studies, 23*(4), 715-736.

Roth, K., Schweiger, D. M., & Morrison, A. J. (1991). Global strategy implementation at the business unit level: Operational capabilities and administrative mechanisms. *Journal of International Business Studies, 22*(3), 369-402.

Rugman, A. M. (2001). The myth of global strategy. *International Marketing Review, 18*(6), 583-588.

Samiee, S. (1994). Customer evaluation of products in a global market. *Journal of International Business Studies, 25*(3), 579-604.

Samiee, S., & Roth, K. (1992). The influence of global marketing standardization on performance. *Journal of Marketing, 56*(2), 1-17.

Schlie, E., & Yip, G. (2000). Regional follows global: Strategy mixes in the world automotive industry. *European Management Journal, 18*, 343-356.

Schooler, R. D. (1965). Product bias in the central American common market. *Journal of Marketing Research*, *2*, 394-397.

Shoham, A. (1995). Global marketing standardization. *Journal of Global Marketing, 9*(1/2), 91-119.

Simmonds, K. (1985). Global strategy: Achieving the geocentric ideal. *International Marketing Review*, *2*(1), 8-17.

Solberg, C. A. (2001). The Perenial issue of adaptation or standardization of international marketing communication: Organizational contingencies and performance. *Journal of International Marketing, 10*(3), 1-21.

Sugiura, H. (1990). How Honda localizes its global strategy. *Sloan Management Review*, *32*(1), 77-82.

Sullivan, D. (1994). Measuring the degree of internationalization of a firm. *Journal of International Business Studies, 25*(2), 325-342.

Szymanski, D. M., Bharadwaj, S. G., & Varadarajan, P. R. (1993). Standardization versus adaptation of international marketing strategy: An empirical investigation. *Journal of Marketing*, *57*(4), 1-17.

van Mesdag, M. (2000). Culture sensitive adaptation or global standardization—the duration-of-usage hypothesis. *International Marketing Review*, *17*(1), 74-84.

Verlegh, P. W. J., & Steenkamp, J. B. E. M. (1999). A review and meta-analysis of country-of-origin research. *Journal of Economic Psychology*, *20*, 521-546.

Wind, Y., Douglas, S. P., & Perlmutter, H. V. (1973). Guidelines for developing international marketing strategies. *Journal of Marketing*, *37*(2), 14-23.

Yip, G. S. (1989). Global strategy…in a world of nations. *Sloan Management Review*, *31*(1), 29-42.

Yip, G. S. (1992). *Total global strategy*. New Jersey: Pearson Prentice Hall.

Yip, G. S. (2000). Global strategy in the internet era. *Business Strategy Review, 11*(4), 1-14.

Zhang, Y. (1997). Country-of-origin effect. *International Marketing Review*, *14*(4/5), 266-287.

Zou, S., & Cavusgil, S. T. (1996). Global strategy: a review and integrated conceptual framework. *European Journal of Marketing, 30*, 52-69.

Endnotes

[1]   For many years developing and newly independent countries have tried to achieve economic advancement through the export of commodity-like primary agricultural products. Although this policy was successful in promoting export, it has been highly unsuccessful, with precious rare exceptions, in fostering economic growth and development.

[2]   Medina and Duffy (1998), Shoham (1995), Lemark and Arunthanes (1997) all provide thorough reviews of the past literature on the adapt/standardize issue. Duffy and Medina further provide a chronological listing of articles and categorize them according to the position taken by the authors. Soldberg (2001) provides a literature review that is more inclusive chronologically than the others, although it is somewhat less comprehensive in scope.

[3]   Proff (2002) cites studies claiming that a strategy combining low-cost and differentiation is possible (Miller & Dess, 1993; Miller & Friesen, 1986a, 1986b) and can be profitable (Buzzell & Gale, 1987; Phillips, Chang & Buzzell, 1983). He also cites studies empirically illustrating the profitability of a joint-strategy (Proff, 2000). In the global context, Proff interprets "stuck in the middle" to mean regionalization that combines both low-cost and a degree of customization as an optimal strategy in so me cases. Tailoring products to the specific needs of individual markets may not be cost effective, while catering to blocks of countries, or regions, may adequately meet minimum customization requirements, while still affording the pursuit of a low-cost strategy. Automotive heating and cooling systems, for example, may require adaptation to differing climates, but regional adjustments should obviate the needs for more specific modifications on a country-by-country basis.

[4]   This is the well-known concept of economic theory generally known by the Latin expression ceteris paribus.

[5]   The latter concept is what Porter (1985) calls the "value chain."

Chapter VII

Genetic Algorithm and Other Meta-Heuristics:
Essential Tools for Solving Modern Supply Chain Management Problems

Bernard K.-S. Cheung,

GERAD & Ecole Polytechnique of Montreal, Canada

Abstract

Genetic algorithms have been applied in solving various types of large-scale, NP-hard optimization problems. Many researchers have been investigating its global convergence properties using Schema Theory, Markov Chain, etc. A more realistic approach, however, is to estimate the probability of success in finding the global optimal solution within a prescribed number of generations under some function landscapes. Further investigation reveals that its inherent weaknesses that affect its performance can be remedied, while its efficiency can be significantly enhanced through the design of an adaptive scheme that integrates the crossover, mutation and selection operations. The advance of Information Technology and the extensive corporate globalization create great challenges for the solution of modern supply chain models that become more and more complex and size formidable. Meta-heuristic methods have to be employed to obtain near optimal solutions. Recently, a genetic algorithm has been reported to solve these problems satisfactorily and there are reasons for this.

Introduction

During the early eighties, when Supply Chain Models just began to take shape, many important problems in logistics such as the Facility Planning and Vehicle Routing Problems were found to be NP-hard. The conventional mathematical programming methods fail to solve these complex problems satisfactorily, especially when they are under time constraints. Researchers began to use meta-heuristic methods such as genetic algorithm, simulated annealing and the Tabu search to handle these problems, since they are often able to find a near global optimal solution in a reasonable time.

Recently, due to the intensive efforts in globalization undertaken by the big corporations, the modern supply chain models at both the strategic and operational level are becoming more complex and size-formidable with thousands of variables. The computation complexity of most of the analytic algorithms are at least of the order n(logn) so that the computation time is really enormous.

The advent of the age of advanced information technology and e-commerce call for distribution models to be more dynamic and readily responsive to all changes in market situations. Because of this immense increase in complexity, one would encounter great difficulty in formulating these models so that they can be solved by well known analytic methods. Furthermore, the requirement of close to real-time solution of supply chain models imposes further restrictions to the application of these methods. This leads to the development of powerful meta-heuristic algorithms that are more appropriate to be applied in this circumstance.

The organization of this chapter is as follows. The first section describes the real case scenarios where meta-heuristics have to be employed in solving present-day supply chain management problems. The next section discusses the controversies in solution methods and the emergence of some powerful meta-heuristics, such as the Tabu Search. The problem dependency of some of these methods leads to the genetic algorithms that are population-based and random-ization in their approaches being chosen as the appropriate tool. An in-depth analysis of the entire genetic search scheme is given. How the restructurings of GA can be performed so that its inherent weakness of being time consuming due to ineffectiveness and redundancy of its basic operations can be overcome is also described in this section. Next, the chapter attempts to explain with simple examples that GA can best be employed as a solver for modern supply chain management problems. This is followed with an outlines how our proposed modified genetic algorithm can be enhanced to a more efficient tool for solving complex optimization problems through combining (or hybridizing) other well-known algorithms.

Because of the large amount of complex mathematical expressions in the context, the reader is advised to refer to the table of important notational conventions in Appendix 2 for easy following of all the arguments in the next section.

Controversy in Solution Methods for Solving Supply Chain Management Problems

There have always been controversies in solving complex optimization prob-lems of large scale. The use of exact solution methods or meta-heuristics, the integrated solution for the entire model or decomposition into simpler and smaller sub-problems that can be solved readily, and in the case of using a meta-heuristic method, the choice between an intensified search scheme or a reliable scheme which ensures high probability of convergence to the true global optimal solution, are all hotly debated. These controversies become more apparent for modern Supply Chain Models that are normally very large and complex. The time constraints and the requirement for their responsiveness to the changes in market situation favor the application of simple and quick methods. There are powerful deterministic methods like column-generation and branch-and-bound, etc., but their applications, however, are restricted to certain specific types of problems (say, for example, linear problems). Traditional heuristic methods, despite of their inherent weakness, do have their advantages in getting sometimes good, approximate solutions and the simplicity of their structures easily lends themselves for computer implementation.

Fortunately, modern meta-heuristics, like the Tabu Search by Glover (1997) have been found capable of obtaining near optimal solutions for a number of important problems in logistics within a reasonably short time. In fact, there have been reports of successful applications of Tabu Search in solving some logistic problems such as the Hub Location problems (see Skorin-Kapov & Skorin-Kapov, 1994). The problem with Tabu Search lies in its difficulty in determining the "Tabu tenure" and the length of "Tabu list" correctly, so that its performance is optimized. It is quite problem dependent. On the other hand, the Genetic Algorithm and the Simulated Annealing being in randomization approach tends to be less problem-dependent, and more reliable in their general applications in spite of their being relatively slow in comparison with the Tabu Search. Genetic (or evolutionary) Algorithm differs from Simulated Annealing by being population-based possesses in a richer structure where individuals are allowed to interact with each other for improvement. The disadvantage of Genetic Algorithm is that it has no memory. However, this can be in some way compensated with enhancing procedures.

Genetic algorithm, with its interesting algorithmic structure, searches for an optimal solution through the evolution of a population of candidate solutions via crossover, mutation and selection operations. The weaknesses of genetic algorithms are the redundancy and the disruptive nature of its crossover and mutation operations. There have been a large number of articles on the study of their convergence properties (see Rudolph, 1999, for a review), but there are only a few papers devoted to the restructuring of the genetic algorithm for performance improvement. Cheung et al. (2001) introduced some effective treatments for enhancing the performance of the traditional genetic algorithm. An intensive study on the probability of success in converging to the global optimum by Yuen and Cheung (2003) reveals some characteristic behaviors of the genetics search scheme that pave some possible avenues for further performance enhancement. We shall give a more elaborate and comprehensive development of those ideas in the following section.

Development of a New GA for Performance Enhancement

The performance of GA in terms of probability of success within a given number of generations can be improved significantly in the following ways: (i) the re-design of crossover for more effective operations; (ii) the introduction of an adaptive mutation rate; (iii) a well designed search scheme that optimally integrates the crossover, mutation and selection process; and (iv) a simple but effective procedure which dynamically enlarges our domain of search. To see how this can happen, we shall make a full analysis of each of the key operations and how they interact with each other.

Issues Affecting the Effectiveness of a Crossover Operation

It was discussed in the papers by Cheung et al. (2001) and Yuen and Cheung (2003) that for any pair of chromosomes of length γ, where the elements (or genes) of each chromosome may take up a given range of integral values, they may contain some genes that are identical to the optimal chromosome, assuming that this optimal chromosome is unique. Let Z_1 be the subset of genes in the first chromosome which are identical to the optimal chromosome and let Z_2 be the subset of genes in the second chromosome that are identical to that of the optimal chromosome. A crossover of any design (1-point, 2-point or uniform, etc.) normally exchanges two corresponding subsets of the same cardinality, each belonging to one of the given chromosomes. This crossover operation can only be effective in producing an offspring closer in resemblance to the optimal chromosome, if this exchange involves in swapping of genes in $Y_2 = Z_2 \setminus (Z_1 \cap Z_2)$ with genes in the complement of Z_1 in the first chromosome or vice versa. This operation fails if the subset S_1 of genes selected for crossover in the first chromosome does not contain genes in Z_1 or the subset S_2 in the second string does not contain genes in Z_2. Even if the previous case is true, this operation may be entirely redundant if those genes in S_1 and that in S_2 all belong to $Z_1 \cap Z_2$. (See diagrammatic illustration below and refer to the case of 2-point crossover towards the end of this section for a better understanding of the idea.) Furthermore, let $i = |Z_1|$ and $j = |Z_2|$, if a crossover operation gives two children with k attributes and l attributes identical with that of the optimal chromosome, we must have $i + j = k + l$. Thus, if the number of attributes of one of the offspring (say k) is higher than both of that of its parents, then we must have $k > i > j > 1$ (assuming $i > j$ for convenience).

To analyze the effect of crossover operation on a pair of binary chromosomes, one can reduce a lot of complication by confining consideration to the following standard case as illustrated below. Since for fixed i, j and overlap m, this case is unique up to a permutation of their relative positions.

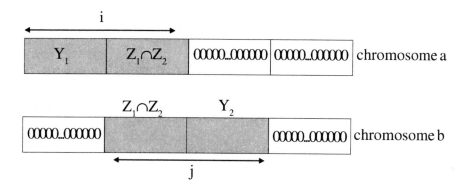

Following from this, one obtains:

(1)   If two distinct chromosomes both have approximately half the number of attributes of the optimal chromosome, then the probability of reproducing an offspring closer in resemblance to the optimal chromosome is high.

(2)   On the other hand, if the overlapping (i.e., the size of $Z_1 \cap Z_2$) is large, then the chance of producing an offspring closer to the optimum is low. Hence, one should consider crossing-over pairs of chromosomes that are very distinct (as measured by their hamming distance). Hence, any procedure which helps avoid selecting very similar pair of chromosomes for cross-over is beneficial in both ways.

(3)   From (1) and (2), it can be seen that, if most of the chromosomes in a given population contain about one half of the attributes of the optimal string, then the crossover between any pair of them tends to produce one offspring significantly closer to the optimal chromosome. This is true for a population with binary strings where over 80% of the initial population lies within the hamming distance of ¼ to ¾ of the total length of the string to the optimal string. Notice that, in general, for a chromosome of length γ, where each of its genes assumes m integer values 1, 2, 3, …, m. The

probability distribution E of the number of optimal solution attributes in the initial population is given by

$$X = \binom{\gamma}{x}\left(\frac{1}{m}\right)^x (1-\frac{1}{m})^{\gamma-x}.$$

(See Appendix 1 for the detail.) It can be seen that the maximum of X lies between $1/m$ and ½ of the length of the chromosome from the left end. Hence, the crossover operation tends to be very effective at the early stages of reproduction. The highest number of attributes obtained, however, cannot exceed $i + j$. More precisely, if chromosomes **a** and **b** produce offspring $\mathbf{c} \in R_k$ and $\mathbf{d} \in R_l$ under this crossover, where R_k denotes the set of all chromosomes with k attributes of the optimal solution and t is the total number corresponding gene-positions being swapped, then $k = i + t_b - t_a$ and $l = j + t_a - t_b$, where t_a and t_b are the respective numbers of attributes of the optimal chromosome selected from Y_1 and Y_2 for swapping. Notice that if $k > i > j$, then $l < j$ and if $i > k > j$, then $l > j$. Also, observe that **this probability of obtaining an offspring in R_k through crossover is zero, if $k > i + j$.**

Let $m = |Z_1 \cap Z_2|$ and we have, the number of ways for t_a bits to be contained in the portion is determined by $Y_1 = \binom{i-m}{t_a}$, the number of ways for t_b bits to be contained in the portion determined by $Y_2 = \binom{j-m}{t_b}$, and the number of ways for $t-t_a-t_b$ bits to be contained in the remaining portions is given by $\binom{\gamma-i-j+m}{t-t_a-t_b}$. Hence, the total number of ways for obtaining

$\mathbf{c} \in R_k$ is $\binom{i-m}{t_a}\binom{j-m}{t_b}\binom{\gamma-i-j+m}{t-t_a-t_b}$.

It is clear from the last statement in the second paragraph of this section that for fixed overlap m, there exist the above number of pairs of elements $\mathbf{a} \, \varepsilon \, R_i$ and $\mathbf{b} \, \varepsilon \, R_j$ (or none), such that any $\mathbf{c} \, \varepsilon \, R_k$ can be obtained by crossover between $\mathbf{a}$ and $\mathbf{b}$. This probability is given by

$$\sum_{t_a, t_b} \binom{i-m}{t_a} \binom{j-m}{t_b} \binom{\gamma-i-j+m}{t-t_a-t_b} \phi(m),$$

where $v = \min\{i, j\}$,

$$\phi(m) = \frac{\binom{\gamma}{m}\binom{\gamma-m}{i-m}\binom{\gamma-i}{j-m}}{\binom{\gamma}{i}\binom{\gamma}{j}}$$

is the probability of having m overlaps and the first summation is taken over t_a and t_b, satisfying $t_a + t_b \leq t$ and $k = i - t_a + t_b$.

One can see clearly that this probability depends on i, j, m and t only and is independent of the positions of those attributes in pattern $\mathbf{a}$ and $\mathbf{b}$. This indicates that the appearance of each chromosome c in R_k produced in this manner in next generation is equally likely.

Simplifying, we have,

$$\phi(m) = \frac{(\gamma-i)!(\gamma-j)!i!j!}{\gamma!(i-m)!(j-m)!(\gamma-i-j+m)!m!}$$

Substituting $t_b = k + t_a - i$, we have, the probability $p(i, j, k, t)$ of obtaining a chromosome $\mathbf{c} \, \varepsilon \, R_k$ by a uniform crossover which swaps t elements between chromosomes $\mathbf{a} \, \varepsilon \, R_i$ and $\mathbf{b} \, e \, R_j$ is given by

$$p(i, j, k, t) = \sum_{m=0}^{v} \sum_{t_a=0}^{\mu} \binom{i-m}{t_a} \binom{j-m}{k-i+t_a} \binom{\gamma-i-j+m}{t+i-k-2t_a} \phi(m) =$$

$$\sum_{m=0}^{v}\sum_{t_a=0}^{\mu}$$

$$\frac{(\gamma-i)!(\gamma-j)!i!j!}{\gamma!m!(i-m-t_a)!(i+j-k-m-t_a)!(\gamma-2i-j-t+k+2t_a)!(i+t-k-2t_a)!(k-i+t_a)!t_a!}$$

where $m = \min\{t, i-m\}$ and $n = \min\{i,j\}$.

(4) Under repeated crossover operations on a given population, the sum total number of attributes of the optimal chromosome is constant. (i.e., $|Y_1| + |Y_2| + ... + |Y_n| = K$, for some real constant K, where Y_i is the subset of Z_i of chromosome i that are distinct from Z_j for all $j \neq i$). If K is less than the chromosome length, the search will never converge to the optimal solution. This explains why appropriate mutation operations have to be employed to make this happen. When the reproduction process reaches its late stages, a large proportion of chromosomes in the population are very close to the true optimal chromosome, any crossover action may become very ineffective, as the overlaps (i.e., the size of $Z_1 \cap Z_2$) between these two corresponding sets of attributes are large. One could perhaps reduce the crossover rate relative to the mutation rate so as to enhance the speed of convergence.

We shall describe a simple and effective but less time consuming method introduced by Cheung et al. (2001) for a conventional 2-point crossover in the following paragraph.

Normally, a 2-point crossover operation on a pair of chromosomes is to be defined as follows. Given two chromosomes of length n:

$a_1, a_2, ..., a_{i-1}, a_i, ..., a_j, a_{j+1}, ..., a_n$
$b_1, b_2, ..., b_{i-1}, b_i, ..., b_j, b_{j+1}, ..., b_n$

a pair of positive integers i, j with $1 \leq i \leq j \leq n$ is randomly generated, and the resulting offspring are obtained by exchanging the middle part of the chromosomes lying between i and j:

$a_1, a_2, ..., a_{i-1}, b_i, ..., b_j, a_{j+1}, ..., a_n$
$b_1, b_2, ..., b_{i-1}, a_i, ..., a_j, b_{j+1}, ..., b_n$

Notice that a single point crossover results, when i = 1 or j = n.

Observe that for this 2-point crossover, the redundancy occurs: (i) when all the corresponding elements (or genes) in both chromosomes lying between these crossover points are identical, or (ii) when all the corresponding elements lying on the end sections outside the section bounded by the two cut-points are identical. If the two strings selected for crossover are distinct, the occurrence of case 2 is only one eighth of all the possible occurrences. Thus, most of the redundancy cases can be avoided, if the sections of both strings between the two crossover points are checked to ensure that they are different. In those cases where the chromosomes are relatively short, one should perhaps check for the occurrence of case 2 as well. Moreover, if the genes of chromosome **a** lying between i and j contains a large number of attributes of the optimal solution that do not belong to chromosome **b** (or vice versa), then one of the offspring produced will contain more attributes than either of its parents. Thus one can make the crossover even more efficient, if we only crossover those sections of the pair of chromosome having at least a prescribed number of pairs (say three or four) of corresponding elements different.

Another well-known crossover is the uniform crossover. It is defined as: select each position along the string from the beginning till the end with a fixed probability (say, χ). Thus a random selected subset of genes in chromosome A is to be swapped with genes at corresponding positions in chromosome B. The average number of genes being swapped is $\chi\gamma$, where γ is the length of the chromosomes. One can consider the 2-point crossover as a special case of the uniform crossover. The latter, however, is more general and more random. It has been shown with test examples that the uniform crossover is more effective than the 2-point crossover at the beginning of the reproduction process (Cheung et al., 2001).

Effect of Mutation Rate on Convergence Rate

Like the crossover operation, the mutation operation tends to be disruptive as well as constructive. Suppose the 1-bit flip mutation where one gene-position is chosen at random for flipping is applied, the probability of changing any specific position on a binary string k/n, where n is the length of the string and k the number of position that need a flip of bit value from 0 to 1 or vice versa. However, this flip will be disruptive, if it is positioned on the genes corresponding to the attributes of the optimal string, the probability of this disruption is given by $(n-k)/n$. This disruption, however, is very small, and it may not be large enough to shake off the search point from the local optimal position. Nevertheless, it helps to improve the fitness of certain chromosomes, especially when it is applied at the end of the reproduction stages.

Suppose the uniform mutation where each gene-position is selected in turn for flipping with probability μ applied, the probability of changing any specific l positions on a binary string is given by $\mu^l(1-\mu)^{\gamma-1}$. By differentiating the expression with respect to μ, it is easy to see that this probability will be maximized if $\mu = (l/\gamma)$. That is, $l = \mu\gamma$ bits will be most likely to be mutated in this case. We shall see that appropriate rate of mutation will allow those chromosomes to be mutated to have a higher probability of improving their fitness value. For instance, when the search is at its earlier stages, the number of attributes of most of the chromosomes in common with the optimal solutions is not so large (probably, about ¼ to ½ of the total length the chromosome), a higher mutation rate is favorable in producing offspring with high resemblance to the optimal chromosome. Moreover, such a mutation rate will cause more disruptive effects to prevent premature termination at a local optimum. When the search is close to the optimal point, most of the chromosomes in the population will be very similar to the optimal chromosome. Only a few bits of changes are necessary to transform them to the optimal one. Hence, one should adaptively reduce the uniform mutation rate when this scenario occurs. However, if the selection rule discards the weaker chromosome after mutation, the single mutation operation often fails to bring about any change in fitness value and repeated mutation operations on this chromosome may then be needed. Thus the frequency of application of mutation operation must be higher relative to those of crossover at these late stages. More precisely, let us consider the case where the chromosomes are binary. For any chromosome $\mathbf{a} \in R_i$, let l_a and l_b be the respective numbers of positions on the set of "0"s and "1"s on the chromosome $\mathbf{a}$ selected by the uniform mutation operator of l bits. That is, $l = l_a + l_b$. If the resulting chromosome $\mathbf{c}$ is in R_k, we must have $k = i + l_a - l_b$. Now, the number of ways such that this will happen is given by

$$\binom{\gamma - i}{l_a}\binom{i}{l_b}.$$

Since the uniform mutation operator mutates '*l*' bits of any chromosome randomly, the probability of having any specific mutation pattern is equal and is given by $\mu^l(1-\mu)^{\gamma-l}$, it follows that the probability of obtaining any chromosome **c** in R_k is equal and is given by

$$\sum_{l_a,l_b}\binom{\gamma-i}{l_a}\binom{i}{l_b}\mu^l(1-\mu)^{\gamma-l}$$

where the summation is taken over all l_a and l_b such that $l_a+l_b=l$ which depends only on i and *l* and is independent of the positions of those attributes.

Summing over all possible mutating bit values, we have the probability of obtaining any $\mathbf{c}\,\varepsilon\,R_k$ is given by

$$m_\mu(i,k)=\sum_{l=1}^{\gamma-1}\sum_{l_a=0}^{l}\binom{\gamma-1}{l_a}\binom{i}{l-l_a}\mu^l(1-\mu)^{\gamma-1}$$

where l_a satisfies k = i - *l* + 2l_a (or *l* = i-k+2l_a) . Hence, if k > i, the above expression reduces to

$$=\sum_{l_a=k-i}^{m}\binom{\gamma-1}{l_a}\binom{i}{i-k+l_a}\mu^{i-k+2l_a}(1-\mu)^{\gamma-i+k-2l_a}$$

where m = min{ $\gamma-i$, $2i-k$ }. Similar expression for $m_\mu(i,k)$ can be deduced for the case i > k.

From the last expression, one sees that if i is large, then μ must be sufficiently small so that the probability of improvement (i.e., the probability of obtaining a chromosome closer to the optimum) is non-negligible. In particular, if k = n, then $l_b = 0$, this implies that $l_a = l$, and hence, l = n − i. The probability of this occurrence is given by $\mu^{n-l}(1-\mu)^i$. It follows that this probability is maximized when $\mu = (n-i)/n$. In any case, μ must be small in the final stage of reproduction. However, at the earlier stages, μ must be sufficiently large in order to avoid being trapped in a local optimum point. Thus an adaptive mutation rate that can be changed dynamically as the search progresses is recommended.

Controversy between Intensification and Avoidance of Being Trapped in a Local Optimum Point

If we examine more closely about how a population of chromosomes may change under the action of crossover, mutation and subsequent selection as described in the previous sections, we may observe that there is a controversy between speeding up the process of convergence and the increasing risk of termination at a local optimum. If we discard the weaker chromosomes by an aggressive selection after crossover and mutation, then it becomes more likely that the search terminates prematurely. Of cause, it may terminate at the true optimum, if we are lucky enough. It might be a good idea, if we replace both the parent chromosomes by the children after a successful crossover, as the total good solution attributes are preserved (see remark (4) under section 2.3), even though the searching process may be somewhat slower. The reduction in mutation rate at the late stages may be more helpful in bringing about more rapid convergence. But too small a mutation rate may not be sufficiently disruptive to shake off the search from the local optimum. A similar situation occurs in Tabu Search and other heuristic searches as well. We propose that the newly mutated chromosome that is evaluated to be inferior should be allowed to stay in the population for a short period of time (say after two to three more generations) before being replaced. This arrangement is very similar to the "Tabu tenure" in the Tabu Search heuristics. Thus, a good adaptive scheme can be developed so that the genetic search can be intensified while sufficiently diversified to have an optimal enhancement in performance.

Unfavorable function landscapes practically render all known meta-heuristic search techniques useless. For example, the function $f(\mathbf{x})$ defined on a domain in R^n by $f(\mathbf{x}_0) = 1$ at a certain point $\mathbf{x}_0$ and zero elsewhere, cannot be solved more efficiently using any meta-heuristics than the simple random search. Also, Wolpert and Macready (1997), in their paper on "No Free Lunch Theorems for Optimization," mentioned a genetic algorithm that gives a trajectory traversing the problem domain such that each solution point is never revisited. However, how such an algorithm can be designed has not been discussed. In any case, based on what we have described in the previous sub-sections under Section 2, one can always design a good genetic scheme that reduces the redundancy and that can avoid some unnecessary or repetitive moves so that that it can still perform under the worse case scenarios.

The population size affects the degree of diversification as well as the speed (or rate) of convergence (not to be confused with the probability of converging to the true optimal solution within a prescribed number of generations). It is not difficult to see that in a single reproduction stage, the number of crossover operations is directly proportional to

$$\binom{n}{2}$$

where n is the population size. Hence, the time required for fitness evaluation in terms of crossover operations increases in the order of square of n. On the other hand, the degree of enlargement of our search space increases linearly with n. Thus, we have to work with a small population but large enough to maintain high probability of success. Other than diversifying the search by mutation operations, which have to be controlled as described in the previous section, there is a relatively economic way of enlarging the search space virtually. This is to be described in detail in the following section.

Partial Reshuffling Procedure

The partial reshuffling procedure as described in Cheung et al. (2001) is implemented for allowing the good mature chromosomes to crossover with some newly generated ones so that the genetic search can be diversified considerably. This procedure allows us to perform a genetic search operation effectively using a much smaller population size. The conventional way of doing this is to repeat the genetic scheme over a new randomly generated population when there is no detectable improvement in the original population after a certain number of generations. This reshuffling procedure enlarges the search space, but it is very time consuming.

Our procedure takes advantage of the fact that a considerable number of attributes of the optimal chromosome might have been acquired previously by some chromosomes throughout the process of reproduction. These chromosomes having good candidacy potential should be allowed to recombine with some new chromosomes for further improvements. Clearly, there is a considerable time saving when compared with the usual reshuffling procedure which requires an actual restart over from the very beginning. The detail of this procedure is described as follows.

For a given population of size 3n, the following steps are performed.

1.   Generate n new chromosomes $\{a_1, a_2, \ldots\ldots, a_n\}$, which are different from all the chromosomes in the original population, and arrange them in descending order of fitness, i.e., the best fitted first.

2.   For j = 1, 2, 3, ..., n, if the fitness value of a_j is better than the worst chromosome in the original population, then replace the worst string with this a_j. Otherwise, crossover a_j with all the chromosomes in the original population and then with all other a_i's not equal to j. Update the population by replacing the worst chromosomes with the best obtained each time.

3.   If no more than 50% of the total replacement has been made possible, then generate more new chromosomes and repeat Step 2 until some more (say about 80%) of the less fitted original chromosomes are replaced.

Assuming that the generation process is random, and that the probability of obtaining improved new offspring when a mature chromosome crossovers with a new chromosome should be approximately the same as that when two new chromosomes crossover with each other, it can be seen that the total number of crossovers in a partial replacement procedure at each generation for a population of size n = 3m is $m\cdot(5m-1)/2$. While in the total reshuffle operation, the total number of crossovers is $0.6\cdot(3m)(3m-1)/2$ for a reproduction rate of 0.6. These two numbers are not very different even for large n, since the ratio $[m(5m-1)/2]/[3m(3m-1)] = (5m-1)/[3(3m-1)]$ tends slowly to a limit 5/9 as n increases. Thus the degree of improvement in fitness value at each generation in both cases should be comparable. However, the total reshuffle requires the process to start over from the very beginning. This means that our partial replacement procedure actually requires much less time to reach the same improved fitness value.

Further Performance Enhancement by Parallel Computation Implementation

The population-based genetic search scheme lends itself easily for partial parallel computation implementation in a modern multi-processor computer for speed enhancement. The fitness evaluations after crossover operations in each reproduction stage can be performed in parallel. Similarly, the fitness evaluations after a mutation operation can also be computed in parallel. Using multi-thread coding on a Sun Workstation with eight processors, the computer time for some problems was shown to be reduced to almost 1/6 of the original (Cheung et al., 2001). This technique can also be applied, when a large complex optimization problem is capable of being decomposed into simple sub-problems (or independent sub-routines) that can be handled simultaneously at some stage of the solution routine.

Some Illustrative Examples for Application of GA in Logistics and Supply Chain Management

Important examples in logistics, like location and sizing of logistic terminals, solution of some distribution models, etc., are to be discussed with various new methods in problem formulation introduced by Cheung et al. (1997, 2001), Chan et al. (2003), and some recent publications by other authors. Starting with some simple examples, we would further extend this approach to models with larger size and higher complexity. We shall see that the suitability of Genetic Algorithms, and other meta-heuristics that have been explained with theoretical arguments in the second section, for solving more complex problems in logistics and supply chain management will be verified by its modified form in the solution of some simple illustrative examples. These lead to an extended strategic approach to apply our modified Genetic Algorithm in solving different versions of a modern Supply Chain Management Problem which will be elaborated later in this chapter.

Sizing and Location of Facilities

This problem is also called the location and allocation problem. The first attack on this problem was described in Devine and Lesso (1972) as the case of location of oil platforms in the offshore oil field. The wells to be drilled are to be allocated to one of these platforms so that the sum of the linking distances between the platform and each of the wells allocated to it and the total cost of platform building is minimized. The cost of the platform is a function of the number of the wells allocated to it, but this function may not be linear. In a large distribution network, the intermediate warehouses have to be built close to the retailers (or customers) so that the goods from the supplier are delivered to the retailers (or customers) via the intermediate warehouses. One has to find the optimal size of each warehouse and the optimal allocation of customers to one of these platforms so that the total delivery cost and the platform building cost are minimized. In its simplest form, this can be considered as a p-median problem, which was solved by Hansen and Mladenovic (1997), using Variable Neighbourhood Search where the search neighbourhood is systematically modified through acquisition of information at local minima so that its convergence to the global optimal solution is efficiently achieved. (See also Hansen and Mladenovic, 2001.) However, in practice, the length of each delivery route from the warehouse to its dedicated customer may not be Euclidean, and the total cost that includes the facility building cost may not be convex, the method proposed by Cheung et al. (2001), to which uses GA has to be applied.

In this location-allocation problem, the objective is to locate the platforms and allocate wells to the platforms so that the total cost for drilling and platform building is minimized. It is to be formulated as follows.

Let m be the number of wells and n be the number of platforms. The decision variables z_{ij} takes the value 1 if well i is allocated to platform j, and 0 otherwise. Let S_j denote the number of wells allocated to platform j and let (a_i, b_i) be the (known) coordinate of well i and (x_j, y_j) denote the (unknown) coordinates of the platform j. For all value of i and j, let

$$d_{ij} = \sqrt{[(x_j - a_i)^2 + (y_j - b_i)^2]}$$

be the Euclidean distance between well i and platform j. The drilling cost function $g(d_{ij})$ depends on (x_j, y_j) the location of the platform j and the platform cost $P_j(S_j)$ is a function of its size S_j.

This problem can be stated as follows:

$$\min \sum_{i=1}^{m} \sum_{j=1}^{n} z_{ij} g\left(d_{ij}\right) + \sum_{j=1}^{n} P_j\left(S_j\right)$$

subject to $\qquad \sum_{j=1}^{n} z_{ij} = 1, \forall i$

$$\sum_{j=1}^{n} z_{ij} = 1, \forall i$$

where, $\qquad z_{ij} = 0 \text{ or } 1.$

The objective function is the sum of the total drilling cost and platform costs. The first set of constraints requires that each well i is assigned to exactly one platform. The second set gives the number of wells allocated to each platform j. In the practical application considered herein, n takes a value from three to five, and m takes a value between 25 and 300. Our decomposition method allows the value of the z_{ij} to be determined by the genetic algorithm, that is, to determine the allocation and then for each allocation solve the following simplified problem:

$$\min \sum_{j=1}^{n} \sum_{i \varepsilon A} z_{ij} g\left(d_{ij}\right) + \sum_{j=1}^{n} P_{j}\left(S_{j}\right)$$

where

$$A_{j} = \{i \,|\, z_{ij} = 1\}$$

In the tests, we take $d_{ij} = \sqrt{[(x_j - a_i)^2 + (y_j - b_i)^2]}$ and $Pj(S_j) = h + k\sqrt{S_j}$ for all j = 1, 2. The values of h and k were respectively set at 50 and 25 in all our tests.

This offshore oil field problem with concave cost and 200 wells was solved by Cheung et al. in 1997 by coupling GA with a Grid Search method. It was again tried with most of the enhancement procedures described above implemented, and an improved solution was obtained with only a fraction (say about 40%) of the previous computer time. When the parallel computation by multi-threading technique was used, the total computer time was further reduced dramatically (Cheung et al., 2001).

Observe that the above formulation also fits in the design of intermediate warehouses for a large distribution network where the locations of customers (or retailing outlets) are just like that of the wells. However, in real cases, there are only a finite (but fixed) number of possible locations to be chosen for the construction of those warehouses and the actual delivery distance d_{ij} from warehouse i to customer j are non-Euclidean, but determined by a GIS. Thus the problem becomes an integer-programming problem with an objective function similar to above, which in general, is neither linear nor convex. The genetic algorithm with its modified structure will handle them readily.

A more complex but very similar problem of location and sizing of logistics terminals taking into account of the traffic condition on the road networks was considered by Taniguchi et al. in 1999. Goods movement is divided into two parts: line hauls for long distance delivery on expressway and local pick-up/delivery by small trucks. The logistics terminals are the connection between line hauls and local tucks. This elaborate model was reportedly solved successfully by genetic algorithm.

Multi-Buyer Joint Replenishment Problems

The Joint Replenishment Problem (JRP) is the multi-item inventory problem of coordinating the replenishment of a group of items that may be jointly ordered from a single supplier. Each time an order is placed, a major ordering cost is incurred, independent of the number of items ordered. Furthermore, a minor ordering cost is incurred for each item included in a replenishment order. In the application described hereafter, an item corresponds to one category of forms to be ordered regardless of the quantity. Joint replenishment of a group of items reduces the number of times that the major ordering cost is charged, and therefore saves costs. In the deterministic joint replenishment problem it is assumed that the major ordering cost is charged at a basic cycle time and that the ordering cycle of each item is some integer multiple of this basic cycle. The single-buyer JRP has been studied extensively during the last two decades. Goyal (1974) proposed an enumerative procedure, which requires substantial computational efforts to produce an optimal solution. The running time of this procedure grows exponentially with the number of items. Since then, there have been a large number of heuristic procedures developed for generating a near-optimal replenishment policy with a reduced amount of computation. However, it is common practice for a multi-branch firm to have all of its branches ordering the same group of items from a single supplier. Clearly there are opportunities to reduce costs by coordinating the joint replenishments among the buyers. If, as is usually the case, the branches have quite different levels of demand, then the JRP becomes a multi-buyer, multi-item problem. It is an area that has received little attention in the literature.

We shall formulate this problem as the following (the formulation corresponds to the multi-buyer JRP for a route):

let i be the item number, i = 1,2, … , I; and j be the branch number, j = 1,2, … , J. I and J are respectively, the number of items and the number of branches.

Assumptions

1. The demand per unit time of each item is assumed to be known and constant. When this assumption is inappropriate, the decision rules can still be used as guidelines for sizes or time duration of replenishments, in much the same way that the EOQ is still useful, in combination with a safety stock, when demand is probabilistic.

2. The lead time is constant.

3. No shortages are permitted.

Notations

d_{ij} – the demand per unit time of item i in branch j.

S – the major set-up cost, in $

s_{ij} – the minor set-up cost when item i is included in a group replenishment in branch j,

  in $

v_i – the unit variable cost of item i, in $

r – the inventory carrying charge, in % per unit time.

The variables are:

t – the basic cycle time interval between orders, in unit time

k_{ij} – the number of integer multiples of t that a replenishment of i is included in a group replenishment in branch j. Thus, the replenishment cycle time of item i in branch j is equal to $k_{ij}t$. Moreover, $k_{ij} \geq 1$.

Q_{ij} – the order quantity of item i in branch j. Thus $Q_{ij} = d_{ij} k_{ij} t$.

The total carrying cost per unit time, C_c, is given by

$$C_c = \sum_i \sum_j \frac{Q_{ij}}{2} \cdot v_i r = r \sum_i \sum_j \frac{d_{ij}}{2} k_{ij} \cdot v_i \cdot t$$

and the total set-up cost per unit time, C_s, is given by

$$C_s = \frac{S}{t} + \sum_i \sum_j \frac{s_{ij}}{k_{ij} \cdot t}$$

Thus, the total relevant cost per unit time, C, is $C_c + C_s =$

$$r \sum_i \sum_j \frac{d_{ij}}{2} k_{ij} \cdot v_i \cdot t + \frac{S}{t} + \sum_i \sum_j \frac{s_{ij}}{k_{ij} \cdot t}$$

Our objective is to determine the k_{ij}'s and t so that the total relevant cost is minimised. It should be noted that the cost function is non-convex. However, for each fixed set of k_{ij}'s, the cost is convex in t, and the optimal value of t is given with the corresponding objective value equal to $2\sqrt{AB}$, where

$$A = r \sum_i \sum_j \frac{d_{ij} k_{ij} v_i}{2}$$

and

$$B = S + \sum_{i} \sum_{j} \frac{S_{ij}}{k_{ij}}.$$

One can now search over all possible choices of k_{ij}'s so that the objective is minimized.

Chan et al. (2003) solved this multi-buyer, joint replenishment problem. Their approach is based on a modified genetic algorithm with some of the modifications suggested in our previous sections. For the multi-buyer JRP, each route is treated separately. The solution of a given route is encoded as a $I*J$ matrix of integers, each integer representing the value of the corresponding k_{ij}, the number of integer multiples of t that a replenishment of item i is included in a group replenishment in branch j.

The above problem was solved successfully showing significant reduction of cost by coordinating the replenishments from various buyers ordering a variety of items. A comparison test on a set of single joint replenishment problems with a large number of items was made by applying the modified GA and Goyal's enumerative method, The results obtained by using GA were extremely close to that obtained by using Goyal's. However, for the number of items larger than 100, the computer time of the modified GA is only one tenth of that of Goyal's algorithm. (See Chan et al., 2003, for detail.)

This solution method extends to the more complex cases of multi-buyer problems, where the overall costs of production, order set-up and inventory for both the buyers and vendor are minimized. One can derive a model where the total cost for minimization includes the trucking and delivery costs as well. This model consists of a number of 0-1 decision variables in addition to the k_{ij}'s, which take integer values. As seen from the arguments in (3) of section 2, genetic algorithms should work most efficiently with 0-1 variables or variables that take a small number of integer values. Hence, a good solution should be found by using a modified GA as an optimizer.

Solution of Modern Supply Chain Management Problems

Like the proposed model described in the last paragraph of the previous section, a general Supply Chain Model normally contains a large number of decision variables, which are essentially {0, 1} or mixed with other integer variables taking a narrow range of values. Hence, the proposed modified genetic algorithm should work well with this type of problems.

As we have mentioned earlier, planning to set up facilities to serve a number of customers (or retailers) scattered around a given region involves locating the optimal number of facilities of appropriate sizes and allocating customers to be served by these facilities so that the sum of distances from each facility to its dedicated customers plus the total building cost are minimized. This cost function is usually non-convex. A genetic algorithm will certainly be efficient in finding a near optimal solution to this problem like what has been shown in the solution of offshore oil field problem described earlier. In real cases, the distances between each facility and its dedicated customer is often non-Euclidean, while the location of facilities are restricted to a number of possible sites. The use of good meta-heuristics like the proposed modified GA is inevitable in solution of this complex integer programming problem.

At the strategic level where production planning is involved as part of the supply chain, there will be decisions in outsourcing part of the operation, decisions in allocation of resources and the decisions that define customer services. Thus, one would construct an integrated model of considerable scale and the genetic algorithm can be used to find the best strategy that maximizes the utilization of available resources and customer service.

For large distribution networks with intermediate warehouses, advances in information technology enable distribution to be coordinated that allows for deliveries direct from supplier to the customers (retailers), from non-dedicated warehouses to any customer (retailer). Goods in transit can be exchanged through cross docking to cope with all the changes in demands. Moreover, in some regions or sub-regions there are choices of transportation modes or alternative carriers. (An example of this region is the Pearl River Delta that consists of a modern city like Hong Kong with multi-modal transportation facilities and some less developed cities where railways and barges are the most economical and efficient means of transportation.) A large-scale complex virtual distribution model was proposed recently by Ngai and Cheung (2004), which imposes a great challenge to a solution by present-day optimization methods. We expect that a properly designed, modified genetic algorithm will be able to meet this challenge.

Extensions and Further Investigation on Genetic Search Techniques

A not-so-closely-related application of genetic algorithm is in an Object Location Problem in Computer Vision. This is an essential aid for the robots working along the assembly line to recognize the noisy image of an object (a tool or a component part) subject to an affine transformation. Yuen et al. (2001) proposed a location method that can locate an object with a high success rate using repeated GA. However, the number of repeated runs has to be large for successful location with a high confidence level, if the probability of success for a single run GA is low for some difficult objects. Recently, Cheung et al. (2004) experimented using a genetic algorithm with all the proposed modifications described earlier. A dramatic increase in the probability of success from a mere 5.7% to 43.4% for a single run was observed using a difficult noisy image. As a consequence, only a few repeated runs are required to locate this type of object with a high probability of success.

There have been publications about possible hybridization of GA with other meta-heuristic methods. GA with some strategic searches has been tried with some success in Multi-stage Flow-shop Scheduling Problems (Oguz & Cheung, 2000), as the random rearrangement of any job sequence emerges after the first stage may cause considerable waiting time. We have to develop some strategic moves on these so that any job rescheduling that causes a large amount for waiting time is avoided.

Genetic algorithms seem to work well with Simulated Annealing. The cooling effect can easily be introduced through the transformation of the original objective function, while the usual random heuristic moves can be replaced by a well designed population-based Genetic Search Scheme. For the positive objective function $f(x)$, the usual replacement by the new object function $\phi(x) = e^{f(x)/t}$, where t is the temperature parameter, may serve as a good starting point for our exploration in this hybridization process.

Ideas similar to that used in Constraint Programming can be applied to reduce our search space. Proper transformation and the special encoding method like that described briefly is able to simplify our algorithm structure to a great extent. The highly constrained problem is reduced to an almost unconstrained one defined over a smaller domain which is readily encoded into a chromosome of length n, and each of its genes takes integer values 1, 2,...,5. Further investigation into this methodology will lead to some standard techniques of turning complex problems into simple problems that can readily be encoded and solved by the genetic search method.

There have been reports on development of multi-population genetic algorithms. The idea of competition and exchanging information among population groups similar to that used in Ant Colony Heuristics may help in building up higher fitness solutions within each population groups. One should perhaps devote some effort in understanding more about this, which could be an interesting and promising area of research.

Conclusions

We have presented a full analysis of how the Genetic Algorithm performs as well as its comparison with other meta-heuristics. Possible restructurings of Genetic Search Scheme for enhanced performance have been introduced with detailed discussions on how it will work. These restructurings, however, are not ultimate, but rather open up more avenues for further research on performance improvements. For example, possible hybridization of GA with other meta-heuristics or other optimization algorithms that were described briefly in previous sections have been and will be studied by most of the researchers in this area.

The merits of using meta-heuristics (GA in particular) in solving Supply Chain Models have been thoroughly discussed with illustrative examples. However, we would like to stress that the meta-heuristics are not the only solution to complex Supply Chain Management problems. Good analytical methods that can give an exact solution within a confined time are still preferred. There may even be lucrative methods that employ the combination of both approaches taking full advantage of all the good performance characteristics coming from both of the methods. In the "Scheduling for the Multi-Buyer Joint Replenishment Problems," the genetic algorithm is used to find the basic optimal cycle and their multiples, while the scheduling of the deliveries is modeled as the network flow model that can be reduced and solved readily as an integer programming problem using Cplex (Chan et al., 2004).

When a Supply Chain Model becomes extremely large to be solved as a full model, it would not be too bad an idea to have it decomposed into a number of sub-models where each can be handled most efficiently by an appropriate optimization algorithm (not necessarily a GA or other meta-heuristics). Solution improvement can be obtained by successive iterations between these sub-models. Sometimes, the genetic algorithm may also be used to coordinate the inputs to various sub-models for optimizing the overall objective. An example of this is to coordinate the distributions at various facilities of a large distribution network so that the total distribution cost, including cost of deliveries at various facilities and the incurred inventory costs, etc., is minimized.

References

Chan, C.K., Cheung, B. K. S., & Langevin, A. (2003). Solving multi-buyer joint replenishment problem with a modified genetic algorithm. *Transportation Research part B, 37,* 291- 299.

Chan, C. K., Li, Y. L., Ng, D. C., Cheung, B. K, S., & Langevin, A. (2004). Scheduling of the multi-buyer joint replenishment problems. *GERAD Working Paper, G-2004-18.*

Cheung, B.K.S., Langevin, A., & Delmaire, H. (1997). Coupling genetic algorithm with a grid search method to solve mixed integer nonlinear programming problems. *Computer and Mathematics with Applications, 34*(12), 13-23.

Cheung, B. K. S., Langevin, A., & Villeneuve, B. (2001). High performing evolutionary techniques for solving complex location problems in industrial system design. *Journal of Intelligent Manufacturing, 12 (Special Issue on 'Global Optimisation Metaheuristics),* 455-466.

Cheung, B. K.S., Yuen, S. Y., & Fong, C. K. (2004). Enhancement in performance of genetic algorithm in the object location problem in computer vision. *To appear in forthcoming GERAD Working Paper.*

Devine, M. D., & Lesso, W. G. (1972). Models for minimum cost development of offshore oil fields. *Management Science, 18,* B378-B387.

Goyal, S.K. (1974). Determination of optimum packaging frequency of items joint replenished. *Management Science, 21,* 436-443.

Glover, F., & Laquna, M. (1997). *Tabu search.* Kluwer Academic Publishers.

Hansen, P., & Mladenovic, N. (1997). Variable neighbourhood search for the p-median. *Location Sci., 5*, 207-226.

Hansen, P., & Mladenovic, N. (2001). Variable neighbourhood search: Principle and applications. *European Journal of Operational Research, 130*, 405-413.

Holland, J. (1975). *Adaption in natural and artificial systems*. Ann Arbor, MI: University of Michigan Press.

Ngai, E. W.T., & Cheung, B.K.S. (2004). Virtual distribution systems: Review & a proposed model with research initiatives. *GERAD Working Paper, G-2004-07*.

Oguz, C., & Cheung, B. K-S. (2002). A genetic algorithm for flow-shop scheduling problems with multiprocessor tasks. *Proc. 8th International Workshop on Project Management & Scheduling*, pp. 282-287.

Rudolph, G. (1998). Finite Markov chain results in evolutionary computation: A tour d'horizon. *Fundamenta Informaticae, 35*, 67-89.

Skorin-Kapov, D., & Skorin-Kapov, J. (1994). On Tabu search for the location of interacting hub facilities. *European Journal of Operational Research, 73*, 502-509.

Taniguchi, E., Thompson, R. G., Yamaha, T., & van Duin, R. (2001). *City logistics-network modelling and intelligent transport systems*. Pergamon Press.

Wolpert, D.H., & Macready, W.G. (1997). No free lunch theorems for optimization. *IEEE Trans. on Evolutionary Computation, 1*(1), 67-82.

Yuen, K.S.Y.. & Cheung, B. K.S. (2003). Bounds for probability of success of simple genetic algorithm based on Vose-Liepin model. *GERAD Working Paper, G-2003-14*.

Appendix 1

Let $\mathbf{e} = (e_1, e_2, \ldots\ldots\ldots\ldots, e_n)$ be the optimal chromosome for an objective function $f(\mathbf{x})$ on the entire set of strings $\mathbf{x} = (x_1, x_2, \ldots\ldots\ldots\ldots, x_n)$ with $x_i \in \{0, 1\}$ and let $R_i = \{ \mathbf{x}: |\mathbf{x} - \mathbf{e}| = i \}$, $i = 1, 2, \ldots\ldots\ldots, n$.

Now, any neighbourhood $U_k = \{ x : |x - e| \leq k \}$ can be written as $U_k = R_1 \cup R_2 \cup \ldots \ldots \cup R_k$.

We have, for any randomly generated string x, the probability for x to be lying in R_k is given by ${}^nC_k / 2^n$. One sees that this probability is very low when $k \leq n/4$. More precisely, we have

$$ {}^{4m}C_m / 2^{4m} = $$
$$ \{[1/4(4-1/m)][1/4(4-2/m)]\ldots\ldots\ldots\ldots[1/4(4-(m-1)/m)]\}/2^{2m} $$

which tends to 0 as $m \to \infty$.

Furthermore, one can show $m[{}^{4m}C_m / 2^{4m}] = (m/2^m)[{}^{4m}C_m / 2^{3m}] \to 0$ as $m \to \infty$.

Hence, one infers that the probability p for any randomly generated chromosome to be lying within a neighborhood of e of the radius equal to ¼ of the length of the string is in fact very low. For example: if m=3, then, $p = ({}^{12}C_3 + {}^{12}C_2 + {}^{12}C_1)/ 2^{12} = 0.07075$ and if

$$ m=4, \quad p = ({}^{16}C_4 + {}^{16}C_3 + {}^{16}C_2 + {}^{16}C_1)/ 2^{16} = 0.0384. $$

Also, from above, we have, $p \to 0$ as $m \to \infty$.

By symmetry, one can also infer that the probability for a randomly generated string lying outside the neighborhood of e with radius equal to ¾ of the length of the string is equally very low.

Hence, most of the population composed of randomly generated chromosomes is lying within the region at a distance between ¼ to ¾ of the length of string from e.

(For example, for a population of string of length 16, the probability for any of these strings to lie within this region is 1- 2 x 0.0384 = 0.9232. I.e., over 90% of the population lies within this region.)

Note: For a chromosome of length γ, where each of its genes assumes m integer values 1, 2, 3, ……..., m. The probability distribution of the number x of optimal solution attributes in the initial population is given by

$$p(x) = \binom{\gamma}{x}\left(\frac{1}{m}\right)^{x}\left(1-\frac{1}{m}\right)^{\gamma-x}.$$

Here, the maximum of x should lie between 1/m and ½ of the length of the chromosome.

Appendix 2

A Table of Notational Conventions

Z_i – the subset of genes in chromosome i which are identical to the optimal chromosome

Y_i – the subset of Z_i whose elements are distinct from Z_j for all $j \neq i$.

μ – the uniform mutation rate

χ – the crossover rate for uniform crossover

$\mathbf{a} = a_1, a_2, …a_g$ – the representation of a chromosome of length g, it can also be regarded as a γ-dimensional vector with a_i taken integer or binary values

t – the number of gene positions to be swapped for a given pair of chromosomes $\mathbf{a}$ and $\mathbf{b}$, thus one can denote t_a to be the number of positions so selected where the gene-value in chromosome $\mathbf{a}$ is identical to that of the optimal chromosome. Similarly, one denotes t_b the corresponding number with respect to chromosome $\mathbf{b}$. It is clear that $t \geq t_a + t_b$.

R_k – the set of all chromosomes with k attributes of the optimal solution. If the chromosomes are binary, and $\mathbf{x}_0$ is the global optimal chromosome, then $R_k = \{\mathbf{a} : |\mathbf{a} - \mathbf{x}_0| = \gamma - k\}$ for all k = 1, 2, ……..., γ.

$\begin{pmatrix} a \\ b \end{pmatrix}$ – Combination: the number of ways of taking b objects from a distinct objects

$p(i,j,k,t)$ – the probability of obtaining a chromosome $\mathbf{c} \in R_k$ by a uniform crossover which swaps t elements between chromosomes $\mathbf{a} \in R_i$ and $\mathbf{b} \in R_j$

Chapter VIII

Understanding and Managing the Intrinsic Dynamics of Supply Chains

Toru Higuchi, Sakushin Gakuin University, Japan

Marvin D. Troutt, Kent State University, USA

Abstract

Both academically and practically, one of the most interesting aspects of supply chains is their intrinsic dynamic behavior. Dynamic interactions can cause unexpected and undesirable results. There are both external and internal reasons for this. Externally, severely competitive environments, consumer behavior and technological innovations are major concerns for supply-chain management. These affect both the structure and behavior of the supply chain and force it to be more flexible and agile. Internally, the supply chain is a multi-echelon system composed of a scratched-together and shifting set of players whose preferences and intentions often differ. This may create and amplify the information distortions, lags, and tricks of business within the supply chain. The combined effects of these external and internal factors make Supply Chain Dynamics (SCD) active and complex. In this chapter, we discuss the influences, mechanisms, and effects of SCD.

Supply Chain Dynamics

"A supply chain is dynamic and involves the constant flow of information, products and funds between different stages. Each stage of the supply chain performs different processes and interacts with other stages of the supply chain." (Chopra & Meindl, 2001, pp. 4-6)

This statement points out the essence of SCD. It is an interaction of processes among participants from different companies and levels. The purpose of supply chain management is to maximize supply chain profitability, which is total profit to be shared across all supply chain stages. It can be concluded that the essence of the supply chain is its dynamics and that how to manage it is one of the most important tasks to maximize supply chain profitability.

SCD features arise from external and internal factors. External factors are drivers for the supply chain to change its structure and therefore have a close relationship with the planning and designing process. Major external factors are the intensity of competition, consumer behavior and technological innovations. Severe competition in the market puts pressure on manufacturers, distributors and retailers to cut costs while maintaining the same quality or service level (or increase the quality or service level under the same costs). The supply chain becomes the major arena for competition in modern business because it is often inefficient for any single company to produce a whole product and maintain the entire, often global, distribution channel (Bradley et al., 1999). As supply chains become worldwide, they must cross the boundaries between company groups. Hence, severe competition in the market makes the supply chain very important and forces it to change continuously.

We find the following analogy helpful in connection with these concepts. Consider the first order vector linear differential equation system given by $\mathbf{x}'(t) = \mathbf{A}\mathbf{x}(t) + \mathbf{u}(t)$. Here, $\mathbf{u}(t)$ is an exogenous vector input series that may be regarded as analogous to the external influences on the system. While the autonomous term **A**x(t) may be regarded as representing the internal dynamics of the system. Although the supply chain is more complex, nonlinear, and involves stochastic as well as deterministic aspects, this model may help to clarify the distinction between internal and external influences.

Customers tend to become more and more demanding and capricious in their wants and needs as the variety and availabilities of goods increase. Supply chains must deal with this routinely. It takes time and a lot of transactions to produce and deliver goods from the raw materials because of the nature of the production and distribution process. Often, this process involves long distances between the retailers and the manufacturer and a multi-echelon system. This may amplify the effects of customer behavior and can cause the well-known problems called the bullwhip effect (Lee et al., 1997a) and boom and bust (Paich & Sterman, 1993). On the other hand, increasing customer needs requires the performance of the supply chain to continuously improve. Successful supply chains must be ever more responsive to customers according to their needs and requirements (Ballou, 1992). To keep up with growing customer needs, the supply chain should enhance its collaborations or change its structure by the making the most of strategic alliances.

Technological innovations, especially radical innovations, are very disruptive and change the nature and balance of the market. They can make obsolete the existing technologies and product categories (Abernathy et al., 1983). In order to avert the risk that another company succeeds in a radical innovation, it is better not to cover all the related area. The auto industry is a good example. A vast number of materials and parts are required to produce a car. Ford, GM, Toyota and other automakers are called the set makers or integrators because they have key suppliers or sub-integrators. It is impossible for them to be in the forefront of the all materials and parts. In addition, they are competing with others to commercialize the hybrid car and Intelligent Transportation System. These advanced technologies cost too much and are too risky for most of them to do R&D by themselves. Therefore, technological innovations enforce the strategic alliances among the different industries and former rivals and make the players of the supply chain fluid. Thus, due to external factors, the first essence of the supply chain is its dynamic nature and the concomitant requirement of flexibility.

Internally, the supply chain is a multi-echelon system composed of scratched-together players whose intentions may and often do differ. To fulfill a customer's needs, a lot of stages and people, retailers, wholesalers, warehouses, transporters, manufacturers, and suppliers are needed. It is natural for everyone in a supply chain to attempt to maximize their own profits by deciding combinations of the selling and buying prices, the production, inventory, and transportation costs, and so on. The accumulation of these individual behaviors makes supply-chain management very difficult. The geographical and mental distances and the differences of the viewpoints and individual self-interests worsen the situation because the supply chain is a loosely coupled organization. This is in sharp contrast to *Keiretsu*, a traditional Japanese company group, whose members are related companies and long-term partners, and in which members are strictly controlled by a headquarters firm.

In addition, the supply chain can also globalize easily and dramatically. Globalization enhances the production at the right place for the right cost and sales promotion, tax avoidance, and so on. On the other hand, globalization lengthens the geographical and mental distance among the players. This amplifies information distortions (Lee et al., 1997b), lags, and tricks of business within the supply chain, and makes its management much more difficult than before. From the internal factors, the second main influence on SCD is the autonomous decision making of the players in the system.

SCD therefore results from the combined effects of these external and internal factors as Figure 1 illustrates. External factors, such as competition, consumer behavior and technological advances, have two aspects, stimulating the supply chain to change its structure and creating the internal supply chain dynamics. Some parts of the former are strategic matters. The purpose of this chapter is how to manage SCD, not how to design or classify it. Hence, in the rest of the chapter, we limit the discussion to the management of internal supply chain dynamics set by the external and internal factors and continue the explanation of SCD from the interactions within the supply chain.

In the following sections, we discuss a number of related issues, including the role of collaboration within supply chains, negative phenomena in SCD, the Theory of Constraints (TOC), and dynamic computer simulation. In the next section, we examine problems that confront supply chains which cannot be handled adequately without collaboration within supply chains. On the other hand, supply chain management is so difficult that it may lead to unpredictable and undesirable results. TOC gives a good framework and dynamic computer simulation is an effective aid in the management of SCD.

Figure 1. Outline of supply chain dynamics

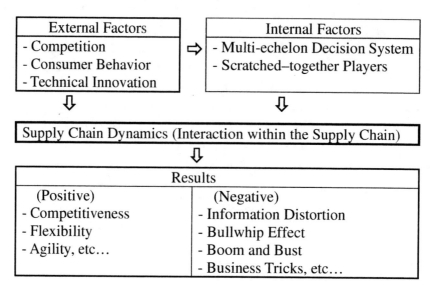

Collaboration within Supply Chains

The supply chain can be an effective and efficient network for satisfying customer needs at appropriate prices with a variety of goods and services at a given level of cost, agility, and risk. It is the modularity and the commitment to enhance collaborations that can guarantee such effectiveness and efficiency. Collaborative commerce is a good milestone, which makes product development and the daily operations more effective and efficient by using a Web site (Bechek & Brea, 2001). It integrates the company's core business processes within the supply chain, including its customers (Gossain, 2002). It is the accumulation of effective and flexible collaborations with appropriate partners that leads to higher competitiveness in the market. This process is called *Supply Chain Synthesis* (Tompkins, 2000). It is a holistic, continuous improvement process of ensuring customer satisfaction through the commitment to the supply chain.

The supply chain faces contradictory requirements, such as providing a wide variety of goods versus lean management, high quality versus low cost, and so on, as in Figure 2. To achieve these tasks simultaneously, modularity (standardization) plays a very important role. A modular system makes sure that the total amount of inventory decreases, that the manufacturer offers a wide variety of

Figure 2. Examples of contradictory requirements for supply chain

Wide Variety of Goods	vs.	Lean Management
High Quality Products	vs.	Low Cost
Quick Response	vs.	Global Manufacturing
Global Compatibility	vs.	Customization

goods with relatively few parts by combinations of modules, and that it localizes the impact of model changes (Abernathy, 1978). Technically, modularity guarantees the feasibility of collaborations within the supply chain.

A player's commitment is a precondition for inducing positive interactions within the supply chain. Sharing the goals, strategy and profits is necessary to enhance such a commitment. The goal is to maximize profitability not only for the supply chain as a whole, but also for the individual players, because the vehicle for competition is the entire supply chain in modern business, as noted earlier. Strategy is an indispensable component of any supply chain in order to achieve higher competitiveness in the market. It also functions as a guide for each player to understand and carry out its role. The policy and rules for profit sharing have a great effect on the incentive and behavior of each player. Sharing these appropriately and fairly will strengthen the unity of the supply chain.

From the point of view of operations, synchronization is the key word in the supply chain. In addition to the above contradictory requirements, and although the supply chain can become geographically complex and global, it is nevertheless required to become increasingly agile. There are two ways to synchronize the supply chain. First, bottlenecks must be identified and eliminated (or reduced) for maximizing throughput (Goldratt & Cox, 1992). Throughput is an important measure of synchronization of the supply chain. The bottleneck, the weakest point in the chain, limits the level of throughput for the entire supply chain. For example, even though a supply chain has a strong distribution channel, it may not achieve optimal performance if its manufacturing and R&D department are not agile enough. On the other hand, a supply chain that has a strong manufacturing and R&D department may not be able to make the most of them without a strong distribution channel. In this sense, it is useful to find the bottleneck and rectify it as quickly as possible. Keeping the network well balanced contributes to higher throughput and increases the ability to synchronize the entire system.

The second way to synchronize is to be a lean supply chain by information sharing on the latest market demands and inventories among the players. The

Figure 3. Collaboration within supply chain

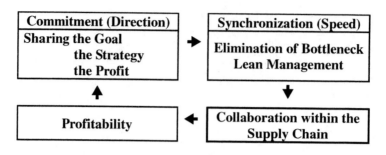

levels of inventories and backlogs are also good measures for the degree to which synchronization is being achieved in the supply chain. JIT is a well-known approach to achieving a lean supply chain. It was originally called the "kanban" system. "Kanban" means a signboard in Japanese. To share information on the latest market demands and the production scheduling with suppliers, Toyota used and sent to suppliers an iron signboard on which the required parts, numbers and times were indicated. Toyota and their suppliers reduced the amounts of inventories dramatically by sharing information through this system[1]. Sharing the information saves costs and time, and makes it possible to synchronize operations within the supply chain.

The stages in Figure 3 might appear to be very different at first, but they are similar. They may be regarded as a pair of dual problems. The first one is to maximize throughput by eliminating the bottleneck and keeping the supply chain well balanced. On the other hand, the second one is to minimize inventories by information sharing. Their goal is to maximize the supply chain's profitability. Both of them incorporate continuous improvement processes, *supply chain synthesis* or *kaizen*, and pursue synchronization throughout the supply chain, whose basis is the customers' wants and needs.

Negative Phenomena in Supply Chain Dynamics

By the term negative phenomena, we mean those obstacles, characteristics and features that work against the goals of shared information, bottleneck reductions, and synchronicity. Most of these come from the independent decision-making at the different stages of the chain because of its multi-echelon nature and the scratched-together players. A *keiretsu* organization or chain is composed of affiliated companies and long-term, established partnerships, and has exclusionary business practices. In contrast, a supply chain is a much more open and flexible network. Ironically, this may aggravate information distortions, various lags, forecasting errors, and tricks of business within the supply chain.

There are a lot of trade-offs in the supply chain (Gopal & Cahill, 1992). For instance, the sales and marketing departments desire a high degree of production flexibility and rapid turnaround to catch up with recent trends and to maximize their sales. From the logistical way of thinking, their behavior is based on the short-term. They would try to dramatically increase the stock of goods that are rising in popularity, but reduce the stock of goods decreasing in popularity. On the other hand, to reduce unit costs or recover sunk costs, manufacturers favor longer production runs, fewer set-ups, smooth schedules and a balanced line. These types of trade-offs have a great influence on supply chain profitability. If each player behaves selfishly to maximize its own performance, overall supply chain profitability would decrease rapidly because the inventories and backlogs increase and cash flows shrink.

Various lags come from the geographical factors, the actual process times, inventory and order policies, decision timing, and so on. The causes of these lags can be divided into an essentially unavoidable one and a managerial one. The delivery times between stages and the manufacturing times at factories are unavoidable. As the supply chain becomes longer and the pressure stronger, the reduction of these times and more efficient management are required. Independent decision-making of players might enlarge the unavoidable lags and, in the worst case, create other lags. The order system is a good example. Both batch and periodic order systems create lags at each echelon. If a supply chain consisted of four stages (retailers, wholesalers, manufacturers and suppliers) and they order weekly, suppliers receive the market demand that actually occurred three weeks before. This leads not only to the mismatch of supply and demand, but also to misguided capacity plans and decisions.

Without sharing the most current market demands, information distortion can be generated and enlarged at each stage in the supply chain. The lack of such information causes tremendous inefficiencies, such as the bullwhip effect, excessive or inadequate estimates of the inventory investment, poor customer service, lost revenues, misguided capacity plans and missed production schedules. From the viewpoint of information distortion, Gavirneni et al. (1999) simulated an overall supply chain model emphasizing the value of information and extended existing inventory theory to the supply chain level. The level of inventory is a further measure reflecting the efficiency of supply chain management.

The following quotes have been offered by various experts to explain the bullwhip effect, which is the exaggerated order swings caused by the information distortion in the supply chain.

"The information transferred in the form of orders tends to be distorted and can misguide upstream members in their inventory and production decisions. In particular, the variance of orders may be larger than that of sales, and the distortion tends to increase as one moves upstream." (Lee et al., 1997b)

"Variations in production are far more severe than variations in demand, and the more levels and stages of production there are, the more violent production level changes become." (Magee et al., 1985, p.42)

The phenomenon called the "shortage game" or "shortage gaming" may be regarded as starting the phantom demand and the boom and bust effects and these can also be escalated or amplified by it (Lee et al., 1997a). Figure 4 summarizes the movement of the supply chain from the view of the flow of orders and products. The shortage game starts when product demand greatly exceeds supply and some customers begin to make duplicate orders with multiple retailers. Retailers and wholesalers misjudge the circumstances, seeing a surge in demand and a shortage of the supply. They may then place excessive orders to the manufacturer. This process is often not very risky for the customer who can accept the first order filled and cancel any outstanding duplicates. Later, when the supply catches up with the real demand, backlogs will suddenly disappear and large excess inventories emerge. Both the retailer and the manufacturer can be victims of the shortage game. Retailers may be stuck with hard-to-sell, excess inventories. While the same is also true of manufacturers, their risk can be even greater if capacity changes are made without a real basis. Based on an inflated picture of real demand, exacerbated by the natural lag in filling orders, the manufacturer might disastrously place larger amounts of capital into capacity expansion. Thus, these overstated demands called "phantom" demands result from the shortage game (Nehmias, 1997). The boom-and-bust phenomenon (Paich & Sterman, 1993) can be the result of the shortage game exaggerated by the bullwhip effect from the viewpoint of the life cycle of the product. These difficulties are well illustrated by the case of the BANDAI Co., Ltd. and the Tamagotchi toy (Higuchi & Troutt, 2003). A seamless information system possessing timeliness, unity and traceability is very useful to estimate phantom demands quickly. Processing orders at several stages and misconnection in the supply chain masks phantom demands and worsen the situation. Without sharing the latest information in an on-time basis, phantom demands are masked so long that they do self-reproduction to a certain level. Hence, sharing the raw information (orders from the customers) throughout the supply chain promptly is a key. If possible, it is very helpful to identify the customers who placed multiple orders at different retailers and grasp their purchase records.

We believe a possible aid to early identification of phantom demand might be based on the sharing of information about cancelled orders. It is known that sharing information about real demand at the customer- or point-of-sale level can be useful in reducing the bullwhip effect (Chopra & Meindl, 2001). Large increases in orders coupled with increases in cancelled orders could be indicative of phantom demand. If demands are inflated, then as these are filled, even partially in the case of rationing, then we can expect a higher level of activity in cancelled orders as well.

Figure 4. Model of the supply chain process (three-echelon)

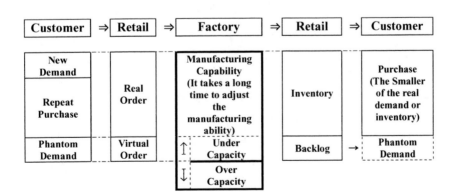

Another possibility for further research would be to compare ratios of returns to orders and look for outlier patterns in the series of ratios. Also, regression models may be similarly useful. Simulation models, as used in Higuchi and Troutt (2004), may be helpful in this regard by expanding such models to include returns assumptions, perhaps some benchmark ratios can be associated with periods of higher or lower over-ordering and returns activity.

Theory of Constraints

Given the potential importance of bottleneck management in supply chains, we discuss in this section some approaches to their management. The Theory of Constraints (TOC) is a system improvement philosophy that focuses heavily on bottleneck management. While TOC is generally well known in the operations management literature, it does not appear to be discussed frequently in the supply chain literature. Also in this section, we discuss a more recent mathematical programming tool of use in bottleneck identification and management.

TOC was developed by Goldratt and others. Some key contributions were also made by: Cox and Spencer (1998), Dettmer (1997), Goldratt (1990a, 1990b, 1990c), Goldratt and Cox (1992), Goldratt and Fox (1986), Kendall (1998), Mabin and Balderstone (2000), McMullen (1998), and Schragenheim (1999). TOC has produced a number of principles and methods for improving the flow of constrained systems. TOC is a kind of common-sense management philosophy. It has continuous improvement as a major feature. It also uses various diagrams for thinking through business problems. Identification and management of bottlenecks is a major feature of TOC. Some general tenets of TOC are:

1. Managers should verbalize their intuitions about business problems and solutions. They probably know the true problems and good solutions. If they don't, then they may do the opposite of what they believe in.

2. Improvements are changes and changes are always perceived as threats.

3. Surface the hidden assumptions. TOC Logic Trees, Compromise or "Evaporating Cloud" diagrams and other diagrams are used in TOC for this purpose. The dice game is a good exercise for this. It goes as follows: Set up a series of "stations" where the output of each station is based on

the roll of a die. Output from one station is input to the next. Everyone assumes that the system output will be 3.5 per period (average of values on a die), but it's actually much less because each station can only output as much as it received from its predecessor. This exercise produces interesting discussion about having equal capacity at all processes, and about making assumptions, more generally.

4.   It is important to understand relationships (correlations) and especially the "why" of relationships (effect-cause-effect).

5.   Concentrating on optimizing the present system may be a dead end. Improvement of the system should be the goal. For example, using EOQ may prevent the search for improvement in setup times.

The major process steps in TOC are:

1.   Identify the major constraint(s) to the system. These are called bottle-necks and limit the system in one way or another. Bottlenecks might be limiting production, information, sales, etc.

2.   Decide how to exploit the constraint.

3.   Subordinate all other activities to the bottleneck.

4.   "Elevate" the constraint, i.e., remove it, reduce it, etc., until it is broken and something else becomes the constraint.

5.   Iterate this process continually.

In addition, TOC suggests scheduling according to the "Drum, Buffer, and Rope." The "Drum" is the bottleneck process. It sets the pace for the whole system. The "Buffer" is a time element for establishing realistic commitment dates for shipments. We want to continually reduce the buffer. The "Rope" is a time element for starting new jobs, like a setup time. The rope pulls new jobs into the process. We want to shorten it as much as possible. TOC addresses other time elements as well.

TOC applications are numerous and are considered in more detail in the above-cited references. Here we mention a few examples of how TOC thinking can be insightful and beneficial. What one may think is a bottleneck, often is not. For example, a process may have sufficient capacity for average demand, but be unable to handle peak load demand. That process is not necessarily a bottleneck, but may be a resource that does not have enough "protective capacity." There may be other ways to solve the problem than by treating it as a bottleneck. Policies and procedures often create situations in which the bottleneck is not fully exploited. Before examining ways to increase the capacity of the bottleneck, it is important to examine these policies and procedures to see whether they should be changed to fully exploit the bottleneck. For example, transferring work to the bottleneck in smaller lot sizes could improve the flow to the bottleneck, thus insuring that the bottleneck does not lose time waiting for work. Also, changing set-up procedures could reduce lost time due to set-ups at the bottleneck (Goldratt, 1990c; Goldratt & Cox, 1992; Goldratt & Fox, 1986). Subordinating other processes to the bottleneck can often increase system flow. This may mean changing the scheduling procedures to ensure that the bottleneck is never idle (Goldratt & Fox, 1986).

As noted above, use of optimization models comes with cautions. In fact, early work by Zeleny (1981, 1986) noted the difference between optimizing a poorly designed system and designing an optimal system. Nevertheless, several useful connections between Linear Programming (LP) and TOC are potentially important tools for the management of bottlenecks in supply chains (Luebbe & Finch, 1992; Mabin & Gibson, 1998). Luebbe and Finch (1992) compare the steps of LP to those of TOC. Mabin and Gibson (1998) stress how LP and TOC were used together effectively in a system with product mix features. Troutt et al. (2001) show how LP-based maximal flow network modeling can help both with bottleneck identification and with capacity expansion decisions for improving system throughput.

Dynamic Computer Simulation

The supply chain, especially in the multi-echelon inventory system case, is too complex to control effectively as a whole without the aid of computer simulation (Ballou, 1992). Computer simulation is very useful, if not essential, for analyzing SCD. Computer simulations can be divided into two types: static and dynamic. Queuing and inventory theories are the bases of both. Static simulations provide the foundation for the dynamic ones. Dynamic simulations incorporate feedback mechanisms that change the structure or behavior of the supply chain. The following statement highlights a difference between them:

"The primary difference between them is the manner in which time-related events are treated. Whereas dynamic simulation evaluates system performance across time, in static simulation no attempt is made to structure time-period interplay. Dynamic simulation is performed across time so that operating dynamics may impact the planning solution." (Bowersox et al., 1986)

Static simulations set the framework for dynamic simulations. They help identify and model the key issues, elements and relations among them in the supply chain. Under specific conditions, they also propose the optimal solutions, such as EOQ, the timing of orders, the level of inventory, the number of warehouses and so on, and the effect of the key factors, such as the lead-time and the cost structure (Vendemia et al., 1995; Takeda & Kuroda, 1999; Schwarz & Weng, 1999; Pidd, 1984).

Dynamic simulations are necessary to analyze the supply chain because it is interactive and contains hierarchical feedback loops. The merits of dynamic simulations are that they can combine these feedback loops with static simulations. There are two major approaches to simulating SCD. One way is to simulate movement of a supply chain by focusing on the dynamic features from the system perspective. The other approach is to demonstrate the mechanisms related to the information distortion.

Systems dynamics is a typical method to analyze dynamic systems from the viewpoint of the whole system. It was called Industrial Dynamics at the beginning because it focused on the shifting nature and behavior of the companies over the passage of time. Forrester (1961) built a system dynamics model of the three-echelon production distribution system and demonstrated how market demands are amplified through the transactions in the supply chain. After that, it has been applied to wide ranging areas from the social to the natural sciences. In fact, many supply chain models have been built by using System Dynamics. Some System Dynamics models are integrated models that simulate the effects of interactions within the supply chain. Paich and Sterman (1993) provide a typical one. They analyzed the "boom-and-bust" process by simulating the diffusion process of a new product. This is caused by the fact that the product life cycles become very short, diffusion and obsolescence occur, and these forces are amplified by SCD. There are time lags everywhere for catching the latest market demands, expanding or reducing the manufacturing facilities according to revealed demands, and so on. Due to the lack of stability of diffusion speed and obsolescence, the players, retailers, wholesalers and manufacturers tend to overestimate the demand when the demand is growing rapidly, and underestimate it when it is decreasing. However, their levels of agility are quite different. Retailers are most agile and, on the other hand, manufacturers are least agile in the supply chain. System Dynamics is a powerful tool to simulate SCD, particularly the combined effects of these lags and differences.

Conclusions

In this chapter, we reviewed some of the principal dynamics features of supply chains. Often, supply chains require a large number of members to provide a wide variety of products at desired cost and service levels. The competitiveness of the supply chain has a close relation with its intrinsic dynamics, with both positive and negative aspects. These dynamics make the supply chain not only flexible and agile, but also complicated and unpredictable. Management of supply chains should therefore generally attempt to capitalize on the positive aspects, while minimizing the effects of the negative aspects.

Profitability is considered to be the primary goal. From the logistical perspective, total system stocks (Winker et al., 1991) and throughput (Goldratt & Cox, 1992) are the keys for improving the performance of the entire supply chain. Both in practice and in theory, various phenomena, such as information distortion, the bullwhip effect, and the shortage game are observed. To increase the supply chain profitability, synchronization of the players and minimization of information distortion within the supply chain is essential. To achieve these, commitment, coordination and information sharing play important roles.

Commitment to the Supply Chain

Commitment to the supply chain encourages the players to recognize the overall strategy and to see the importance of their assigned roles in the context of the whole system. Without recognition of these, each player may behave inconsistently with each other and the results may be far from the plan. It is natural for each player to be tempted to sub-strategies. For example, even though a supply chain (integrator) has a strategy to sell a product at high price using a brand, some retailers may decide to sell it as a loss leader. Such behavior increases the chance of negative effects, such as business tricks, the bullwhip effect and phantom demands. As a result, a supply chain fails to execute its strategy. Hence, enhancing the commitment to the supply chain is an important first step to increasing profitability.

Coordination within the Supply Chain

Coordination is fundamental to the effective operation of a successful supply chain. Its function is to embody commitment and to smooth the collaboration within the supply chain. To make sure that each player takes a consistent direction, sharing of the strategy, profits and risks is very useful. In addition to the direction, adjusting the speed (agility) is also essential to collaboration within the supply chain. Even though some players are very agile, the throughput is decided by the slowest part (stage) in the chain. In this case, a supply chain might suffer from excessive inventories or backlogs. So coordination of both direction and speed is the next step. We note next that coordination also plays an important role in information sharing.

Information Sharing Among Supply Chain Players

Information distortion in the supply chain can start from and be amplified by independent decision-making. Multi-echelon systems tend to create time lags in knowing about the latest market demand and unnecessary phantom-demand order swings in the supply chain. For minimizing information distortion, the coordination process becomes very important in the sharing of information effectively and efficiently and by use of an appropriate information system. Bowersox and Closs have noted that:

"Coordination is the backbone of overall information system architecture among value chain participants." (Bowersox & Closs, 1996, p.37)

References

Abernathy, W.J. (1978). *The productivity dilemma.* Baltimore, MD: Johns Hopkins University Press.

Abernathy, W.J., Clerk, K.B., & Kantrow, A.M. (1983). *Industrial renaissance.* New York: Basic Books.

Ballou, H.R. (1992). *Business logistics management.* Englewood Cliffs, NJ: Prentice Hall.

Becheck, B., & Brea, C. (2001). Deciphering collaborative commerce. *Journal of Business Strategy, 22*(2), 36-38.

Bowersox, D.J., & Closs, D.J. (1996). *Logistical management: The integrated supply chain process.* New York: McGraw-Hill.

Bowersox, D.J., Closs, D.J., & Helferich, O.M. (1986). *Logistical management: A systems integration of physical distribution, manufacturing support, and materials procurement (3rd ed.).* New York: Macmillan.

Bradley, P.J., Thomas, T.G., & Cooke, J. (1999). Future competition: Supply chain vs. supply chain. *Logistics Management and Distribution Report, 39*(3), 20-21.

Chopra, S., & Meindl, P. (2001). *Supply chain management: Strategy, planning and operation.* Upper Saddle River, NJ: Pearson Prentice Hall.

Cox, J., & Spencer, M. (1998). *The constraints management handbook.* Boca Raton, FL: St. Lucie Press/APICS Series on Constraints Management.

Dettmer, H. (1997). *Goldratt's theory of constraints: A systems approach to continuous improvement.* Milwaukee, WI: ASQC Quality Press.

Forrester, J.W. (1961). *Industrial dynamics.* Boston, MA: MIT Press.

Gavirneni, S., Kapuscinski, R., & Tayur, S. (1999). Value of information in capacitated supply chains. *Management Science, 45*(1), 16-24.

Goldratt, E. (1990a). *The theory of constraints.* Croton-on-Hudson, NY: North River Press.

Goldratt, E. (1990b). *The haystack syndrome: Sifting information out of the data ocean.* Great Barrington, NY: North River Press.

Goldratt, E. (1990c). *What is this thing called the theory of constraints and how is it implemented?* Croton-on-Hudson, NY: North River Press.

Goldratt, E., & Cox, J. (1992). *The goal: A process of ongoing improvement (2nd ed.).* Croton-on-Hudson, NY: North River Press.

Goldratt, E., & Fox, R. (1986). *The race.* Croton-on-Hudson, NY: North River Press.

Gopal, C., & Cahill, G. (1992). *Logistics in manufacturing.* IL: Richard D. Irwin.

Gossain, S. (2002). Cracking the collaboration code. *Journal of Business Strategy, 23*(6), 20-25.

Higuchi, T., & Troutt, M.D. (2004). Dynamic simulation of the supply chain for a short life cycle product - Lessons from the Tamagotchi case. *Computers & Operations Research.*

Kendall, G.I. (1998). *Securing the future: Strategies for exponential growth using the theory of constraints. APICS series on constraints management.* Boca Raton, FL: St. Lucie Press.

Lee, H.L., Padmanabhan, V., & Whang, S. (1997a). The bullwhip effect in supply chains. *Sloan Management Review, 38*(3), 93-102.

Lee, H.L., Padmanabhan, V., & Whang, S. (1997b). Information distortion in a supply chain: The bullwhip effect. *Management Science, 43*(4), 546-558.

Luebbe, R., & Finch, B. (1992). Theory of constraints and linear programming: a comparison. *International Journal of Production Research, 30,* 1471-1478.

Mabin, V., & Balderstone, S. (2000). *The world of the theory of constraints: A review of the international literature. APICS series on constraints management.* Boca Raton, FL: St. Lucie Press.

Mabin, V., & Gibson, J. (1998). Synergies from spreadsheet LP used with the theory of constraints: A case study. *Journal of Operational Research Society, 49*(9), 918-927.

Magee, J.F., Copacino, W.C., & Rosenfield, D.B. (1985). *Modern logistics management: Integrating marketing, manufacturing, and physical distribution.* New York: John Wiley & Sons.

McMullen, T., Jr. (1998). *Introduction to the theory of constraints (TOC) management system. APICS series on constraints management.* Boca Raton, FL: St. Lucie Press.

Nehmias, S. (1997). *Production and operations analysis (3rd ed.)*. New York: McGraw-Hill.

Paich, M., & Sterman, J.D. (1993). Boom, bust and failures to learn in experimental markets. *Management Science, 39*(12), 1439-1458.

Pidd, M. (1984). *Computer simulation in management science (2nd ed.)*. Chichester, UK: John Wiley & Sons.

Schragenheim, E. (1999). *Management dilemmas: The theory of constraints approach to problem identification and solutions. APICS series on constraints management*. Boca Raton, FL: St. Lucie Press.

Schwarz, L.B., & Weng, K.Z. (1999). The design of JIT supply chains: The effect of leadtime uncertainty on safety stock. *Journal of Business Logistics, 20*(1), 141-163.

Takeda, K., & Kuroda, M. (1999). Optimal inventory configuration of finished products in multi-stage production/inventory system with an acceptable response time. *Computers & Industrial Engineering, 37*, 251-255.

Tompkins, J.A. (2000). *No boundaries*. NC: Tompkins Press.

Troutt, M.D., White, G., & Tadisina, S. (2001). Maximal flow network modeling of production bottleneck problems. *Journal of the Operational Research Society, 52*, 182-187.

Vendemia, W.G., Patuwo, B.E., & Ming, S.H. (1995). Evaluation of lead time in production/inventory systems with non-stationary stochastic demand. *Journal of the Operational Research Society, 46*, 221-233.

Winker, J., Towill, D.R., & Naim, M. (1991). Smoothing supply chain dynamics. *International Journal of Production Economics, 22*, 231-248.

Zeleny, M. (1981). On the squandering of resources and profits via linear programming. *Interfaces, 11*(5), 101-117.

Zeleny, M. (1986). Optimal system design with multiple criteria: De Novo programming approach. *Engineering Costs and Production Economics, 10*, 89-94.

Endnote

[1]   In 1989, an electronic information system replaced the "kanban."

Chapter IX

Re-Engineering of Logistics Activities for Electronic Commerce

Nathalie Marcoux, Ecole Polytechnique of Montreal, Canada

Diane Riopel, Ecole Polytechnique of Montreal, Canada

André Langevin, Ecole Polytechnique of Montreal, Canada

Abstract

In order to achieve a successful implementation of electronic commerce (EC), it is necessary to "re-engineer" the logistics activities of the enterprise. This chapter first presents and analyses the features of EC, i.e., the typical content of Web sites and technological and operational requirements, for the implementation of each of the four stages of EC (Brochureware, e-commerce, e-business, and e-enterprise). Then the concepts, techniques, and tools that may contribute to the successful implementation of EC are surveyed. Finally, a self-diagnosis tool is presented to initiate the re-engineering process. The self-diagnosis tool details the company's profile in view of an EC implementation and identifies the operational activities that need to be reviewed, upgraded, integrated or outsourced.

Introduction

The Internet and the World Wide Web (Web) have allowed the advent of new forms of marketing and new possibilities of collaboration and exchange between a company and all its actors. Electronic commerce (EC) is certainly the most prominent application of the Internet. Hoque (2000) presents four stages of EC:

- **Brochureware** (also called *brochures-online Web sites*, Rosen, 2000), which is the static posting of information (e.g., description of the company, product catalogue, employment opportunities);

- **E-Commerce** (associated to *B2C - Business-to-Consumer*, Delfmann, Albers & Gehring, 2002), which includes all the commercial transactions and their supporting activities for a consumer to obtain a product or a service (e.g., online advertisement, billing, customer service);

- **E-Business** (associated to *B2B - Business-to-Business*, Delfmann et al., 2002), which includes all the intra- and inter-enterprises transactions with any types of commercial partners (e.g., suppliers, subcontractors, distributors);

- **E-Enterprise** (associated to the *Virtual Enterprise*, Lefebvre & Lefebvre, 2000), which integrates the previous stages with all the intraorganisational activities.

A number of authors (e.g., Baker, 2000; Chambers, 2000; Dilger, 2000; Norton, 2000; Tinham, 2000b; and Chabli, Chapelet, Deglaine & Dimitriadis, 1999) have pointed out that, in order to achieve a successful implementation of EC, it is necessary to review the logistics activities of the enterprise. This review is defined herein as the *re-engineering* of the logistics activities of the traditional processes for an integration of EC.

Rosen (2000) enumerates a number of questions raised by most businesses when considering the implementation of EC: How should we integrate EC with our business? Where do we start? What resources do we need? What skills do we need? How do we make EC a success for our company? Also, Norris, West, and Gaughan (2000) propose issues to be addressed when automating a supply chain: What are the steps in a given transaction? Who is concerned? What is the activity? However, no details are given to complete the analysis.

Over the last few years, numerous articles have been published which are linked with the recent technological evolution and addressing issues as diversified as:

- the computerisation of information systems;
- the development of the communication technologies and databases;
- the implementation of production management systems;
- the widespread use of simulation and optimisation;
- the integration of agility and adaptability concepts;
- the transformation from a mass market to a customised market;
- the business velocity;
- the consumers' interest for the numerous opportunities offered over the Web.

In that context, this chapter first presents and analyses the Features of EC, i.e., the typical content of Web sites and technological and operational requirements, for the implementation of each of the four stages of EC (next section). The third section, named Inventorying the means for implementing EC, follows with a survey of the concepts, techniques, and tools that could contribute to the successful implementation of the various stages of EC. The implementation of EC is definitely a favourable moment for the re-engineering of the logistics activities of a firm as mentioned by Auramo, Aminoff, and Punakivi (2002). Furthermore, they point out the need to establish how EC impacts a company's logistics operations and supply chain efficiency.

In the fourth section, a self-diagnosis tool is presented to initiate the re-engineering process. The self-diagnosis tool details the company's profile in view of an EC implementation and identifies the operational activities that need to be reviewed, upgraded, integrated or outsourced. This tool, in the form of a questionnaire, contains two levels (strategic and operational) of analysis. The aim of this self-diagnosis tool is to position the firm and to provide an action plan for implementing one or several stages of EC.

Features of Electronic Commerce

Based on the definitions of Hoque (2000), we have listed in Table 1 the most frequent features of the four stages of EC. Those features include the typical content of Web sites and the technological and operational requirements for

Table 1. Features of electronic commerce

Brochureware	
Basic features	
Product catalogue with specifications	Yen (2002), Hall (2000)
Search engines	Yen (2002), Feldman (2000)
"about" (list of stores, branches, etc.)	May (2000)
"contact" (customer service phone number or e-mail)	May (2000)
Information reliability	Gaw (2000)
Optional features	
Sales prices	
Delivery information: schedule, costs	
Technical reports	Davidson (1997)
Graphic portrayal of products	Feldman (2000)
Up-to-date inventory, per store	
Sales promotions, clearance sales, discount coupons	Kleindl (2001)
Competitors' products comparative table	
Customised visits (acknowledgement of previous access to the web site)	Feldman (2000)
E-Commerce	
Basic features	
Sales prices	
Delivery information: schedule, costs	
Technical reports	Davidson (1997)
Graphic portrayal of products	Feldman (2000)
Geographic limits of service area	
Delivery options: regular or fast service	
Information validation	Kimball and Merz (2000)
Order Confirmation	Kimball and Merz (2000)
Secured payment - data security	Gunasekaran, Marri, McGaughey, and Nebhwani (2002), Bitouzet (1999)
Cancellation, exchange, and reimbursement policies	
Procedures for product return	Hall (2000)
On-Line and phone after-sales service	May (2000)
Optional features	
Customer purchase history	Kimball and Merz (2000), Jutla, Bodorik, and Wang (1999)
Request for proposal	Yen (2002)
Auction	Keskinocak and Tayur (2001)
Product sample by mail	Yen (2002)
Tracking	Gunasekaran et al. (2002), Kimball and Merz (2000)
Traceability	

Table 1. Features of electronic commerce (continued)

E-Business	
Basic features	
Customised transactions	Feldman (2000)
Real-Time information sharing	Auramo et al. (2002), Democker (2000), Dilger (2000), Fulcher (2000), Schultz (2000)
Seamless interface (inter-computer communications)	Feldman (2000), Lientz and Rea (2001)
Information integrity	Gaw (2000)
Order Confirmation	Kimball and Merz (2000)
Secured payment - data security	Gunasekaran et al. (2002), Bitouzet (1999)
Optional features	
order scenarios (available-to-promise, capable-to-promise, and make-to-order), delivery dates	Dilger (2000), Fulcher (2000)
Transaction cancellation or modification	Pancucci (2000)
E-Enterprise	
Basic features	
Visibility of the global supply chain	Baker (2000), Dilger (2000), Fulcher (2000), Michel (2000); Ward (2000)
Hardware and software standardisation	Lefebvre and Lefebvre (2000)
Working process elaboration	
Optional features	
Access to simulation software	Sheridan (1996)

EC. They are divided in two categories: basic and optional. We have classified as basic the features that are usually mentioned by most of the authors.

By consulting the Web, it is easy to witness that the first two stages are well implemented in the retail sale industry, but much less in the manufacturing sector where usually only the first stage (Brochureware) is implemented.

The analysis of the features of the four stages of EC reveals that e-commerce can be seen as an evolution of Brochureware and e-enterprise an evolution of e-business. However, e-enterprise is linked to e-commerce. Figure 1 illustrates the links between the stages of EC.

It should be noted, as stated by several authors (e.g., Bean, 2003; Vallamsetty, Kant, & Mohapatra, 2003; and Kuglin & Rosenbaum, 2001), that e-commerce and e-business should be considered as distinct stages of EC. For example, firms in high added-value sectors or in an area with a high level of customisation (e.g., aeronautics) have a lot of incentives to implement e-business, but much less for e-commerce. Some comments on the features needed to implement each stage of EC and listed in Table 1 follow.

Figure 1. Relationships between the EC stages

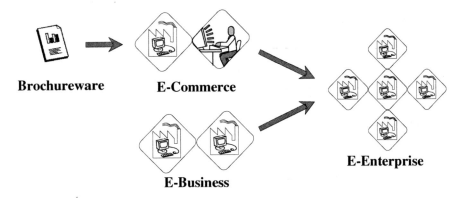

Brochureware

The product catalogue may correspond to the entire range of products offered in traditional commerce, or a subset of those products, or new products specific to EC. Sophisticated search engines allow finding products by names, by reference numbers, or by characteristics. The catalogue may include inventories of each retail point. May (2000) presents the typical elements for a basic commercial Web site, which include *products/services/job/about/contact*. The product characteristics and directions for use may be displayed as graphics, as mentioned by Feldman (2000), but also as pictures, videos, etc. Finally, in order to adequately inform potential customers, information reliability is crucial.

E-Commerce

Data security is an essential element of any financial transaction on the Web. This encompasses four aspects: integrity (including reliability), authentication, non-repudiation (using archive system), and confidentiality. In order to prevent a high level of product returns, it is important that the information on the Web is as accurate and up-to-date as possible. Pictures and videos of products allow the consumers to properly select goods and/or services. Cancellation, exchange, and reimbursement policies should be clearly posted. The customer history may list the purchases of the consumer for a given time period. A more sophisticated tool, the "clickstream" defined by Kimball and Merz (2000), allows a business to analyse in detail the links of the consumer's habits when consulting the site and purchasing products. Yen (2002) also discusses the use of tools to monitor usage patterns. Such analyses may lead to offers of complementary products.

E-Business

Three important characteristics are the real-time visibility, the information sharing, and, as stated by Lientz and Rea (2001), the seamless interface permitting transactions to flow freely across distributed computer systems. The real-time visibility allows a partner to validate the availability of resources such as finished goods, work-in-progress, raw material, machine capacity, tooling, approvals, workforce, services, and so on. Shared documents may be as complex and detailed as drawings, standards, and quality control procedures. This information sharing leads to the problem of semantic reconciliation (King, 2000; Dan et al., 1998; Pancucci, 2000). Semantic reconciliation relates to the standardisation of terminology and product nomenclature. The real-time access to the management system by the partners should be limited. Transactions by the partners could concern fulfilment, acquisitions — material and service — payment, inventory levels, shipments in transit, labour costs and time spent, production schedule, and so on. As mentioned by Auramo et al. (2002), real-time access to information should prevent the bullwhip effect. And here again, the issues of information integrity and data security have to be addressed.

E-Enterprise

The e-enterprise stage includes the three other stages and implies an active involvement of the commercial partners. This stage requires an automation of many business processes. In the e-enterprise, all the logistics activities of the supply chain are integrated. This encompasses both the internal and external logistics activities. Baker (2000) includes the financial, sales, distribution, material management, production planning, and human resources. The partnership may lead to the insourcing of some logistics activities of the partners or, conversely, to the outsourcing of some of the logistics activities of the enterprise. Examples of such partnership activities are: assembly, order picking, distribution, inventory management, or product returns.

Golicic, Davis, McCarthy, and Mentzer (2002) report that interviews with businesses highlight emergent themes specific to the nature of conducting business electronically. Among others are speed (rate of change and pace of decision-making), connectivity (information sharing and market access), information visibility, dynamic market structure, and uncertainty. The very nature of EC requires the systems to have specific features, which are listed in Table 1.

Inventorying the Means for Implementing EC

This section reviews the management and engineering concepts and techniques, and the computer tools that have been proposed for implementing EC. Those means are presented in four groups: industrial engineering concepts, quality management techniques, management techniques, and computer tools. Those concepts, techniques and tools are not specific to EC, but they may contribute at creating winning conditions for implementing EC, as mentioned by several authors listed in Table 2. For example, a highly computerised firm could expect a smoother and quicker implementation of EC. Table 2 summarises the means and lists the references related to each group of concepts, techniques or tools.

Industrial Engineering Concepts

The re-engineering concept includes *streamlining, downsizing, standardisation,* or *restructuring* of business processes. The objectives are to be more agile, to offer better quality, better prices and more customisation. The potential savings are shortening purchasing cycle, decreasing inventories, increasing response time, and so on. The concepts of *reliability* and *agility* are related to the quickness and constancy of response despite fluctuation of demand. The concepts of *adaptability* and *scalability* are related to the facility to adapt to mutations of the company (in the part mix, processes, technologies, organisation, etc.) due to internal or external variations. The concepts of *modularity* and *interoperability* are linked with the growth of the company and the integration of new elements (products, technologies, etc.). To be added to those is *portability*, a new concept related to the mobility of

Table 2. Means for implementing EC

Industrial engineering concepts	
Re-engineering: streamlining, downsizing, standardisation, restructuring	Chambers (2000), Lefebvre and Lefebvre (2000), McGuffog (1999)
Reliability	Krasner (2000)
Agility	Krasner (2000), Tinham (2000a)
Adaptability	Gunasekaran et al. (2002), Kleindl (2001), Hoque (2000), Booty (2000), Fallows (1999)
Scalability	Hoque (2000), Burnson (2000)
Modularity	Krasner (2000)
Interoperability	Hoque (2000), Krasner (2000)
Portability	Bean (2003)
Quality management techniques	
Total quality	McGuffog (1999)
Performance measurement	Collins (2000), Kuglin and Rosenbaum (2001), McGuffog (1999)
Quality Function Deployment (QFD)	Gunasekaran et al. (2002)
Kaizen	Yami (2000)
Management techniques	
Just-In-Time (JIT)	Gunasekaran et al. (2002)
Lean manufacturing	Yami (2000), McGuffog (1999)
Collaborative functions (e.g., engineering, planning, forecasting and replenishment)	Gunasekaran et al. (2002), Kuglin and Rosenbaum (2001)
Concurrent engineering	Gunasekaran et al. (2002), Hsu and Pant (2000)
Product Data Management (PDM)	Auramo et al. (2002)
Vendor Managed Inventories (VMI)	Bauer, Poirier, Lapide, and Bermudez (2001)
Partnership (including outsourcing)	Gunasekaran et al. (2002), Chow and Gritta (2001), Kalpakjian (2001), Lewis (1999), Dan et al. (1998)
Computer tools	
Material Requirement Planning (MRP) and Distribution Requirement Planning (DRP)	
Enterprise Resource Planning (ERP)	Gunasekaran et al. (2002), Huin, Luong, and Abhary (2002), Krasner (2000)
Advanced Planning and Scheduling (APS)	Bauer et al. (2001)
Warehouse Management System (WMS)	Mason, Ribera, Farris, and Kirk (2003)
Transportation Management System (TMS)	Mason et al. (2003)
Computer-Integrated System (CIS)	Kalpakjian (2001), Hsu and Pant (2000)
Computer Aided Design (CAD)	Gunasekaran et al. (2002), Rhodes and Carter (1998)
Data warehousing	
Data mining	
Global Positioning System (GPS)	Bauer et al. (2001)

different actors. Portable computers and cell phones connected to the Web are new technologies from which the company can benefit.

Quality Management Techniques

Product quality is even more important in the EC market, which is characterised by the change from a mass market to a customised market and by the consumer's opportunities to take advantage of deals offered over the Web. As discussed by McGuffog (1999), quality management techniques such as *total quality* and *performance indicators* may be used to fulfil best performances requirements. Other quality management techniques such as *QFD* and *Kaizen* may also have a positive impact on the quality of a product, including the functional, the delay, and the cost aspects of a product and on the efficiency of the activities performed to complete the production cycle.

Management Techniques

A number of authors in the literature suggest using several management techniques for a successful implementation of EC. Techniques such as *JIT* and *lean manufacturing* may be used for the re-engineering of production activities. *Collaborative functions* and *concurrent engineering* are techniques used for other activities. *PDM*, *VMI*, and *partnership* are management techniques which could be applied to all types of activities.

Computer Tools

Three main characteristics could define the computer tools presented in Table 2: resource management, information management, and real-time communication. *MRP*, *DRP*, *ERP*, *APS*, *WMS*, *TMS*, and *CIS* are related to resource (material, equipment, and personnel) management. *CAD*, *data warehousing* and *data mining* are specific to the management of information. Finally, *GPS* is used for the real-time communication of information. Computer tools main goal is to increase flexibility and responsiveness to market demand and change by automating and integrating the majority of business processes, by sharing common data and practices across the enterprise. They favour the real-time visibility of the global supply chain. It should be noted that although some authors (e.g., Krasner, 2000) promote an extensive usage of an ERP system for EC, others (e.g., Pancucci, 2000; Tinham, 2000b) do not agree.

Besides the means in Table 2, a few specific models — conceptual or operational, "embryonic" or detailed — are proposed and aimed at the automation or the integration of various logistics activities in the EC context. Some examples of such models are: an auction model (e.g., Keskinocak & Tayur, 2001), a conceptual simulation model for the integration of WMS and TMS (e.g., Mason et al., 2003), an equation for the integration and the consolidation of logistics activities (e.g., Leung, Cheung, & Van Hui, 2000), an algorithm for the fulfilment activity based on the sales trend (e.g., Stevens & Sharma, 2001), a model for a mix drop shipping distribution system (e.g., Khouja, 2001).

Complementary to Table 2, three notions deserve to be elaborated: the "virtuality" of a company's activities, the distribution system, and the partnership option. All three are analysed next in the EC context. They all have a direct impact on the means selected to perform logistics activities.

Vergnion and Montreuil (2001) depict, for EC in the retail business, five network levels which we summarise in Table 3. These levels are related to the "virtuality" of a company's activities. At the first level, the virtual network conveys only the information flow from the supplier to the consumers. At the last level, the virtual network links all the activities related to the production of finished goods and their distribution. Those various levels necessitate different logistics implementations.

EC has a significant impact on the distribution of products to the consumers. A synthesis of various distribution systems is presented in Figure 2 where six elements of a distribution system are identified: production, storage at facility, distribution center (D.C.), local D.C., retailer, and customer. Those systems have been defined by various authors, such as Bowersox, Closs, and Cooper (2002), Holmqvist, Hultkrantz, Stefansson, and Winggvist (2001), and Khouja (2001). In Figure 2, the responsibility of the material handling for the distribution activities between two facilities is depicted by a full arrow when assumed by the enterprise, and a doted arrow when assumed by its business partners or by the consumers. For some systems, facilities are bypassed for a more direct distribution system to the final customer. As presented by Khouja (2001), in the

Table 3. Levels of a company's activities virtuality

Level	Catalogue	Order	Transport		Finished goods inventory		Production
			Producer-to-Customer	Producer-to-D.C.*	Management	Purchase	
1	✓						
2	✓	✓	✓				
3	✓	✓	✓		✓		
4	✓	✓	✓	✓		✓	
5	✓	✓	✓	✓	✓		✓

Figure 2. Various distribution systems

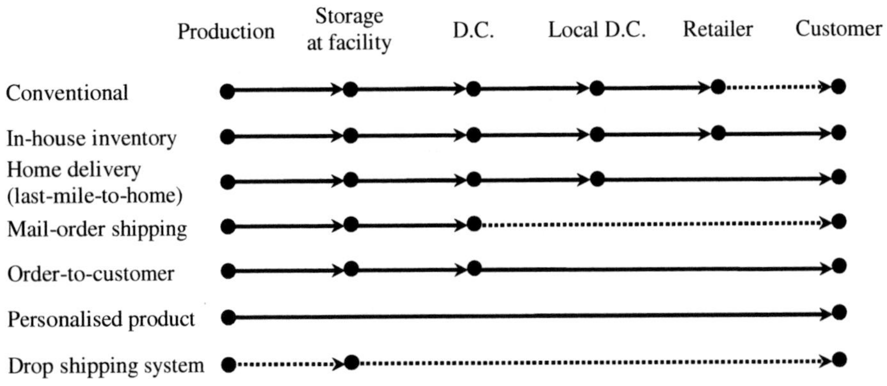

	Production	Storage at facility	D.C.	Local D.C.	Retailer	Customer

drop shipping system, the retailer takes the order and the payment, and the manufacturer fills the order and ships it to the customer.

The type of distribution system has a direct impact on the response time. A company may select one of those distribution systems or a combination of them in order to offer more flexibility for delivery. For example, Khouja (2001) proposes a model for a mixed drop shipping distribution system. His model combines a drop shipping option with an in-house inventory option (with the possibility of switching from in-house inventory to drop-shipping in case of shortage). Parameters of the model include the demand, the cost of each option, the shortage penalty cost of in-house inventory, and the salvage value of unsold in-house inventory. Another impact of the selection of a distribution system is on the packaging. An analysis may lead to its standardisation, rationalisation, or even elimination.

Various partnerships may be used as a leverage of a company's limited skills and resources for increased competitiveness. Within the e-enterprise framework, we identify four types of partnerships:

- **The outsourcing partnership** is the use of a third party for carrying out one or several production or logistics activities. Based on a survey, Chow and Gritta (2001) present the typical third party logistics services and capabilities, including: warehousing, JIT, inventory management, product audit processing, and product life-cycle management.

- **The symbiotic partnership** allows certain companies, which may be competitors, to share common activities. One aspect of this partnership is the "shared manufacturing" concept detailed in Kalpakjian (2001), which aims at production cost reduction. For example, several companies could have access to the service of a common paint shop.

- **The cross-marketing partnership**, which includes the multi-party relationship proposed by Dan et al. (1998), allows the joint sales of products or services of commercial partners. For example, the purchase of an airplane ticket which gives a rebate on a hotel room reservation or on a rental car location.

- **The stickiness partnership**, based on the "network stickiness" concept formalised by Lewis (1999), includes any commercial action aimed at maintaining the loyalty of a customer towards a product, a service, or a trademark. An example of this is the popular AirMiles program.

The successful growth of a company within EC and the success of e-enterprise requires the integration of all its logistics activities. A preliminary step is the re-engineering of the logistics activities for EC. In the literature, authors such as Taylor (2000), Gorbach (2000), Hoque (2000), and May (2000) propose a few rules, steps, concepts, or questions that need to be answered. But none of them present a complete tool for an enterprise diagnosis in regard to the implementation of EC. No checklist has yet been established for a successful implementation of EC. The next section presents a self-diagnosis tool to scrutinise the company's profile in order to analyse its logistics activities.

Self-Diagnosis Tool

The need for an enterprise to be rapidly online to ensure the visibility of its products or services is fulfilled by implementing the first stage of EC - Brochureware. However, the mutation of the enterprise toward another stage of EC implies a competitive repositioning of its business activities, from both the strategic and the operational point of view. Also, as stated by Auramo et al. (2002), Delfmann et al. (2002), and Hall (2000), an enterprise should determine the level of integration of its electronic commerce activities into its traditional business activities.

The self-diagnosis tool presented herein should be used to evaluate the current state of the enterprise and to establish its objectives for implementing EC. It could also be used as an improvement tool within any stage of EC. As stated in "Getting active" (1999), one should keep in mind that the monitoring of processes should not exceed the capacity of the firm to react.

The self-diagnosis tool has the form of a questionnaire, with two levels of analysis:

- **Strategic diagnosis:** an analysis of the company's mission and a search of new business opportunities offered by EC; and
- **Operational diagnosis:** an analysis of the impacts of EC on the company's operational logistics activities, such as: procurement, receiving, manufacturing, assembly, fulfilment, warehousing, material handling, quality control, maintenance, packaging, shipping, distribution, and reverse logistics.

For each level of analysis of the self-diagnosis tool, the classical process analysis questions are used: What? Where? When? Who? How? and Why? The Why? is used as a sub-question for the other questions and allows a revision of every activity. Each question is applied to both the material and the information flows. For each element of the diagnosis, a global analysis can evaluate the logistics activities integration. The answers may indicate that the company integration is not yet suitable for a successful implementation of EC. In that case, a process of standardisation should be initiated before implementing EC.

Strategic Diagnosis

The evolution of a company towards e-enterprise requires an analysis of the company's foundation: its mission and its business opportunities. Based on the classical process analysis, the strategic diagnosis enumerates various issues to be addressed for the implementation of EC. Table 4 summarises the elements of analysis.

What?

The first element to review is the company's mission. This includes defining the range of products or services being offered free of charge or against payment and being exclusive or not to the company's EC.

The second element corresponds to the numerous opportunities that are offered over the Web, the first one being the transfer of information between the company and various parties (suppliers, consumers, distributors and others), which can increase a clientele's satisfaction and promote loyalty-making relationships. There are many other business opportunities, such as customer solicitation, elaboration of a marketing plan including spot discounts for online customers, clearance of manufacturing products and by-products (e.g., obsolete products, stock surplus or remanufactured products), use of electronic tools such as search engines, electronic bulletin boards (internal or external) for the posting of information, and electronic money. Another opportunity is using other companies' innovations, e.g., a multi-supplier type of service. Michel (2000) presents different applications of e-business such as self-service applications, trading exchange, B2B storefronts, indirect procurement, hosted services, collaborative planning, Web-enabled order management, product life-cycle management, Web-based service and support, and a virtual fulfilment network.

A third element is cannibalisation, a term used by authors like Kleindl (2001), Kimball and Merz (2000), Seminerio (2000), and Jordan (1998). Cannibalisation, as self-competition, is defined as the transfer of a company's market share to a new transactional mode. The impact of EC on the traditional business activities should be estimated according to this self-competition, and also according to the relationship with the business's partners such as the resellers. Trebilcock (2001) proposes a way to eliminate cannibalisation in regard to distributors by using a Web site to direct users to the distributor nearest to them.

Kleindl (2001) presents the results of a survey about the online incentives for the loyalty of the customers to their Web site. All the elements cited, such as the ease of use and quick download, are related to the access to the Web site. But other elements linked to the logistics activities should also be considered.

Another element is reverse logistics, discussed by Guide, Jayaraman, and Linton (2003), Dowlatshahi (2000), Johnson, Wood, Wardlow, and Murphy (1999), Minahan (1998), and Giuntini and Andel (1995a, 1995b), and the related issues. Reverse logistics has a significant impact on several operations such as supplying, production, warehousing, and distribution. One has to clearly determine what aspects of reverse logistics have to be implemented and specifies which products are concerned.

Finally, considering the passage to the electronic era, the last element is the identification of the stage of EC the company aims for, i.e., Brochureware, e-commerce, e-business, or e-enterprise.

Where?

The company should determine the level of integration of its EC activities into its traditional business activities, which means an analysis of where the activities should be performed. Both the material flow and the information flow have to be reviewed. For example, the activities related to the completion of an online purchase can be integrated into the logistics activities of the company's traditional business or handled separately (e.g., via another distribution centre). Partnerships, as for example the outsourcing of logistics or production activities, also have implications on where the activities should be conducted.

When?

The company have to determine when to implement EC. According to its competitors' actions, a proactive or a reactive strategy could be adopted. The proactive strategy, associated to a short-term implementation of EC, requires major investments (financial, material and human) but allows the company to define the rules of the game and to become a leader. The reactive strategy, associated to the postponed implementation of EC, allows the company to benefit from the experience gained by other companies. A step-by-step implementation, which spreads out over time the stages of EC, could be appropriate.

Who?

The decision of insourcing or outsourcing is included in the partnership concept. A partner may be a manufacturer, a distributor, a partner-server or partner-master, the head office, a subsidiary company or a customer. As previously presented, there are four types of partnership: outsourcing, symbiotic, cross-marketing, and stickiness. In a competitive environment, the company should consider developing one or more partnerships to reduce its operating costs, to increase its clientele's satisfaction (based on costs, delays, quality and other criteria), or simply to provide a better market exposure.

How?

It is essential, for every business opportunity, to establish a plan of action. For example, information sharing opportunities using the Web may include:

- characteristics of products or services offered by the company or its business partners,
- limitations on the use of products,
- demonstrations,
- comparison with similar products,
- answers to customers' inquiries,
- information related to its business field.

Customer solicitation can be customised or mass-targeted, using a cross-marketing or a stickiness partnership. Solicitation can be done at random, based on the proposed products, or done using a personalised historical analysis. Clearance of manufacturing products and by-products can be managed by the company or by a block-and-mortar or a virtual company specialised in stock clearance. Clearance can be conducted in the company's sale centre or using the Internet on the company's official Web site or on a specialised Web site like an auction site.

The level of integration of its EC activities into its traditional business activities being established, the control and management policies of the direct and reverse logistics activities should be reviewed. For example, the control of input (raw material and products related to reverse logistics), work-in-process, and output should be reviewed, integrated, or distributed. Centralisation of some activities such as inventory management and warehousing should be considered. The potential financial profits being an important incentive for the implementation of reverse logistics, the means laid out should be fast and effective.

Table 4. Strategic diagnosis

		Flow of	
		Material	Information
	WHAT?		
	- What is the company's mission?	x	x
	- Which business opportunities are conceivable for the growth of the company?	x	x
	- What could be the level of cannibalisation (as self-competition) of the EC over your traditional business?	x	
	- Which aspects of reverse logistics the company wants to implement?	x	x
	- Which stage of EC is the company aiming for?	x	x
	WHERE?		
W	- Where will each activity related to EC be performed?	x	x
H	**WHEN?**		
Y	- When each stage of EC will be implemented?	x	x
?	**WHO?**		
	- Who could be a business' partner, and considering what type of partnership?	x	x
	HOW?		
	- Which action strategy is considered for each business opportunity?	x	x
	- How can be managed and controlled the direct and the reverse logistics activities?	x	x
	- How is defined your partners' core business and domains of activities?	x	x
	- How does EC impact your business, both financially and legally?	x	x

The company should review its participation to different partnerships, looking at each party's specialities and domains of activities as well as at the physical, virtual and financial relationships. Finally, financial and legal implications associated to EC should be evaluated.

Operational Diagnosis

The objective of the operational diagnosis is to evaluate the impacts of EC on the company's activities. This operational diagnosis is based on the analysis of issues related to the concepts and techniques used, as well as to the technology implemented. The essence of EC involves knowledge and control of the company's operating parameters and of information on material flow (ideally in real-time).

The success of the company's EC implementation requires an analysis of every element of the operational diagnosis tool. As with the strategic diagnosis, the operational diagnosis is defined for both the material and the information flows. Furthermore, the logistics activities are divided into three classes: the Supplier-to-Company activities (S-to-C), also named pre-production activities, the production activities (P), and the Company-to-Customer activities (C-to-C), also named post-production activities.

The three classes of logistics activities may include respectively:

- **S-to-C:** product specifications, request for proposal, proposal evaluation, purchasing, monitoring, receiving, quality control, and payment;

- **P:** design, prototyping, manufacturing, assembly, packaging, monitoring, remanufacturing, repair, and production support (e.g., quality control, material handling, maintenance); and

- **C-to-C:** answer to inquiry and to request for proposal, order entry, confirmation, modification, cancellation, monitoring and fulfilment, delivery, billing, reverse logistics, and customer service (e.g., use restrictions, products comparison).

It should be noted that in the literature, the activities of the supply chain are usually divided into two parts: the order-entry activities from the customer's point-of-view (front-end applications) and the shipping activities, including order fulfilment, delivery and billing (back-end applications). Both concern the Company-to-Customer activities.

Considering the variability of all the activities performed from one company to the other, an exhaustive list of elements to be analysed, based on all the logistics activities, is not suitable for this operational diagnosis. Therefore, unlike the strategic diagnosis for which each element is described, the operational diagnosis is an overall analysis tool, which can be applied to every logistics activity.

For the operational diagnosis, the classical process analysis questions (What? Where? When? Who? How? and Why?) are still applicable. The possible actions for an activity are: eliminate, combine, change (of the sequence, the place, or the person), improve, or maintain status quo. Tables 5 and 6 present the operational diagnosis. The analysis uses an iterative methodology where, for each activity, a complete operational diagnosis is performed.

Using the self-diagnosis tool allows an enterprise to brush up a portrait of its logistics activities in view of the implementation of EC. Weaknesses are highlighted and an action plan can be established for the enterprise "mutation" (organisational change) toward another stage of EC. Some authors present steps to realise this mutation. For example, Riggins and Mukhopadhyay (1994)

Table 5. Operational diagnosis - Information flow

	Classes of activities		
	S-to-C	P	C-to-C
WHAT?			
- What are the activity objectives?	x	x	x
- What is the level of the terminology standardisation needed?	x	x	x
- What are the new databases characteristics? (e.g., dynamic)	x	x	x
- What is the appropriate supply chain visibility of the company?	x	x	x
- What is the appropriate supply chain visibility of the business partners?	x		x
- What is the traceability need for all raw material used for a given product?		x	x
WHERE?			
- Where is the appropriate place to perform the activity? (integrated with the traditional activity or not)	x	x	x
WHEN?			
- When should one have access to the company's information? (e.g., real-time or postponed, during business hours or on a continuous operating hour basis)	x	x	x
- When should one have access to the business partners' information?	x	x	x
WHO?			
- Who should have access to the information?	x	x	x
- Who should be authorised to update information?	x	x	x
- Who should control the databases access? (internal or external access)	x	x	x
- Who should be responsible of the authorisation for an efficient carrying out of the activity?	x	x	x
- Who should be responsible for the activity? (dedicated or shared responsibility)	x	x	x
- What is the appropriate resource allocation? (e.g., by functions, by products, by data transmission channels)	x	x	x
- Can the activity be automated?	x	x	x
- Is the personnel able to execute the new tasks related to EC?	x	x	x
- Is an expert needed for the EC implementation?	x	x	x
HOW?			
- Are the computer platforms standardised for internal and external communications?	x	x	x
- How secure is the electronic communication protocol?	x	x	x
- How should be integrated the different data transmission channels (Internet, fax, telephone, or mail)?	x	x	x
- How should the activity react to its environment? (passive or dynamic, proactive or reactive)?	x	x	x
- Are the new tasks related to EC properly integrated?	x	x	x
- How should the information be passed on to the personnel?	x	x	x
- How should the information be controlled?	x	x	x
- Can the actual technology support EC activities?	x	x	x

(The left margin of the WHO? block is labelled vertically: **W H Y ?**)

present five levels of business transformations: 1 - Localised exploitation, 2 - Internal integration, 3 - Business process redesign, 4 - Business, network redesign (intra- and inter-networks, scope and tasks), and 5 - Business scope

Table 6. Operational diagnosis - Material flow

		Classes of activities		
		S-to-C	P	C-to-C
W	**WHAT?**			
H	- What are the activity objectives?	x	x	x
Y	- Which range of products or services offered is standardised?	x	x	x
?	- Which production processes are standardised?		x	
	- What is the appropriate technology to use for the product identification? (e.g., bar codes, manually)	x	x	x
	- What is the appropriate unit load to use for the new material flow?	x	x	x
	- What are the appropriate links between the product received and the order form?	x		
	- What is the appropriate allocation type to use for the product received? (e.g., by end user, by warehouse allocation)	x		
	- What is the level of knowledge of the product characteristics and its physical conditions needed prior to the receiving?	x	x	x
	- What information on the product characteristics and its physical conditions needs to be stored?	x	x	x
	- What are the appropriate criteria to use for the identification of the level of completion of an activity?	x	x	x
	- What is the estimated volume increase (or decrease) of products to be processed related to EC?	x	x	x
	- What are the new services offered by the company? (e.g., request for proposal from a customer)		x	x
	- Which aspects of reverse logistics may be implemented?		x	x
	- What is the appropriate product allocation to use? (e.g., by customer's address, by warehouse allocation, FIFO)		x	
	- Does the product or its packaging need to be reviewed in order to satisfy EC constraints?	x	x	x
	- What is the appropriate technology to use for the product monitoring?	x	x	x
	- What are the new parameters to include in the performance measurement program?	x	x	x
	- What are the impacts on the improvement program? (e.g., feedback, implementation of changes)	x	x	x
	- What is the appropriate facility layout for the implementation of EC?		x	
	WHERE?			
	- Where is the appropriate place to perform the activity? (integrated with the traditional activity or not)	x	x	x
	- Where should the consolidation be performed?	x	x	x
	- Can the activity be outsourced? (completely or partly)	x	x	x
	WHEN?			
	- When should the activity be performed? (e.g., in real-time or postponed, during the company's business hours or on a continuous operating hours basis)	x	x	x
	- When should the activity status be updated? (in real-time or per fixed interval)	x	x	x

Table 6. Operational diagnosis - Material flow (continued)

	Classes of activities		
	S-to-C	P	C-to-C
WHO?			
- Who should be responsible for the activity? (dedicated or shared responsibility)	x	x	x
- What should be the resource allocation? (e.g., by product, by function)	x	x	x
- Can the activity be automated? (completely or partly)	x	x	x
- Can the activity be outsourced? (completely or partly)	x	x	x
- Who should be responsible of the authorisation for an efficient carrying out of the activity?	x	x	x
- Is the personnel able to execute the new tasks related to EC?	x	x	x
- Is an expert needed for the EC implementation?	x	x	x
HOW?			
- How should the activity react to its environment (proactive or reactive)	x	x	x
- How can the company integrate new tasks related to EC?	x	x	x
- How should be managed the waiting queue? (e.g., FIFO, time-window by product)	x	x	x
- Can the actual technology support EC activities?	x	x	x

redefinition. Another example is Tinham (2000b) who focuses on four steps: 1 - e-business strategy, 2 - e-procurement, 3 - e-delivery, logistics and supply, and 4 - Web-enabling to link e-buying, e-selling and e-collaboration.

It should be noted that some issues could slowdown the implementation of EC, such as the management and the personnel commitment, data matters (security, limited access, and incompatibility), interoperability problems, performance measurement questions, specialised workforce for the EC development of applications, and training of a company's actual workforce.

Conclusions

The opportunities due to EC, which can increase the company's benefits and the clientele's satisfaction, are countless. The successful growth of a company within EC requires the integration of all its logistics activities. Four stages of EC — and the links between — are presented: Brochureware, e-commerce, e-business, and e-enterprise. For each stage, the most frequent features for EC are inventoried and categorized as various technological and operational requirements for the implementation of EC. Then, means for implementing EC were inventoried. Those means include traditional concepts, techniques or computer tools, and more recent ones, such as portability, lean manufacturing, data warehousing, or GPS. Another important contribution of this chapter is the self-diagnosis tool, which is the first detailed checklist for a systematic analysis of a company's processes. It is the first step in the re-engineering of logistics activities for EC since it allows a company to evaluate its situation within the EC framework. The self-diagnosis tool highlights logistics activities that need to be reviewed, upgraded, integrated, or even outsourced. Based on the results of the detailed analysis, an action plan can be established for implementing the first stage of EC or for the enterprise "mutation" toward another stage of EC. Using the proposed self-diagnosis tool, an action plan specific to each logistics activity may be developed.

For directions of research concerning all aspects of EC, the reader is refer to Auramo et al. (2002) which present a research agenda for e-business logistics. Also, decision support systems are needed to evaluate the required level of integration and consolidation of traditional activities with activities related to EC. Mathematical models could evaluate different choices for a company's part mix. Results for different scenarios of demand (quantity, location) should be generated to analyse the impact of EC on all the logistics activities, including production activities.

References

Anonymous. (1999). Getting 'active': A finger on the pulse. *Manufacturing Computer Solutions, 5*(5), 26-28.

Auramo, J., Aminoff, A., & Punakivi, M. (2002). Research agenda for e-business logistics based on professional opinions. *International Journal of Physical Distribution & Logistics Management, 32*(7), 513-531.

Baker, S. (2000). Global e-commerce, local problems. *IEEE Engineering Management Review, 28*(2), 104-110.

Bauer, M. J., Poirier, C. C., Lapide, L., & Bermudez, J. (2001). *E-Business: The strategic impact on supply chain and logistics*. Oak Brook, IL: Council of Logistics Management.

Bean, J. (2003). *Engineering global e-commerce sites: A guide to data capture, content, and transactions*. New York: Morgan Kaufmann.

Bitouzet, C. (1999). *Le commerce électronique: Création d'une valeur pour l'entreprise*. Paris: Hermès Science.

Booty, F. (2000). Make manufacturing part of the supply chain. *Manufacturing Computer Solutions, 6*(3), 46-47.

Bowersox, D. J., Closs, D. J., & Cooper, M. B (2002). Market distribution strategy. In *Supply chain logistics management* (pp. 93-129). Boston, MA: McGraw Hill.

Burnson, P. (2000, September). The logistics of e-fulfillment. *Logistics Management and Distribution Report*, E14-E16.

Chabli, S., Chapelet, B., Deglaine, J., & Dimitriadis, S. (1999). L'impact du commerce électronique (CE) sur les emplois et compétences en P.M.E.: une méthodologie de l'étude. *Gestion 2000, 16*(5), 35-55.

Chambers, A. (2000). Utilities buy into B2B. *Power Engineering, 104*(6), 28-32.

Chow, G., & Gritta, R. (2001). The growth and development of the U.S. third party logistics industry. *The Ninth World Conference on Transport Research*, Seoul, Korea. July 22-27.

Collins, P. (2000). E-logistics 2000 re-thinking the supply chain. *Management Services, 44*(6), 6-10.

Dan et al. (1998). The Coyote project: Framework for multi-party e-commerce. *Lecture Notes in Computer Science, 1513*, 873-889.

Davidson, W. H. (1997). E-commerce's effect on sales and distribution is only beginning. *Industry Week, 246*(21), 20-22.

Delfmann, W., Albers, S., & Gehring, M. (2002). The impact of electronic commerce on logistics service providers. *International Journal of Physical Distribution & Logistics Management, 32*(3), 203-222.

Democker, J. (2000, December 4). Putting e-business on 18 wheels. *InfoWorld*, S43-S44.

Dilger, K. A. (2000). Keep your promises. *Manufacturing Systems, 18*(4), 79-83.

Dowlatshahi, S. (2000). Developing a theory of reverse logistics. *Interfaces, 30*(3), 143-155.

Fallows, J. (1999). 'Net profits. *Computing & Control Engineering Journal*, *10*(4), 177-180.

Feldman, S. (2000). The changing face of e-commerce: Extending the boundaries of the possible. *IEEE Internet Computing, 4*(3), 82-83.

Fulcher, J. (2000). Stay on track. *Manufacturing Systems, 18*(5), 58-68.

Gaw, B. (2000). Eight ways to improve demand-based manufacturing. *APICS: The Performance Advantage, 10*(4), 60-63.

Giuntini, R., & Andel, T. (1995a). Advance with reverse logistics: Part 1. *Transportation and Distribution, 36*(2), 73-77.

Giuntini, R., & Andel, T. (1995b). Master the six R's of reverse logistics: Part 2. *Transportation and Distribution, 36*(3), 93-98.

Golicic, S. L., Davis, D. F., McCarthy, T. M., & Mentzer, J. T. (2002). The impact of e-commerce on supply chain relationships. *International Journal of Physical Distribution & Logistics Management, 32*(10), 851-871.

Gorbach, G. (2000). Seven fundamentals of e-manufacturing. *Manufacturing Systems, 18*(11), 120.

Guide, V. D. R., Jayaraman, V., & Linton, J. D. (2003). Building contingency planning for closed-loop supply chains with product recovery. *Journal of Operations Management, 21*(3), 259-279.

Gunasekaran, A., Marri, H. B., McGaughey, R. E., & Nebhwani, M. D. (2002). E-commerce and its impact on operations management. *International Journal of Production Economics, 75*(1-2), 185-197.

Hall, J. (2000). Are your processes fit for e-commerce. *Management Services, 44*(4), 12-16.

Holmqvist, M., Hultkrantz, O., Stefansson, G., & Wingqvist, A. (2001). The logistical consequences of e-commerce: Theoretical scenarios for spare-part distribution. *The Ninth World Conference on Transport Research*, Seoul, Korea. July 22-27.

Hoque, F. (2000). *E-enterprise: Business models, architecture, and components*. New York: Cambridge University Press.

Hsu, C., & Pant, S. (2000). *Innovative planning for electronic commerce and enterprises: A reference model*. Boston: Kluwer Academic Publishers.

Huin, S. F., Luong, L. H. S., & Abhary, K. (2002). Internal supply chain planning determinants in small and medium-sized manufacturers. *International Journal of Physical Distribution & Logistics Management, 32*(9), 771-782.

Johnson, J. C., Wood, D. F., Wardlow, D. L., & Murphy, P. R., Jr. (1999). *Contemporary logistics (7th ed.).* Upper Saddle River, NJ: Prentice Hall.

Jordan, J. M. (1998). *Organizing for electronic commerce: Toward lightweight decentralization.* Ernst & Young Center for Business Innovation. [Technical report.]

Jutla, D., Bodorik, P., & Wang, Y. (1999). Developing Internet e-commerce benchmarks. *Information Systems, 24*(6), 475-493.

Kalpakjian, S. (2001). *Manufacturing engineering and technology (4th ed.).* Upper Saddle River, NJ: Prentice Hall.

Keskinocak, P., & Tayur, S. (2001). Quantitative analysis for Internet-enabled supply chains. *Interfaces, 31*(2), 70-89.

Khouja, M. (2001). The evaluation of drop shipping option for e-commerce retailers. *Computers & Industrial Engineering, 41*(2), 109-126.

Kimball, R., & Merz, R. (2000). *Le data webhouse: Analyser les comportements client sur le web.* Paris: Eyrolles.

King, E. (2000). I before E. *Enterprise Systems Journal,* 18.

Kleindl, B. A. (2001). *Strategic electronic marketing: Managing e-business.* Australia: South Western College Publishing.

Krasner, H. (2000). Ensuring e-business success by learning from ERP failures. *IT Professional, 2*(1), 22-27.

Kuglin, F. A., & Rosenbaum, B. A. (2001). *The supply chain network @ Internet speed: Preparing your company for the e-commerce revolution.* New York: Amacom.

Lefebvre, L. A., & Lefebvre, É. (2000). Virtual enterprises and virtual economy: Manifestations and policy challenges. *International Journal of Technology Management, 20*(1-2), 58-71.

Leung, L. C., Cheung, W., & Van Hui, Y. (2000). A framework for a logistics e-commerce community network: The Hong Kong air cargo industry. *IEEE Transactions on Systems, Man, and Cybernetics - Part A: Systems and Humans, 30*(4), 446-455.

Lewis, T. (1999). Something for nothing. *Computer, 32*(5), 118-120.

Lientz, B. P., & Rea, K. P. (2001). *Start right in e-business: A step-by-step guide to successful e-business implementation.* San Diego: Academic Press.

Mason, S. J., Ribera, P. M., Farris, J. A., & Kirk, R. G. (2003). Integrating the warehousing and transportation functions of the supply chain. *Transportation Research Part E: Logistics and Transportation Review, 39*(2), 141-159.

May, P. (2000). *The business of eCommerce from corporate strategy to technology.* New York: Cambridge University Press.

McGuffog, T. (1999). E-commerce and the value chain. *Manufacturing Engineer, 78*(4), 157-160.

Michel, R. (2000). The two faces of e-commerce. *Manufacturing Systems, 18*(2), 34-43.

Minahan, T. (1998). Manufacturers take aim at end of the supply chain. *Purchasing, 124*(6), 111-112.

Norris, M., West, S., & Gaughan. K. (2000). *E-business essentials: Technology and network requirements for electronic marketplace.* Chichester, UK: Wiley.

Norton, J. (2000). The relevance of e-commerce. *Manufacturing Engineer, 79*(3), 90-91.

Pancucci, D. (2000). Making the plant beat to a new drum. *Manufacturing Computer Solutions, 6*(3), 16-17.

Rhodes, E., & Carter, R. (1998). Electronic commerce technologies and changing product distribution. *International Journal of Technology Management, 15*(1-2), 31-48.

Riggins, F. J., & Mukhopadhyay, T. (1994). Interdependent benefits from interorganizational systems: Opportunities for business partner reengineering. *Journal of Management Information Systems, 11*(2), 37-57.

Rosen, A. (2000). *The e-commerce question and answer book: A survival guide for business managers.* New York: Amacom.

Schultz, G. (2000). Factory floor data fuels true e-commerce. *APICS - The Performance Advantage, 10*(6), 38-43.

Seminerio, M. (2000, January 24). Spin to win: Large companies are spinning off e-com ventures to maximize valuations, but such moves don't always pay off. *PC Week*, 59.

Sheridan, J. H. (1996). Gearing up for e-commerce. *Industry Week*, *245*(21), 43-50.

Stevens, C., & Sharma, K. (2001). Hbc.com mise sur une chaîne d'approvisionnement intégrée et des capacités de fulfillment innovatrices. *Logistics Magazine*, *5*(1), 18-23.

Taylor, S. (2000). E-commerce best practices. *APICS - The Performance Advantage*, *10*(11), 38-44.

Tinham, B. (2000a). What place MRP II in the new world? *Manufacturing Computer Solutions*, *6*(1), 14-18.

Tinham, B. (2000b). Above all, get set for e-business. *Manufacturing Computer Solutions*, *6*(3), 11-15.

Trebilcock, B. (2001). Buy it online. *Modern Materials Handling*, *56*(3), 60-64.

Vallamsetty, U., Kant, K., & Mohapatra, P. (2003). Characterization of e-commerce traffic. *Electronic Commerce Research*, *3*(1-2), 167-192.

Vergnion, J., & Montreuil, B. (2001). Réseau logistique de la e-entreprise de détail. *Gestion 2000*, *18*(2), 129-148.

Ward, A. (2000). E-business and the Web in manufacturing. *Manufacturing Computer Solutions*, *6*(3), 26-27.

Yami, Z. (2000). Lean means cycle times. *European Semiconductor Design Production Assembly*, *22*(8), 23-24.

Yen, B. P.C. (2002). Electronic commerce front-end in apparel supply chain. *Computers & Industrial Engineering*, *42*(2), 471-480.

Chapter X

Studies on Interaction and Coordination in Supply Chains with Perishable Products: A Review[1]

Xiping Song, The Chinese University of Hong Kong, Hong Kong

Xiaoqiang Cai, The Chinese University of Hong Kong, Hong Kong

Jian Chen, Tsinghua University, P.R. China

Abstract

We review the recent literature on supply chain management of perishable products. Our emphasis is placed on the interaction and coordination between inventory and marketing, financing, distribution, and production. We survey the recent research progress in this area, by discussing the motivations, features and extensions of various models.

Introduction

Perishable products are common in the contemporary world. Fresh fish decays in a few days. The value of novel electronic products quickly decreases because of technological development. Photographic film can be used only before the expiry date, subsequently becoming valueless. For these kinds of products, traditional inventory models that assume the inventory can all be used to fulfill the future demands are no longer applicable. Hence, many researchers have developed specific models on the inventory of perishable products. Some articles study the situation where all items in an inventory become obsolete simultaneously at the end of a period. Many such studies are reported in the field of yield management, such as airline management, which will not be included in our review here. In this chapter we focus on models in the manufacturing area, where we must handle material flow problems.

An early work on a perishable inventory problem was described by Whitin in 1957, where fashion goods deteriorating at the end of certain storage periods were considered. Since then, considerable attention has been attracted to this line of research. Nahmias (1982) provides a comprehensive survey of the research works published before the 1980s, where perishable products were divided into two categories; products with a fixed lifetime and those with a random lifetime. For products with a fixed lifetime there is a fixed expiry date. Before this date, they are assumed to be fresh and can be used without any decrease in their quality or quantity. After that, the products will have expired and become valueless. For products with a random lifetime, their quality or quantity decreases with time. More recent studies on the deteriorating inventory models can be found in Raafat (1991) and Goyal et al.'s (2001) reviews, where relevant literature published in 1980s and 1990s was reviewed respectively.

While inventory is an important element in supply chain management (SCM), focusing on inventory models without considering its interactions with other elements is not sufficient. It is clear that the relationship of the manufacturer, the supplier, the retailer, and the consumers may directly affect efficiency and effectiveness of the whole supply chain system. For example, the pricing mechanism and promotion strategy will affect the demand, which is the main parameter that affects the order quantity. The order quantity will affect the optimal production strategy, and in all these processes the financial element is always an important factor to be considered. The specific properties of deteriorating products make their supply chain management very different from the traditional one. For instance, because the product deteriorates, the quantity produced may be significantly different from the quantity that can be sold. These issues may affect financial strategy, especially in times of high inflation or when high interest rates are incurred. It is important, but complicated, to find a tradeoff among the different parts in the supply chain and to build an efficient SCM system for products that deteriorate.

In this chapter we will survey mainly those studies published since the 1980s. Unlike other reviews that focus largely on deteriorating inventory, we emphasize the interfaces of different supply chain parts, in particular the interaction and coordination between inventory and marketing, inventory and financial planning, inventory and distribution, and inventory and production.

Joint Inventory-Marketing Decisions

Finding an optimal pricing strategy to maximize profit is always the core objective of the marketing function of any manufacturing firm. A marketing department may adopt different promotional strategies to attract more consumers, which may make the demand less constant than most inventory models assume. There has been some research on joint strategies for marketing-inventory systems with deteriorating products. In what follows, we classify these studies into two categories, based on the demand types: (1) the demands are deterministic, which are assumed to be predictable in advance; and (2) the demands are random, which may fluctuate stochastically over time.

Deterministic Demands

The work of Eilon and Mallaya (1966) was among the earliest studies that integrates pricing into the deterministic inventory model. They extend Ghare et al.'s work (1963), by considering a price-dependent demand. Cohen (1977) investigates a model with a constant deteriorating rate and a constant price. He examines cases without shortage and with a complete back-ordering shortage, respectively. In this research, it had been assumed generally that the demand was affected only by price and only a single period model was considered. As is well known, for a perishable product, the demand is not only determined by price, but also related to time, because customers may prefer to purchase a new product because the quality (or the functionality) of the old one has deteriorated. This motivates studies with different demand functions, which are discussed in the following subsections.

Models with Special Demand Functions

Wee (1995) considers a problem where the initial demand rate is a linear function of price. Let $A(s)$ be the demand rate at time 0 and s be the price. Wee's model assumes $A(s) = a - bs$. The demand rate at any given time t is then modeled by $d(t,s) = A(s)^{-\alpha t}$. The deteriorating rate is assumed to be constant. The system operates only for a prescribed period of H years. Wee (1999) extends this model by introducing a discount for quantity, where he assumes that the distribution of the time that an item takes to deteriorate is a Weibull. The solution method in these two articles is similar. Supposing the life cycles are equal, first he optimizes the price and inventory cycle for a given number of life cycles. Then, with marginal analysis, he arrives at the optimal number of life cycles in the planning period H. Since there exists a discount for quantity in Wee (1999), by comparing the profit for different price breaks, Wee reaches the optimal strategy with a discount for quantity. Papachristos et al. (2003) extend Wee's model (1999) by assuming the demand rate is any convex decreasing function of the price and that the partial backlogging rate is variable. With an iterative method, they obtain the optimal time period and price, and the time point when the inventory equals zero. They also point out that Wee (1999) omits the sales lost in the revenue function.

Models with General Demand Functions

Rajan et al. (1992) study the situation where a monopolistic retailer must decide both the order quantity and the price. Their model deals with a random lifetime with deterministic demand and continuous decay. The demand decreases in price and time, which implies that the older the product, the lower its value. In their model the optimal dynamic price is independent of the choice of cycle length, which suggests that the solution of this problem can be decomposed into two stages. In the first stage, the optimal price can be computed with a given cycle length. In the second stage, the best cycle length can then be derived using the optimal price. Shortage is not allowed. When the inventory reaches zero, fresh products will arrive.

For products with a high deteriorating rate, it is expensive to maintain the inventory. Some researchers suggest that, if the consumers are willing to wait a while for fresh products, backlogging demand should be a useful way to avoid deteriorating cost. Abad (1996) extends Rajan et al.'s model by allowing a back-order. In this model, part of the demand is back-ordered. Because most consumers are reluctant to wait for too long, he assumes that the back-order rate is a decreasing function in the waiting time. With a procedure similar to that of Rajan et al., he decomposes the problem into two parts. By solving a two-variable nonlinear programming problem, he derives the optimal back-ordering period. Then he reconsiders the example of Rajan et al. and finds that, with the back-order the price will be lower and the profit will be higher. Abad (2003) extends this model again by supposing that the production rate is finite and larger than the demand rate. In this model, the optimal price is dependent on the best cycle length, which means that the problem cannot be decomposed as Rajan et al. have tried to do. Abad first studies the inventory problem with a fixed price, then uses an iterative method to tackle the case with the price p as a decision variable.

Models Considering Suppliers' Promotion Strategy

In practice, a supplier may provide a special offer to promote his products, e.g., a discount for quantity, or a special credit term. These promotions affect the cost to the retailers, making them adopt different strategies to sell the goods. The different strategies adopted by the retailers will also affect the consumers, so that the demand function may become more complicated (Figure 1).

Figure 1. Relationship among different stages in the supply chain

Hwang et al. (1997) study the problem to determine the retailer's pricing and lot sizing policy for exponentially deteriorating products, under the condition of a permissible delay in payments. They assume that the demand function is known as $D=KP^{-B}$, where P is the price, K and B are positive constants, and the deterioration rate is constant. The supplier allows a certain fixed credit period. Since the profit function is complicated, they simplify the problem by using a truncated Taylor series expansion for the exponential term.

Arcelus et al. (2002) consider a model to jointly determine the retailer's pricing, credit period, and inventory policies for deteriorating items in response to temporary price/credit incentives. They assume that the supplier may use different price and credit incentives to promote his products. Their model deals with a constant rate of deterioration, and a deterministic demand function $D(p,t) = ap^b t^r$, where p is the price, t is the credit time, and a, b and r are constants. It is assumed that $a > 0; b < 0$, which implies that the demand is decreasing in price. In addition, it is assumed that $r \geq 0$, and therefore the demand is increased with extra credit time. Optimal solutions are not obtained in this article. Some useful managerial insights are, however, provided with numerical studies.

Stochastic Demands

Research on joint inventory-marketing decisions is still quite rare for problems involving stochastic demands for perishable products. There are, nevertheless, some interesting models which handle this kind of problems elegantly. Stochastic models on marketing-inventory systems can be divided into two categories: (1) the demand is random, but the distribution is known; (2) the demand is random and the distribution is unknown.

Stochastic Models with Known Distributions

These models assume that the demand follows a known distribution. The distribution may be derived from past experience or may be estimated following opinions of experts. Unlike deterministic models, even when all the decision parameters are given, the demand is not known exactly. This variability in demand will directly affect the pricing and inventory strategy in different periods of time.

In most models for deteriorating products, it is assumed that deterioration begins when there is a positive inventory if the product has a random lifetime, or deterioration occurs at a fixed period if the product has a fixed lifetime. However, Rahim et al. (2000) study a single-period perishable inventory model, where they assume the deterioration begins at a random point in time. The customers arrive according to a Poisson process at a rate dependent on the item's selling price. It is natural to divide the life cycle into two phases: the phase without deterioration and the phase with deterioration. In the first phase, since the products are fresh, the authors assume the price is constant, and the demand rate is constant, too. However, in the second phase, the price will vary with time and the demand rate will change accordingly. They apply dynamic stochastic programming to analyze the dynamic property of this system. They first use the Fibonacci search technique to determine the optimal price when the time left and the quantity left are known. Then, by comparing the expected profits for different order quantities, they obtain the optimal one.

Some researchers analyse the demand from another point of view. They first investigate the value consumers attach to a product. By adding the demand of consumers whose values are higher than the price, they get the demand quantity. Chun (2003) studies an optimal pricing and ordering policy for perishable commodities. In his model, no shortage, no inventory cost, and no back-orders are considered. He supposes that the value every buyer attaches to the product is drawn from a special distribution. Each consumer's demand is 1. Hence, the demand quantity is the number of buyers whose values attached to the item are not lower than the post price. This assumption is very similar to that used in studies of auctions. He proves that dividing the selling period into several sub-periods, in which the seller can set a specific price, will bring the seller more profit.

Integrating the demand of every buyer to get the demand function is a useful way to study a pricing mechanism. Since in different pricing mechanisms, the buyer may act using different strategies, assuming a fixed demand function may be invalid at some point in time. Especially in dynamic pricing such as in an auction, the buyers' strategy will apparently affect the demand. Chun's paper (2003) is a good beginning for introducing buyers' strategies to the marketing-inventory system.

Studies on Interaction and Coordination 229

Stochastic Models with Unknown Distributions

In the real world, the demand distribution may not be known to the retailer. Hence, retailers tend to estimate the demand distribution from their former sales' history. For new products, the demand distribution is more uncertain, which becomes clearer gradually after some rounds of sales. Finding an optimal strategy when the demand is still not very clear is important, but difficult. Burnetas et al. (2000) study a problem with an unknown demand distribution. The seller does not know the demand distribution. However, using the information of previous sales' history, he updates his knowledge on the demand distribution gradually. No inventory is carried over from one period to the next. Hence the model is more like a newsboy problem with a price parameter. They first use a pricing algorithm based on the policy developed for the multi-armed bandit problem, with an average expected reward. Then, with an adaptive ordering policy, they derive the order quantity. They prove the convergence of their policy and extend it to situations where the parameters of the demand's distribution are unknown. This article offers some ideas for pricing and ordering methods in an uncertain market.

Summary

Table 1 is a brief summary of the main features of the studies on joint marketing–inventory models for deteriorating products.

Generally, studies of marketing-inventory models for deteriorating products are still quite limited. The majority of the relevant literature has focused on one-period models with deterministic demands. In multi-stage cases, most articles suppose that the deterioration will occur only at the end of the inventory period. Moreover, it appears that strategies of the buyers have not been taken into account. In practice, since the values and prices of deteriorating products change rapidly, it may be more rational to consider the possibility that buyers will determine whether and when to purchase a product, based on the different strategies of the retailer. In this way, dynamic pricing becomes a game model with the buyers and the sellers as players, instead of a decision model where only the sellers can make decisions.

Table 1. Summary of marketing-inventory models for deteriorating products

Articles	Demand	Replenishment	Backordering	Deterioration
Rajan et al. (1992)	Deterministic and decreasing in time	Infinite	No	Deterministic and dependent on time
Abad (1996)	Deterministic and decreasing in time	Infinite	Partial and variable	Deterministic and dependent on time
Abad (2003)	Deterministic and decreasing in time	Finite	Partial and variable	Deterministic and dependent on time
Wee (1995)	Deterministic and decreasing in time	Infinite	Partial	Constant
Wee (1999)	Deterministic and decreasing in time	Infinite	Partial	Random
Hwang et al. (1997)	Deterministic	Infinite	No shortage	Constant
Papachristos et al. (2003)	Deterministic	Infinite	Partial and variable	Random
Arcelus et al. (2002)	Deterministic	Infinite	No	Constant
Rahim et al. (2000)	Nonstationary Poisson process	Infinite	No	Beginning at a random point in time
Chun (2003)	Random	Infinite	No	At the end of the period
Burnetas et al. (2000)	Random with unknown Distribution	Infinite	NO	At the end of each period

Joint Inventory-Financial Decisions

It is well known that the value of money changes over time. On the other hand, the value in terms of quantity or quality of a perishable product is also a time-varying function. Thus, for deteriorating products, how to combine the financial instrument with the inventory policy so as to generate the maximal profit is a very interesting problem. A representative work in this area is Jaggi et al. (1994), who study an economic ordering quantity (EOQ) model with deteriorating items in the presence of trade credit. They use a cash-flow (DCF) approach to introduce the time value of money to a perishable inventory model. Other research is discussed next.

Models with Permissible Payment Delays

In many situations a supplier may allow a delay for payment by the retailer without charging interest. This delay gives some flexibility to the retailer for arranging his own cash flow. This results in the problem of how cash flow should be managed to coordinate with the material flow so that the overall cost is minimized. In general, the permissible payment delay may be longer or shorter than the inventory cycle. Figure 2 shows two such scenarios, where M is the permissible delay and T is the inventory cycle.

If the payment delay is longer than the inventory cycle, no interest will be payable for the inventory and the retailer can earn interest in the time gap between payment and the inventory cycle. However, if the payment delay is shorter than the inventory cycle, the retailer will have to pay interest for the inventory left after the permissible payment delay runs out. Aggarwal et al. (1995) study the ordering policies of deteriorating items under permissible delays in payment, where they consider constant demand rate and deterioration rate, and a fixed permissible period for payment delay. They assume the cost function is convex, based on which they derive the optimal strategy. With a sensitivity analysis, they point out that:

1. The unit costs of the products are important for setting the credit period;
2. The increase of the deterioration rate will incur a significant decrease in the cycle length and order quantity and a sharp increase in total cost.

Figure 2. Payment time and inventory cycle

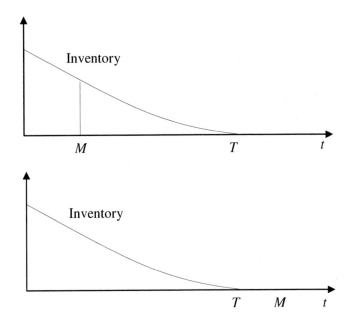

Aggarwal's work (1995) on integration of suppliers' financial credit with retailers' inventory strategy has become the basis for many studies focusing on permitted delay of payment. Chu et al. (1998) generalize Aggarwal et al.'s model. They study the convexity of the variable cost function for deteriorating products and prove that the overall cost function is piecewise-convex in general. With this conclusion, Chu et al. improve Aggarwal et al.'s solution procedure.

Jamal et al. (1997) extend Aggarwal et al.'s model by allowing for shortages with back-orders. Considering the ordering cost, holding cost, deterioration cost, interest and the back-order cost, they develop a function for the variable cost per unit time. Since this cost involves a higher order exponential function, they determine the convexity of the function in the feasible ranges indirectly. They then use an iterative search approach to determine the optimal payment time and cycle period. Sarker et al. (2000) extend Jamal et al.'s (1997) model by introducing the factor of inflation. They consider the time value of money with continual investment, and study scenarios with inflation and shortages respectively. Liao et al. (2002) consider the problem where the consumption rate is related to the initial stock. Interest cost is also considered. Similar to Aggarwal et al. (1995), they propose an algorithm to compute the optimal order quantity for cases where the inventory cycle is shorter or longer than the permissible payment delay, respectively.

Jamal et al. (2000) consider a model where there is an interest-free period allowed by the wholesaler to the retailer. The retailer's objective is to decide an optimal time (which may be longer than the interest-free period) to complete the payment to the wholesaler, by considering various costs and interest rates involved. Their idea of determining an optimal payment time is quite novel. Unfortunately, as indicated by Song and Cai (2003), there are a number of flaws contained in their development, on the convexity of the total unit cost function, the negativity of the interest cost, and the interest that should be paid for the deteriorated item.

Models considering permission of delay in payment capture a common feature in wholesaler-retailer supply chains. Because any cash can also be reinvested, the timing for payments plays an important role. In particular, since the value of a perishable product is time-varying, how to make use of the permissible delay may have an important impact on the retailers' order strategy when products to be sold are deteriorating.

The results developed in the articles reviewed above may also help the supplier to determine the optimal payment delay. Since suppliers have the right to set the credit period and amount, models on how to determine optimal credit periods are certainly also useful for them. However, it appears that little attention has been paid to the strategy on the suppliers' part. This is an interesting direction for future study.

Models Considering Inflations

Bose et al. (1995) consider a model with demand rate $f(t)=a+bt$, where $(a,b)>0$, which implies the demand rate increases in time t. Moreover, inflation rate, holding cost and shortage cost for the internal (company) and external (general economy) systems are taken into account. They first develop the first-order optimality condition, and then derive the optimal order quantity for a given inventory cycle. By comparing the costs of different inventory cycles in the planning horizon, they obtain the optimal solution.

Chung et al. (1997b) study a model considering continuous time value of money. The demand is time-dependent and all shortages are back-ordered. They analyze the present value of all the costs, and use a bisection algorithm to search for the optimal inventory period. Chung et al. (2001) extend their model (1997a) to an inventory system which begins and ends with a shortage. They divide the plan horizon into m equal life cycles. First they study the model without a shortage, and find that the cost function is convex. They then study the scenario with complete backlogging. They assume the no-shortage time in the life cycle is KT, where T is the length of the life cycle and $0<K<1$. With the Newton-Raphson method, they find the optimal K for the given m. Then by comparing the NPV in different life cycles, they obtain optimal m.

In practice the deterioration rate may also change randomly. Chen (1998) supposes that the deterioration rate is a two-parameter Weibull distribution and the demand is a linear function of time. By applying a dynamic programming method, he finds the optimal replenishment schedule.

Summary

Table 2 is a brief summary of joint inventory-financial studies for deteriorating products.

In traditional studies, the inventory cycles can always be assumed to be equal because of the symmetry of the parameters. However, with the time value of

Table 2. Summary of inventory-financial models for deteriorating products

Articles	Interest rates for borrowing and lending	Inflation	Backordering	Deterioration rate
Aggarwal et al. (1995)	Different	No	No shortage	Constant
Chu et al. (1998)	Different	No	No shortage	Constant
Jamal et al. (1997)	Different	No	Yes	Constant
Sarker et al. (2000)	Different	Yes	Yes	Constant
Liao et al. (2000)	Different	No	No shortage	Constant
Jamma et al. (2000)	Different	No	No shortage	Constant
Bose et al. (1995)	Equal	Yes	Yes	Constant
Chung et al. (1997b)	Equal	No	Yes	Constant
Chung et al. (2001)	Equal	No	Yes	Constant
Chen (1998)	Equal	Yes	Yes	Random

money, and in particular the time-varying nature of perishable products, the symmetry in time is broken. Consequently, for perishable products, the optimal inventory cycles during the planning horizon may be unequal. Nevertheless, because of the complexity of the problems with unequal inventory cycles, it appears that most studies so far still carry the common assumption of equal inventory cycles. This is a topic that needs further investigation.

Joint Inventory-Distribution Decisions

The process of distribution of perishable products may result in substantial loss if not managed properly. The problem has received considerable attention in the literature. Two main issues are involved: one on transportation, and the other on allocation. First, we have to find the right route and timing to transmit the products in order to minimize their deterioration during the process of transportation. Second, we must allocate the right products to the right places, and therefore the age of the products to be allocated and the inventory in the sales outlets should all be taken into consideration. To achieve better coordination of the supply chain, a joint decision with transportation and allocation being considered in one integrated model is desirable. All these make the problem very challenging.

Transportation of Perishable Products

The transportation problem with deteriorating products is not an easy one. This is complicated by the needs to determine the optimal decisions based on:

1. The quantity of a product to be transported (due to deterioration during the process of transportation, the initial amount to be delivered must be higher than the demand at the destination).

2. The route and timing of transmission (different amounts of time and cost may be required over different seasons/periods).

Diaby (1991) studies a generalized fixed-charge transportation problem with perishable products. He supposes that the loss of the perishable products is different if the transportation route is different and the loss is deterministic and known for each route. Evans and Norback (1985) describe the implementation of a heuristic-based decision-support system for vehicle routing of food service delivery at Kraft, Inc. Rowe et al. (1996) describe a deport-bookings system to automate the vehicle planning and scheduling process to deliver perishable commodities. Iijima, Komatsu and Katoh (1996) report a Just-In-Time logistics system for the distribution of food products. Tarantilis and Kiranoudis (2001) consider a distribution problem of fresh milk, and develop a meta-heuristic solution method.

Allocation of Perishable Products

Because of the possibility of deterioration, the age of perishable products is an important factor that must be considered in allocation. How to allocate the right quantity of products with appropriate ages is a key problem.

Some researchers classify the products into two categories: the old one, which will decay after one cycle; and the fresh one, which can also be used in the next cycle. This assumption implies that the products have a fixed life cycle, after which they will decay. But before their life cycle expires, the products can be used as fresh ones.

Prastacos (1981) studies the allocation of a perishable product inventory. He assumes that there is a distribution center to allocate the perishable products to n locations. Each product has a fixed lifetime and the demand at each location

Figure 3. Allocation of deteriorating products

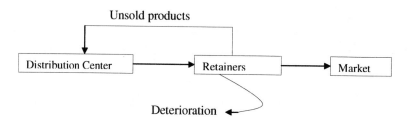

is i.i.d. Any unsold amount of the product will be returned to the center. Figure 3 illustrates this system.

He constructs an optimal myopic policy, which minimizes the one-period expected cost, but is not optimal in general for the long run. He also provides the bounds for the performance of an optimal long-run policy. Lin et al. (2003) study the dynamic allocation of an uncertain supply for a perishable commodity supply chain. They suppose that there are *m* suppliers and *n* retailers, and the problem is to distribute the products of the suppliers to the *n* retailers. First, they establish a model to formulate the problem, and then they apply a two-stage extended-Genetic Algorithm (EGA) to control the orders and allocation quantities. They also give a numerical study which shows that the EGA outperforms the traditional approach.

Integrated Models

Katagiri et al. (2002) consider an integrated delivery and inventory problem for perishable products with fuzzy shortage costs. The products have a fixed lifetime. The demands in different regions are treated as a set of independent random variables. Based on an LIFO (Last In, First Out) issuing policy, the center aims to allocate the products to different regions, with transportation costs taken into account. They give the optimal solution for this problem, with a concept of least "ambiguity."

Federgruen et al. (1986) study an allocation and distribution model for perishable products. They also suppose that each product has a fixed life cycle.

The system consists of three costs: a shortage cost, an out-of-date cost and a transportation cost. First, they divide the products into old items that will deteriorate in one time unit, and fresh ones. Then they integrate the routing and inventory allocation into one model, and obtain the optimal allocation strategy. They consider two delivery patterns, individual deliveries and combined deliveries. They provide an algorithm for the problems of both patterns. Computational results are also reported, based on which they point out that the travel costs of the combined deliveries are much lower.

Morales et al. (1999) study a more general mode, which involves production, inventory, and distribution of perishable products. They assume that there are q facilities, m warehouses, and n customers. The products are assumed to have a fixed lifetime. They propose to split the planning horizon into smaller periods. During each of the periods, the dynamic demand is approximately constant. This problem can easily be formulated as an integer programming one. However, even to determine whether a given problem has a feasible solution is an NP-complete problem. Hence in this article a heuristic approach is suggested to solve the problem.

Partially because of their complexity, studies on joint inventory-distribution decisions for products that deteriorate at a random rate are still quite rare. In the majority of the literature, it is assumed that each product has a fixed life cycle. This assumption also makes the routing problem much easier. For perishable products, the rates of deterioration in different routes may be different. This property should be taken into account when determining distribution and inventory decisions. However, it does not seem that it has been emphasized and addressed in the existing literature.

Joint Inventory-Production Decisions

Production planning is a key component in supply chain management. To make a good production plan, we must also consider the inventory, the demand, and the possible decay of perishable products. From the point of view of supply chain management, the production and the inventory are linked so closely that it is natural to consider them together. In addition to deterioration in inventory, decay may also occur when perishable products are being produced. These make joint production-inventory decision models for perishable products quite different from traditional ones.

Single-Period Problem

The life cycles of certain perishable products are so short that the producer will only need to make a one-cycle production plan. On the other hand, studies of the single-period problem may capture the basic essences of the inventory-production system, and therefore provide useful insights for studies of more general multi-period problems.

Yan and Cheng (1998) study a production-inventory model for deteriorating products, where they assume that the production, demand and deterioration rate are all time-dependent. The objective is to find the optimal producing strategy, so as to minimize the cost per unit time. In their model, the inventory life cycle begins and ends at shortage. During the shortage period, the demand is partially backlogged at a constant rate. They give the conditions for a feasible stationary point to be optimal. Since this model is quite general in production rate, demand rate, deterioration rate and the backlogging rate, the result can be used in other cases, such as problems with a constant production rate and full backlogging.

Balkhi (2000) and Balkhi et al. (2001) indicate that Yan et al.'s model can be improved by including the setup cost and the backlogging cost when the inventory is negative. Skouri and Papachristos (2003) extend Yan et al.'s model, by assuming that the backlogging rate is also a time-dependent function. The planning cycle is divided into four stages as shown in Figure 4:

1.   The inventory is negative and begins to build up until it reaches 0.

2.   The inventory is positive and builds up until the maximal point, where the production stops.

Figure 4. Inventory level fluctuation in Skouri et al.'s model

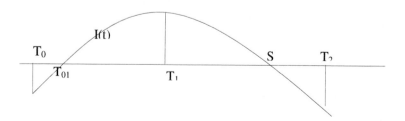

3.   The inventory is positive and decreases to 0.

4.   The inventory is negative and shortages begin.

Note that the slope in each stage is different even when the rates of deterioration, production and demand are constant in the life cycle. By analyzing the costs of these four stages, Skouri and Papachristos give the sufficient conditions for a minimized cost and then study the case with no shortages, where they also point out the mistakes in Yan et al.'s solution. They give the conditions under which Yan et al.'s results become valid. They do not find, however, conditions for existence and uniqueness of the optimal solution.

While many unresolved issues still remain on single-period models, the idea of dividing the inventory cycle into four stages is useful for analysis of the dynamic properties of the system.

Multi-Period Problem

Yang et al. (2002) study an integrated production-inventory model with a deteriorating item. They assume that there is one vendor and n buyers. The demand rate is different for each buyer. The production rate and deterioration rate are constant. No shortage is allowed. They prove that the overall cost of the system is convex. Because the demand, production and deterioration rates are all constant, the only decisions that need to be determined are the inventory cycles for the different participators. Since the solution of this problem is quite complicated, they suggest a heuristic solution procedure, in which they assume that all the buyers require the same delivery times. Based on results computed from a numerical example, they claim that the heuristic solution closely approximates the optimal solution.

Yang et al. (2003) investigate a multi-lot-size production-inventory model with deteriorating items. Unlike Yang (2002), the system investigated in this article includes the raw materials cost, the cost of the producer and the cost of the buyers. The cost of raw materials is important, especially for deteriorating products, because the raw materials may also deteriorate. The deterioration rates of the raw materials and products are assumed to be different but constant. The buyers' demand rates are also different but constant. No shortage is allowed. With these assumptions, the optimal product cycle of the producer and the optimal order cycle for the buyer are considered together.

The method they use is similar to Yang et al. (2002). Based on numerical results, they point out that the integrated strategy may yield a lower cost.

Balkhi (2001) studies the optimal solution for a finite-horizon production-lot-sizing with deteriorating items. The demand, the production and the deteriorating rates are assumed to be continuous functions of time. Shortage is allowed and is completely backlogged. It is further assumed that the inventory at the beginning and at the end of the horizon is zero, and that the planning horizon is divided into n equal cycles. By analyzing the costs of the four stages as shown in Figure 4, he obtains the function of total cost. He first finds the optimal strategy with a fixed number of cycles. Then, by comparing the costs for different numbers of cycles, he derives a strategy, which he proves to be globally optimal. Finally, he uses an example to illustrate his solution.

Zhou et al. (2003) develop a model for an integrated production and inventory system with deteriorating items, where time-varying demands and partially backlogged shortages are considered. They use a two-stage procedure to find the optimal strategy, which works as follows:

1.   For a given number of production cycles in the planning horizon, it optimizes the production and ordering plans.

2.   By a marginal analysis method, it then optimizes the number of production cycles.

They obtain conditions for the solution to be a global optimal point.

Since the problem of finding the optimal stopping and restarting times for production is difficult, some researchers have attempted to use numerical methods to search for the optimal strategies. Wee et al. (1999) study a variable production scheduling policy for deteriorating items with time-varying demands. They consider a system with a constant deterioration rate and a constant production rate. Shortage is allowed and demand is time-dependent but deterministic and known. Production may take place at any time in the planning horizon. They first analyze the total cost function of this system. Then, they suggest using a heuristic approach to find the decision. Since the cost function is unimodal convex with respect to the number of production cycles, their search method is valid, although it does not seem to be very efficient. They use numerical examples to analyze the performance of their model, where they suppose the demand rate

$$R(t) = \begin{cases} a \exp(bt) & if \ 0 \le t \le H \\ 0 & otherwise \end{cases} \quad \text{or} \quad R(t) = \begin{cases} a + bt, & if \ 0 \le t \le H \\ 0 & otherwise \end{cases},$$

where H is the planning horizon. They find that the optimal production cycle increases with the inventory cost, production rate, deterioration rate, planning horizon, and b. The increase in value of a will not, however, affect the optimal production cycle but will increase the optimal cost.

While the majority of the inventory-production literature on perishable products considers deterministic deterioration rates, there has also been some work that takes randomness into account. Wee et al. (1999) study an economic production lot sizing problem with deteriorating items, which considers the time-value of money. They assume the life cycle of the products follows a two-parameter Weibull distribution. The demand rate is a decreasing linear function of the selling price. The production rate is constant and known. The production life cycles are equal in the planning horizon. Shortage is allowed and completely backordered. The inventory levels at the beginning and end times are all zero. All costs and revenue are discounted to the present value. They propose a heuristic procedure similar to that of Wee (1999). They use numerical examples to compare the profits of this model under different assumptions, e.g., without considering the time value of money, without deterioration, etc.

Applications of Control Theory

Control theory has been applied to study the optimal policy for production-inventory systems, since a production-inventory supply chain also exhibits a kind of system dynamics.

Andijani et al. (1998) analyze an inventory/production system with deteriorating products, using a linear quadratic regulator. They seek to find the optimal control for the production-inventory system with the objective to minimize

$$J = \int_0^T \{h[I(t) - \hat{I}]^2 + c[p(t) - \hat{p}]^2\}dt,$$

where $I(t)$ is the inventory at time t, $\hat{I}$ the desired inventory level, $p(t)$ the production rate, $\hat{p}$ the satisfactory production rate, h the inventory holding cost and c the unit cost. After some development, the problem is shown to become a standard linear-quadratic control problem. Based on the setting of the control problem, they find the optimal policy. With a sensitive analysis, they conclude that the objective function is less sensitive to the change in the inventory holding cost than to the change in the unit cost.

Boukas et al. (1999) also apply the control theory to an inventory-production control problem with a stochastic demand. It is assumed that the demand rate is a continuous-time stochastic Markov process with a finite state space and the rate of deterioration depends on the rate of the demand. They try to find an optimal control for the production system with no setup cost, under the objective to minimize

$$J_u(x_0, a, 0) = E[\int_0^T [c_1 x^2(t) + c_2 u^2(t)]dt \mid x(0) = x_0, v(0) = a],$$

where c_1 is the inventory holding cost or shortage cost, and c_2 is the production cost. This objective function infers that the inventory cost is equal to the shortage cost.

Extensive studies have been published on joint production-inventory decisions on perishable products. They carry, however, a common assumption that the products have a constant deterioration rate. An interesting topic for future study is to relax this assumption, by considering models with stochastic deterioration rates.

Conclusions

Perishable commodities are produced in numerous industries, in particular in food, biochemical, and electronic industries. It has long been recognized that a remarkable challenge in these industries is how to make the proper decisions by taking perishability into account. As we have discussed above, a large amount of the literature has been devoted to the study of the management of perishable products. The majority of the literature, however, has focused on inventory only. This is not sufficient for supply chain management. Obviously, interaction and coordination of the related components (functionalities) in the supply chain are the key in achieving the overall objective of the system. This requirement is perhaps more prominent for industries producing perishable products, because the time-varying value of perishable products demands not only coordination in space, but also in time.

We have, consequently, placed the emphasis of our chapter here on the studies of interaction and coordination of supply chains with perishable products. We have reviewed published research studies that consider the interfaces between the inventory with marketing, finance, distribution, and production. The main results/contributions of the previous literature in these areas have been reviewed and summarized. Some possible topics that need further investigation have also been discussed above. Here are two general remarks that we would like to highlight:

1. The majority of the literature we have reviewed still carries the common assumption that the deterioration rate of the product is deterministic, which is known and fixed in advance. In practice, the deterioration rate may fluctuate due to changes of environmental factors, and may also be affected by decisions such as transportation routing and timing. It would be very interesting if the deterioration rate could be modeled as a random variable or process, which depends not only on uncertain/uncontrollable factors, but also on the decisions of the decision-maker.

2. Most studies consider interactions only between a pair of components in the supply chain (such as inventory/marketing; inventory/finance; inventory/distribution; and inventory/production, as we have reviewed above). Future studies may extend to consider interaction and coordination of more functionalities/components in the whole supply chain.

References

Abad, P.L. (1996). Optimal pricing and lot-sizing under conditions of perishability and partial backordering. *Management Science, 42,* 1093-1104.

Abad, P.L. (2003). Optimal pricing and lot-sizing under conditions of perishability, finite production and partial backordering and lost sale. *European Journal of Operational Research, 144,* 677-685.

Aggarwal, S.P., & Jaggi, K.C. (1995). Ordering policies of deteriorating items under permissible delay in payments. *Journal of the Operational Research Society, 46*, 658-662.

Andijani, A. & Dajani, M.A. (1998). Analysis of deteriorating inventory/ production systems using a linear quadratic regulator. *European Journal of Operational Research, 106*, 82-89.

Arcelus, F.J., Shah, N.H. & Srinivasan, G. (2002). Retailer's pricing, credit and inventory policies for deteriorating items in response to temporary price/credit incentives. *International Journal of Production Economics, 81*(2), 153-162.

Balkhi, Z.T. (2000). Viewpoint on optimal production and restarting times for an EOQ model with deteriorating items. *Journal of the Operational Research Society, 51*, 999-1003.

Balkhi, Z.T. (2001). On a finite horizon production lot size inventory model for deteriorating items: An optimal solution. *European Journal of Operational Research, 132*, 210-223.

Balkhi, Z.T., Goyal, S.K. & Giri, B.C. (2001). Viewpoint some notes on optimal production and restarting times for an EOQ model with deteriorating items. *Journal of the Operational Research Society, 52*, 1300-1301.

Bose, S., Goswami, A. & Chaudhuri, S.K. (1995). An EOQ model for deteriorating items with linear time-dependent demand rate and shortages under inflation and time discounting. *Journal of the Operational Research Society, 46*, 771-782.

Boukas, E.K., Shi, P. & Andijani, A. (1999). Robust inventory-production control problem with stochastic demand. *Optimal Control Applications and Methods, 20*, 1-20.

Burnetas, N.A, & Smith, E.C. (2000). Adaptive ordering and pricing for perishable products. *Operations Research, 48*, 436-443.

Chen, J.M. (1998). An inventory model for deteriorating items with time-proportional demand and shortages under inflation and time discounting. *International Journal of Production Economics, 55*, 21-30.

Chu, P., Chung, K.J. & Lan, S.P. (1998). Economic order quantity of deteriorating items under permissible delay in payments. *Computers & Operations Research, 25*, 817-824.

Chun, Y.H. (2003). Optimal pricing and ordering policies for perishable commodities. *European Journal of Operational Research*, *144*, 68-82.

Chung, K.J., & Lin, C.N. (2001). Optimal inventory replenishment models for deteriorating items taking account of time discounting. *Computers & Operations Research*, *28*, 67-83.

Chung, K.J., & Tsai, S.F. (1997a). Inventory systems for deteriorating items taking account of time value. *Engineering Optimization*, *27*, 303-320.

Chung, K.J., & Tsai, S.F. (1997b). An algorithm to determine the EOQ for deteriorating items with shortage and a linear trend in demand. *International Journal of Production Economics*, *51*, 215-221.

Cohen, M.A. (1977). Joint pricing and ordering policy for exponentially decaying inventory with known demand. *Naval Research Logistics*, *24*, 257-268.

Diaby, M. (1991). Successive linear-approximation procedure for generalized fixed-charge transportation problems. *Journal of the Operational Research Society*, *42*, 991-1001.

Eilon, S., & Mallaya, R.V. (1966). Issuing and pricing policy of semi-perishables. *Proceedings of the 4th International Conference on Operational Research*. New York: Wiley-Interscience.

Evans, S.R., & Norback, J.P. (1985). The impact of a decision-support system for vehicle routing in a foodservice supply situation. *Journal of the Operational Research Society*, *36*, 467-472.

Federgruen, A., Prastacos, G. & Zipkin, P.H. (1986). An allocation and distribution model for perishable products. *Operations Research*, *34*, 75-82.

Ghare P.M., & Schrader, G.F. (1963). A model for exponentially decaying inventory. *Journal of Industrial Engineering*, *14*, 238-243.

Goyal, S.K., & Giri, B.C. (2001). Recent trends in modeling of deteriorating inventory. *European Journal of Operational Research*, *134*, 1-16.

Hwang, H., & Shinn, S.W. (1997). Retailer's pricing and lot sizing policy for exponentially deteriorating products under the condition of permissible delay in payments. *Computers & Operations Research*, *24*, 539-47.

Iijima, M., Komatsu, S. & Katoh, S. (1996). Hybrid just-in-time logistics systems and information networks for effective management in perishable food industries. *International Journal of Production Economics, 44,* 97-103.

Jaggi, C.K., & Aggarwal, S.P. (1994). Credit financing in economic ordering policies of deteriorating items. *International Journal of Production Economics, 34,* 151-155.

Jamal, A.M.M., Sarker, B.R. & Wang, S. (1997). An ordering policy for deteriorating items with allowable shortage and permissible delay in payment. *International Journal of Production Economics, 48,* 826-833.

Jamal, A.M.M, Sarker, B.R. & Wang, S. (2000). Optimal payment time for a retailer under permitted delay of payment by the wholesaler. *International Journal of Production Economics, 66,* 59-66.

Katagiri, H., & Ishii, H. (2002). Fuzzy inventory problems for perishable commodities. *European Journal of Operational Research, 138,* 545-553.

Liao, H., Tsai, C. & Su, C. (2002). An inventory model with deteriorating items under inflation when a delay in payment is permissible. *International Journal of Production Economics, 63,* 207-214.

Lin, C.W.R. & Chen, H.Y.S. (2003). Dynamic allocation of uncertain supply for the perishable commodity supply chain. *International Journal of Production Research, 41,* 3119-3138.

Morales, D.R, Nunen, J.A.E.E.V. & Romeijn, H.E. (1999). Logistics network design evaluation in a dynamic environment, new trends in distribution logistics. *Lecture Notes in Economics and Mathematical Systems, 480,* 113-135.

Nahmias, S. (1982). Perishable inventory theory: A review. *Operations Research, 30,* 680-708.

Papachristos, S., & Skouri, K. (2003). An inventory model with deteriorating items, quantity discount, pricing and time-dependent partial backlogging. *International Journal of Production Economics, 83,* 247-256.

Prastacos, G.P. (1981). Allocation of a perishable product inventory. *Operations Research, 29,* 95-107.

Raafat, F. (1991). Survey of literature on continuously deteriorating inventory models. *Journal of the Operational Research Society, 42,* 27-37.

Rahim, M.A, Kabadi, S.N. & Barnerjee, P.K. (2000). A single-period perishable inventory model where deterioration begins at a random point in time. *International Journal of Systems Science, 31*, 131-136.

Rajan, A.R., & Steinberg, R. (1992). Dynamic pricing and ordering decisions by a Monopolist. *Management Science, 38*, 240-262.

Rowe, J., Jewers, K., Sivayogan, J., Codd, A. & Alcock, A. (1996). Intelligent retail logistics scheduling. *AI Magazine, 17,* 31-40.

Sarker, B.R., Jamal, A.M. & Wang, S. (2000). Supply chain models for perishable products under inflation and permissible delay in payment. *Computers & Operations Research, 27*, 59-75.

Skouri, K., & Papachristos, S. (2003). Optimal stopping and restarting production times for an EOQ model with deteriorating items and time-dependent partial backlogging. *International Journal of production Economics*, 81-82, 525-531.

Song, X.P., & Cai, X. (2003). On optimal payment time for a retailer under permitted delay of payment by the wholesaler. Working Paper, Chinese University of Hong Kong.

Tarantilis, C.D, & Kiranoudis, C.T. (2001). A meta-heuristic algorithm for the efficient distribution of perishable foods. *Journal of Food Engineering, 50*, 1-9.

Wee, H.M. (1995). Joint pricing and replenishment policy for deteriorating inventory with declining market. *International Journal of Production Economics, 40*, 163-171.

Wee, H.M. (1999). Deteriorating inventory model with quantity discount, pricing and partial backordering. *International Journal of Production Economics, 59*, 511-518.

Wee, H.M., & Law, S.T. (1999). Economic production lot size for deteriorating items taking account of the time-value of money. *Computers & Operations Research, 26*, 545-558.

Wee, H.M., & Wang, W.T. (1999). A variable production scheduling policy for deteriorating items with time-varying demand. *Computers and Operations Research, 26*, 237-254.

Whitin, T.M. (1957). *Theory of inventory management.* Princeton University Press.

Yan, H., & Cheng, T.C.E. (1998). Optimal production stopping and restarting times for an EOQ model with deteriorating items. *Journal of the Operational Research Society, 49,* 1288-1295.

Yang, P.C., & Wee, H.M. (2002). A single-vendor and multiple-buyers production-inventory policy for a deteriorating item. *European Journal of Operational Research, 143,* 570-581.

Yang, P.C., & Wee, H.M. (2003). An integrated multi-lot-size production inventory model for deteriorating item. *Computers & Operations Research, 30,* 671-682.

Zhou, Y.W, Lau, H.S., & Yang, S.L. (2003). A new variable production scheduling strategy for deteriorating items with time-varying demand and partial lost sale. *Computers & Operations Research, 30,* 1753-1776.

Endnote

[1]   This work was partially supported by NSFC Research Fund No. 70329001 and 70321001, and RGC of Hong Kong under an Earmarked Grant No. CUHK 4170/03E.

About the Authors

Chi Kin Chan is an assistant professor of the Department of Applied Mathematics at the Hong Kong Polytechnic University. He received his Ph.D. in management science from Lancaster University, UK, under the supervision of Professor Brian G. Kingsman. He has published in journals such as *Transportation Research, Part B, European Journal of Operational Research, Annals of Operations Research and International Journal of Operations and Production Management.* His current research areas include inventory control, supply chain management, forecasting and optimization.

Heung Wing Joseph Lee obtained his BSc (Hons) and PhD from The University of Western Australia (1994 and 1997, respectively). His PhD was awarded with 'Distinction', an accolade that is rarely bestowed by the Board of Postgraduate Studies at the University of Western Australia. He is currently an assistant professor at the Department of Applied Mathematics at the Hong Kong Polytechnic University. He is specializing in the computational studies of optimal controls and several other areas in operations research. He has published in Automatica, International Journal of Bifurcation and Chaos, Journal of Optimization Theory and Applications (JOTA), and other reputable international journals.

*   *   *

William Acar (DiplIng; MASc Waterloo, CA; PhD, Wharton-UPenn, USA) teaches management and information systems at Kent State University (USA). The author of numerous published articles, Dr. Acar has developed a causal mapping method for the analysis of complex business situations and coauthored a book, *Scenario-Driven Planning*. Currently, his method is being used to develop a computerized GDSS for solving strategic problems. He has published in journals such as: *Strategic Management Journal, INFOR, Decision Sciences, OMEGA, Information Systems, Journal of Management, Behavioral Science, Strategic Change* and *INTERFACES*.

Paul J. Ambrose is an assistant professor of management information systems at the University of Wisconsin – Milwaukee (USA). He received his PhD in MIS from Southern Illinois University at Carbondale. His current research interests include the impact of Internet technologies on knowledge intensive work processes, e-business and information systems success, information systems downsizing, and object-oriented systems development. He has published several papers in refereed academic journals, practitioner journals, and conferences. He is a member of the Association for Information Systems, the Decision Sciences Institute, the Association for Computing Machinery, IN-FORMS, and Beta Gamma Sigma and Phi Kappa Phi Honors Societies.

Xiaoqiang Cai received his BEng from the Harbin Shipbuilding Engineering Institute (1982) and his MEng and DEng degrees from Tsinghua University (1985 and 1988, respectively). He is currently a professor of the Department of Systems Engineering and Engineering Management at the Chinese University of Hong Kong. His research at present concentrates on scheduling and logistics management, portfolio optimization, and time-varying network optimization. He has published extensively in leading journals in these areas, such as *Operations Research, Management Science, Naval Research Logistics, IIE Transactions,* and *IEEE Transactions.* He is on the editorial boards of several international journals, including *IIE Transactions on Scheduling and Logistics, Journal of Scheduling, and Fuzzy Optimization and Decision Making.*

Jian Chen received a BSc, MSc, and PhD from Tsinghua University (1983, 1986 and 1989, respectively). He is currently professor and chairman of the Management Science Department, and co-director of the Research Center for

Contemporary Management, Tsinghua University. He has more than 100 technical publications and has been a principal investigator for over 20 grants or research contracts with National Science Foundation of China, governmental organizations and companies. His main research interests include supply chain management, e-commerce, modeling and control for complex systems, decision support systems and information systems, forecast and optimization techniques. He is an associate editor of IEEE Transactions on Systems, Man and Cybernetics: Part A, and Part C, and serves on the editorial board of International Journal of Electronic Business, Systems Research and Behavioral Science, and Journal of Tsinghua University.

Bernard K-S. Cheung is an adjunct professor at the Ecole Polytechnique de Montreal (Canada) and a collaborator of GERAD Research Centre, Montreal, Canada. He is a founding member of Polygistique — a research group in industrial logistics at the Department of Mathematics and Industrial Engineering of the above university. He received his MSc and PhD from the University of Toronto. Recently, he is investigating in some new global optimization meta-heuristics and their applications in modern logistics and has been collaborating with the faculty members of several universities in Hong Kong. He has published a number of articles related to these areas.

Toru Higuchi is a full-time lecturer of logistics at the Department of Community Development, Sakushin Gakuin University in Utsunomiya, Tochigi prefecture, Japan. He is an associate editor of the *Journal of Public Utility Economics*. He received an MA from the School of Management at Gakushuin University (1996). From 1999-2000, he studied in the PhD program at the Graduate School of Management at Kent State University. His publications have appeared in *Computers & Operations Research, Journal of Public Utility Economics*, and others. His current research interests include supply chain management, business logistics, global logistics, and transfer pricing.

Brian G. Kingsman (1939-2003) was professor of operational research and operations management at the Department of Management Science, Lancaster University, UK. He received a first class bachelor's degree in mathematics from Cambridge University, UK, and his PhD in operational research from Lancaster University, UK. He has published in journals such as *Journal of Operational Research Society, International Journal of Production Re-*

search, *European Journal of Operational Research, Annals of Operations Research and International Journal of Production Economics.* His research areas included production planning, inventory control, supply chain management and purchasing.

André Langevin is a professor at the Department of Mathematics and Industrial Engineering, École Polytechnique, Montreal, Quebec, Canada. He holds a BSc in mathematics from UQAM, Montreal, Quebec, Canada. He received an MScA in industrial engineering and a PhD in operations research from École Polytechnique. His research interests encompass logistics, distribution, and mathematical optimization. His articles have appeared in *International Journal of Production Research, Transportation Science, Network*, and other journals.

Nathalie Marcoux is a research associate at the Department of Mathematics and Industrial Engineering, École Polytechnique, Montreal, Quebec, Canada. She holds a PhD in industrial engineering from École Polytechnique. Her research interests include logistics, facilities layout, and e-commerce.

Brian A. Polin is currently a lecturer (assistant professor) in the Department of Technology Management & Marketing at the Hochstein School of Industrial Management at the Jerusalem College of Technology (Israel). His PhD is in the fields of strategic management and international business. He holds additional degrees in mathematics, transportation and operations research. Dr. Polin has worked on two continents as an engineer, business operations consultant, and the principal of a consulting firm. He has published research in the areas of strategy, supply chain management, and international studies. His current research interests include supply chain globalization, the role of assets in competitive advantage, and the application of operations research tools in strategic management.

I Nyoman Pujawan is currently a lecturer in operations management in the Manchester Business School, The University of Manchester, UK. He is temporarily on leave from his job as a lecturer in the Department of Industrial Engineering, Sepuluh Nopember Institute of Technology (ITS), Surabaya – Indonesia. He received a bachelor's degree in industrial engineering from ITS, MEng in industrial engineering from the Asian Institute of Technology (AIT),

Bangkok – Thailand, and a PhD in management science from Lancaster University, UK. His research interests are in the area of operations and supply chain management. His papers have been published or will appear in the *International Journal of Production Economics, European Journal of Operational Research, International Journal of Operations and Quantitative Management, International Journal of Integrated Supply Management*, and in a number of national journals in Indonesia.

Diane Riopel is a professor at the Department of Mathematics and Industrial Engineering, École Polytechnique, Montreal, Quebec, Canada. She holds a BEng and an MScA in industrial engineering. She received a doctorate in industrial engineering from École Centrale de Paris, France. Her research interests are in the areas of logistics, facility layout, material handling, and warehousing. Her articles have appeared in *International Journal of Production Economics, International Journal of Production Research, International Journal of Flexible Manufacturing Systems*, and other journals.

Xiping Song received a BSc in management information systems from Tsinghua University, Beijing, China (2001), and an MSc in management science and engineering from the same university (2003). He is currently a doctoral student at the Chinese University of Hong Kong, China. His current interest of research is in supply chain management, online auction, and group-buying. He has published in journals such as IEEE *Trans. on Systems, Man and Cybernetics: Part A,* and *Systems Engineering: Theory and Practice.*

Marvin D. Troutt is a professor at the Department of Management & Information Systems and at the Graduate School of Management, Kent State University (USA). He is an associate editor of *Decision Sciences* journal and a fellow of the Decision Sciences Institute. He received a PhD in mathematical statistics from the University of Illinois at Chicago. His publications have appeared in *Decision Sciences, Management Science, Journal of the Operational Research Society, European Journal of Operational Research, Operations Research, Decision Support Systems, Naval Research Logistics, Statistics*, and others. His current research interests include supply chain management, operations strategy, efficiency, and applications of optimization methods.

K.H. Wong was born in Hong Kong on March 1, 1950. He obtained his BSc (Honours) from London University (1979). He received his MSc and PhD from the University of New South Wales (1981 and 1984, respectively). In 1985, he was employed to work as a lecturer with the University of the Witwatersrand. He was promoted to senior lecturer in 1988 and reader in 1999 at the same university. His research areas include optimal control theory, stability theory, classical optimization and global optimization and numerical analysis. Thus far, he has more than 40 publications in international journals, together with a book which appeared as a research monograph. His publications have attracted more than 150 citations worldwide.

Index

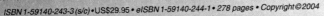